SUNDAY SCHOOL

Sunday School

THE FORMATION OF

AN AMERICAN INSTITUTION

1790–1880

ANNE M. BOYLAN

YALE UNIVERSITY PRESS
NEW HAVEN AND LONDON

Some of the material in this book first appeared
in *American Studies*. Copyright 1979 by Midcontinent
American Studies Association (Mid-America
American Studies Association). Used by permission.
Designed by Sally Harris
and set in Kennerly type by
The Composing Room of Michigan, Inc.
Printed in the United States of America by
Murray Printing Co., Westford, Massachusetts.

Library of Congress Cataloging-in-Publication Data

Boylan, Anne M., 1947–
Sunday school : the formation of an
American institution, 1790–1880 / Anne M. Boylan.
p.   cm.
Bibliography: p.
Includes index.
ISBN 0–300–04019–9 (cloth)
0–300–04814–9 (pbk.)

1. Sunday-schools—United States—History.   I. Title.
BV1516.A1B69 1988
268′.0973—dc19   87–34588
CIP

The paper in this book meets the guidelines for
permanence and durability of the Committee on
Production Guidelines for Book Longevity
of the Council on Library Resources.

2   4   6   8   10   9   7   5   3

For my mother
Brigid Lanigan Boylan
and in memory of my father
John F. Boylan

CONTENTS

𝕱𝕴𝖁𝕰

Conversion and Christian Nurture: Children and Childhood
in Sunday Schools

ILLUSTRATIONS

ACKNOWLEDGMENTS

It is a pleasure to acknowledge the assistance I have received on this project over the years. The staff of the Presbyterian Historical Society in Philadelphia, particularly Gerald Gillette, Norotha Robinson, and Frederick Shalow, were cordial and extremely helpful in guiding me through the society's rich Sunday school collection. Edward C. Starr of the American Baptist Historical Society in Rochester, New York, gave me a key, access to a Xerox machine, and the freedom to explore the society's collections. Librarians at the Congregational Library in Boston were similarly generous. In Nashville, Gladys Beasley at the Methodist Publishing House Library was interested and helpful. The holdings of the following libraries proved indispensable to my work: the State Historical Society of Wisconsin; the New York Public Library; Swift Library of the University of Chicago; Garrett Theological Seminary Library in Evanston, Illinois; Union Theological Seminary Library; Lovely Lane Methodist Museum in Baltimore; the Brooklyn Historical Society; the Historical Society of Pennsylvania; the Boston University School of Theology Library; and the Dargan-Carver Library of the Southern Baptist Historical Commission in Nashville.

Portions of chapters 3, 4, and 5 have appeared in very different form in *Feminist Studies, American Studies, Church History,* and *The Journal of Presbyterian History.* I am grateful to those journals for permission to reproduce the material here.

Many friends and colleagues have read and commented on this book in its various incarnations. At the University of Wisconsin, where I wrote the first version as a dissertation, Carl F. Kaestle, Joe Lukonic, and especially Stanley K. Schultz provided many helpful suggestions. James F. Findlay, Jr., of the University of Rhode Island and Robert T. Handy of Union Theological Seminary also read the dissertation with care, offering encouragement and valuable suggestions. I am especially grateful for the assistance of Robert Wood Lynn, Jr., of the Lilly Endowment, who has sustained his interest in and enthusiasm for this project over many years. Other individuals—particularly Paul Boyer, Joseph Hawes, Janet Wilson James, David

Macleod, Daniel Rodgers, Mary Ryan, Anne Firor Scott and Ralph Smith—read article drafts or simply encouraged me at various times. I want them to know how much their interest meant to me.

Jon Butler and two other readers reviewed the manuscript; their incisive critiques improved the finished book substantially. At Yale University Press, Chuck Grench was a supportive editor and Harry Haskell wielded a sharp pencil to hone my prose.

Margaret Thornton and Donna Merwick, my teachers at Mundelein College, inspired my interest in history and provided extraordinary models of commitment to scholarship and teaching. At the University of Wisconsin, Paul K. Conkin (now of Vanderbilt University) became my mentor and friend. He guided the original dissertation to completion, all the while pressing me to strive for the precision of thought and expression for which he is so admired.

My family has been and continues to be my lifeline. My parents, John and Brigid Boylan, never doubted that I could do anything I set out to do, and my sisters and brothers carried on the family tradition. Kate and Ellis Kolchin offered me shelter, refreshment, encouragement—and that most precious commodity, time—without stinting. But without my husband, Peter Kolchin, I know I would never have finished this book. He has read more versions of these chapters than he would care to remember, and has provided unfailingly good suggestions and advice. Most of all, though, it was his faith in my ability to get it done that enabled me to persevere.

SUNDAY SCHOOL

INTRODUCTION

The nineteenth century was an era of institution building. The long list of familiar modern institutions that trace their origins to the last century includes political parties, corporations, prisons, hospitals, and asylums. Institutions for children proliferated, too, as Americans established orphanages, reform schools, houses of refuge, and free public schools. Some of these agencies were residential and exerted almost total control over their clients; others, such as common schools, affected larger numbers of children in a much less comprehensive fashion. Insofar as modern Americans accept institutional solutions to the problems of educating and disciplining the young, they owe a large debt to their nineteenth-century forebears.

This book is a study of one such institution: the Sunday school. It examines the creation and evolution of Sunday schools in five evangelical Protestant denominations (Baptist, Congregationalist, Low Church Episcopalian, Methodist, and Presbyterian) and through the interdenominational American Sunday School Union. Each chapter analyzes some aspect of the nineteenth-century Sunday school: its origins and rapid expansion, its educational functions in the era of the common school, its response to changing perceptions of adolescence and childhood, and the creation of national organizations that provided curricular materials and spurred the proliferation of schools. From this perspective, I hope to illuminate the entire process of institution building and to connect it to the economic and social changes that transformed the United States in the nineteenth century.

The importance of institutions in American history has long been the subject of scholarly contention. Pursuing themes articulated by Alexis de Tocqueville and Frederick Jackson Turner, historians have debated whether Americans are essentially rugged individualists or, in Arthur M. Schlesinger's phrase, "a nation of joiners." Stanley Elkins has characterized antebellum society as one in which "the power of so many institutions had . . . melted away" as traditional sources of stability—the church, the bar, and the state—became fragmented and lost their authority to provide "both organized social power and internal discipline." The proliferation of religious sects, the democratization of politics, and the rise of un-trammeled free enterprise contributed to making American society one in which "individual drives rather than institutional needs" prevailed—a society, as David Donald writes, "so new and so disorganized that its nerves were rawly exposed." Many historians have concluded that this institutional rudderlessness contributed largely to the republic's crackup in 1861 on the shoals of slavery. The notion that institutional breakdown was the defining characteristic of antebellum America and that some Americans, notably the abolitionists, were positively hostile to institutions, provided historians with a convincing explanatory model of early nineteenth-century politics and religion.[1]

This model could not, however, account for the behavior of many Americans in the antebellum years. In a recent book on the abolitionists, for example, John R. McKivigan found that only a small proportion exhibited the anti-institutionalism often ascribed to them. Despite their attacks on "the proslavery religion" of Ameri-can churches, most abolitionists remained committed church members. Then, too, Elkins's thesis flew in the face of mounting evidence that pre–Civil War Americans (especially northerners) were in fact joiners. This characteristic became clear as historians chronicled the extraordinary growth of associative activity that began in the 1790s, accelerated during the 1810s and 1820s, and continued throughout much of the century. During precisely the same decades when many historians saw the growth of unrestrained individualism and social anomie, others discovered Americans forming and joining voluntary societies at an unprecedented rate.[2]

Although some voluntary societies were purely social in nature and others disap-peared after a time, many made indelible markes on history by creating institutions and weaving them permanently into the American social fabric. If much of the modern "institutional state" which we take for granted today originated in the nineteenth century, its creators were generally people who associated together voluntarily to cope with some perceived social need. Thus, the first houses of refuge, reform schools, orphanages, old-age homes, and modern hospitals were begun by groups of men and women who formed voluntary societies and raised donations from among friends, relatives, acquaintances, and strangers. In many cases, the state assumed the functions of these institutions only after decades of management by private volunteers. In other cases, as with schools, lobbying by associations of citizens forced the state to transform privately run free schools into publicly supported common schools. The results of this institutionalizing tendency are all around us. As Michael Katz has pointed out, modern Americans "respond to a widespread problem through the creation of an institution, the training of spe-cialists and the certification of their monopoly over a part of our lives."[3]

Schools, asylums, hospitals, and Sunday schools are not, of course, "institutions" in the sense that established churches or monarchies are. To historians who con-trasted the decentralized social organization of antebellum America with the centuries-old national loyalties of many European countries, the United States did indeed appear institutionless. But the importance of institutions can be measured as much by their ability to maintain social order, promote social cohesion, and enforce social control as by their longevity. By that standard, the United States was far from rudderless. Millions of children imbibed a shared Protestant nationalism as part of the standard curriculum in both common and Sunday schools. Political parties taught basic rules in the exercise of power, and economic institutions initiated Americans into the ways of free enterprise. By giving Americans a common fund of experience, whether it be reading Morse's *Geography* or voting for a political candidate, nineteenth-century institutions united disparate people in a shared American-ness.

Like monarchies and state churches in other nations, then, the institutions that Americans created in the early nineteenth century assumed the social tasks of maintaining order, cohesion, and control. Precisely how they did so is a matter of controversy among historians. Some analysts, examining the language that reformers used to explain the need for schools, prisons, and asylums, have found common threads of fear and coercion. They argue that fear—of immigration, urban growth, and social disorder—was the primary motive behind the formation of new institutions, and that coercion of the urban poor was the primary objective. Moreover, the religious phraseology adopted by the reformers cloaked darker impulses. In this interpretation, "social control" represents an effort to hold back the tide of history and preserve or restore traditional patterns of social order based on deference and hierarchy.

Other historians have questioned this view, not only because it distinguishes artificially between the reformers' religious and secular goals (which were inseparable) but, more important, because it discounts the dynamic, modernizing drive behind the reformers' programs and lives. The men and women who devised institutions to deal with poverty, ignorance, and intemperance were not merely an old elite struggling to keep alive a dying social order; they were themselves part of an emerging leadership class with close ties to the urban mercantile and manufacturing economy. From this perspective, evangelical Protestantism can be seen as closely allied with the new middle-class vision of an expanding free labor economy and a democratic state. "Social control" is then better described not as a process of coercing recalcitrant urbanites to adopt alien behavioral patterns, but as a process of transmitting to others the personal qualities and values—self-control, delayed gratification, self-improvement—that reformers believed essential to individual and national progress.[4]

This interpretation has a great deal to recommend it. By taking full account of early nineteenth-century reformers' commitment to evangelical Protestantism, it enables us to understand how they managed, in Daniel Walker Howe's words, to "promot[e] values conducive to industrialization" and help "create a modern capitalist social order" while working to save souls. Just as they "assumed that without religion one could not rise in the world," as Carroll Smith Rosenberg writes, they "could not but assume that a secular by-product of this spiritual change would be universal thriftiness, temperance, prudence—and hence social stability." From individual regeneration and social stability would come national progress, temporal as well as spiritual. This interpretation also illuminates the connections between nineteenth-century evangelicalism and the republicanism of the Revolutionary era. For the virtues that evangelical institution-builders urged upon their clients were not alien importations but quintessentially American values. During and after the Revolution, evangelical religion came to be associated with the virtues of re-publican citizens: simplicity, lack of sophistication, honesty, temperance. As Rhys Isaac has demonstrated, the Baptist sect in Virginia grew rapidly because Baptists capitalized on small-farm folks' disdain for the style of life followed by their wealthier gentry neighbors. Thus, revival religion came to be identified with a class protest against gambling, intemperance, luxurious display, and high living. The success of the republican experiment became inextricably linked in the minds of evangelicals with the progress of religion, particularly because evangelical sects increasingly emphasized moral behavior as a criterion for continued good standing in the congregation. By the 1820s many looked forward to a millennial age when America would be, as Robert Handy has written, "a Christian civilization rooted in a Protestant morality."[5]

Although now primarily an instrument of denominational education, the Sunday school first became an American institution because it promised to fulfill the broad millennial expectations of evangelical reformers. Only over the course of decades did it acquire its denominational character and adopt a curriculum emphasizing sectarian training. Like the other institutions created in the nineteenth century, it began as a project of voluntary societies and eventually became institutionalized and bureaucratized. Unlike most of them, however, it never lost its essentially voluntary nature. Although many congregations today employ religious education directors, Sunday school teaching remains one of the most ubiquitous types of volunteer work in the United States.

This book is not a history of the Sunday school; readers looking for a comprehen-sive examination of the school's evolution in individual denominations will not find it here. Nor have I attempted to establish who started the first Sunday school and where—questions to which there are no definitive answers. Readers who want to pursue these issues may turn to the works of writers cited in the notes. Although blessed with many chroniclers, the Sunday school has had few historians. That is to say, most works on the subject have been written by individuals whose lives revolved around the Sunday school and whose major interest was to celebrate or preserve its historical record. I have written about Sunday schools because they seem to me an important but neglected piece of American history, and because a great deal more was transmitted in them than hymns and prayers. Like the common school, the Sunday school taught more than the lesson plans revealed. Along with the Ten Commandments and the Lord's Prayer, students absorbed the values and precepts of evangelical Protestantism. More important, they imbibed their teachers' expectations and learned the behavioral manifestations of religious conversion.

The story of the Sunday school concerns changing concepts of childhood and adolescence (and child and adolescent behavior) as much as prayer and piety, the power of denominational publishers and their competitors as much as catechisms and lesson books. It is the story of an American institution.

Chapter One

THE ORIGINS OF
EVANGELICAL SUNDAY SCHOOLS

Sunday schools first appeared on the American scene in the 1790s. Inspired by British examples, most were designed to provide rudimentary instruction to poor working children on their only free day of the week. Robert Raikes and other British evangelicals had pioneered this model during the 1780s by collecting children off city streets, cleaning them up, and keeping them in school for two long Sunday sessions. American organizers soon set up Sunday schools in several East Coast cities, as well as in factory towns like Pawtucket, Rhode Island, where Samuel Slater organized one for the benefit of his child workers. In these schools, children "prevented from receiving the benefit of instruction on any other day" were taught basic reading and writing (and sometimes arithmetic) by hired teachers who used the Bible as their text.

Although their format was novel, the premise that underlay these early schools was not. The belief that children should be educated in the faith of their fathers was deeply rooted in American history. Colonial Americans provided for the religious instruction of children in a variety of ways, ranging from family instruction to town schools and ministers' catechizing classes. In the 1790s, however, Sunday school founders were less concerned about the recipients' religious indoctrination than about the growing numbers of working children who seemed to be slipping through the cracks in the educational system, receiving neither the literacy training nor the religious knowledge that potential citizens of the new republic needed. Gathering in noisy groups to play on Sundays, these children were perceived as a social problem because they were under the control of no visible authority—no parent, no master—and because they violated accepted standards of public behavior on "the Lord's day." To their founders, Sunday schools represented an effort to fill the cracks, to offer poor working children opportunities to become educated in basic reading and religion, while also tackling the social problem posed by their Sunday behavior.[1]

By 1830, however, these first American Sunday schools had all but disappeared. In their place arose a new type of Sunday school, taught by volunteers and offering a specifically evangelical Protestant curriculum.[2] These schools, from which modern church schools developed, were remarkably successful, soon enrolling tens of thousands as teachers and students. They spawned local, state, and national associations devoted to establishing new schools and furnishing them with curricular materials. The phenomenal growth of evangelical schools, as compared with the limited success of their predecessors, illuminates some of the conditions that caused institutions to succeed or fail in post-Revolutionary America.

The prototypes of the first American Sunday schools were those begun in Philadelphia in 1791 under the auspices of a group called the First Day Society. Two concerns motivated the founders of First Day schools. Alarmed by the disintegration of the apprenticeship system—which, in theory at least, had provided basic education to all children who went through it—they wanted First Day schools to provide "proper opportunities of instruction" to "the offspring of indigent parents . . . previously to their being apprenticed to trades." They were also bothered (as Robert Raikes had been in England) by the tendency "among the Youth of every large city" to spend Sundays "employed in the worst of purposes, to the depravation of morals and manners." In other words, the society's members proposed both to change the way their clients used leisure time and to improve the tone of public life by removing unruly children from the streets on Sundays.

To carry out their plans, the founders of the First Day Society recruited two Philadelphia schoolteachers, John Ely and John Poor (head of the Young Ladies' Academy of Philadelphia), to teach "persons of each sex and of any age . . . to read and write." Students were to spend their time "reading in the Old and New Testaments, and . . . writing copies from the same." One founder argued that "no other book would have been proper" in a school that met on Sunday. The teachers were also to enforce proper behavior, reprimanding children for "lying, swearing, talking in an indecent manner, or other misbehaviour."[3] These men did not question their right to set behavioral standards for their schools' clientele.

The founders of the First Day Society were an ecumenical group who would perhaps have described themselves as enlightened republican gentlemen. They included Episcopalians, such as Bishop William White and the physicians Benjamin Rush and William Currie; Friends, such as the merchants Thomas Pym Cope and his uncle Thomas Mendenhall; and a Catholic, the publisher Matthew Carey.

Most were middle-aged or nearly so; all were well established in prominent careers; and all possessed an Enlightenment-bred faith in progress and human rationality.[4]

Their shared republicanism encompassed their views on the nature and functions of education, but did not extend to political uniformity (some were Federalists, some Republicans). They believed that education was, as Carey wrote in a petition to the Pennsylvania legislature, "the surest preservative of the Virtue, liberty, and happiness of the people." The United States, so recently embarked on an experiment in republican self-government, had no other recourse for the success of that experiment than the "virtue" of her citizens. Without an educated populace, public virtue would soon disappear, liberty would degenerate into anarchy, and the republican experiment would fail. Education, defined not in the narrow sense of intellectual training but in the broad sense of cultivation, would "promote good order and suppress vice" because learning good habits, fundamental among which was religious practice, was as much a part of education as reading or ciphering. Thus, education inculcated self-control and respect for authority. Educating the poor promoted "habits of order and industry" and qualified them to become "good servants [and] good apprentices." None of the society's founders would have denied his belief in the hierarchical nature of society, the need for every person to know his or her place, and the indispensability of deference to authority. Yet in stating their collective hope that First Day students would become "good masters and good citizens," they were also expressing a conviction that only through good habits learned in school could children become happy and useful adults, capable of fulfilling their talents, and worthy of participating in the republic. Believing that education should not be available merely to the wealthy, the First Day Society founders petitioned the Pennsylvania legislature to provide for the establishment of free schools. Believing that education should also be religious, the Society's teachers regularly escorted their charges to church services, as well as teaching them almost exclusively from the Bible.[5]

The structure of the society revealed something of the founders' educational views and purposes. The managers, who met approximately every month, solicited funds, hired teachers, paid bills, made policy, and recruited students. They also served, on a rotating basis, on the Board of Visitors, whose function was to visit the schools regularly and report back on problems and progress. The managers supervised the schoolmasters (usually there were two or three) who ran the schools, employing student monitors in a system similar to that developed by the British educator Joseph Lancaster. The managers remained relatively remote from the actual operations of the schools, except during periodic examinations at which they presented rewards in the form of books to deserving scholars. Although they tried to raise funds for schoolroom rentals, supplies, and teachers' salaries, the managers themselves were always the primary donors.[6]

Around 1800 the First Day Society began to experience declining enrollments, a recurring problem the managers at first attributed to the growth of free charity day schools in Philadelphia. By 1810 the city had more than a dozen of these schools, most of which were run by individual Protestant congregations. By 1817 the managers were also attributing enrollment difficulties to "the introduction of . . . Sunday schools by . . . religious Societies." The last remaining First Day school closed its doors in 1819; although the society continued to exist as a legal entity, its managers met with decreasing frequency, and then only to disburse its funds to the new Sunday schools.[7] A similar trend emerged in other cities, as Sunday schools with paid teachers were gradually eclipsed by the free day schools and new evangelical Sunday schools.

The process was not entirely linear, however. Both types of schools coexisted for about two decades as schooling opportunities expanded in the new republic, especially in the North. Amid the jumble of free schools, pay schools, charity schools, subscription schools, and common schools, Sunday schools fulfilled a variety of functions. Some used paid teachers to impart basic literacy to working children; others were staffed by volunteers who taught reading, writing, and religion to poor or black children, many of whom were excluded from other schools; still others were essentially variants on catechism classes for church members' children. A Boston schoolmaster named Oliver Lane established a subscription Sunday school in 1791, and five years later the Methodist evangelist Francis Asbury urged his fellow preachers to "establish Sabbath schools, wherever practicable, for the benefit of the children of the poor." Joanna Graham Bethune and her mother, Isabella Graham, began a Sunday school in New York in 1803. They hired teachers for the reading and writing classes, but gave the religious instruction themselves as volunteers. Many Congregationalist, Baptist, and Presbyterian ministers in New England catechized the children of church members at weekly meetings, some of which convened on Sunday.[8] In some localities, Sunday school supporters sought and won public funds to advance their work. In 1824, for example, school commissioners in Richmond, Virginia, appropriated thirty cents for each Sunday school pupil, adding a supplement the following year for books and supplies. Arguing that Sunday schools provided cheap education without interfering with regular working hours, promoters in Delaware secured legislation in 1821 allocating twenty cents for each white pupil to schools that met for at least three months in the year. By 1852 the appropriation was forty cents. In North Carolina, similar legislation was introduced and debated several times during the 1820s, but failed.[9]

The new evangelical Sunday schools differed fundamentally from the First Day schools and others like them in their founders' purposes and personal backgrounds and in their appeal to potential pupils. Although all Sunday schools provided an education centered on Christian belief, the founders of the evangelical schools placed paramount emphasis on the religious aspects of teaching, which they defined in a specifically evangelical Protestant manner. For them, teaching reading and writing was only a means to a greater end, not an end in itself. That greater end—an evangelical interpretation of the Bible—was to be achieved by teaching students to read the Bible, familiarizing them with its contents, and leading them to interpret it as their teachers did. Thus, the religion that these Sunday school founders hoped to impart was much more specific than the mere teaching of belief in God, the immortality of the soul, and the need for religious practice. It encompassed the evangelical doctrines of innate depravity, future punishment, and, most important, the need for a personal experience of regeneration. In the words of one teacher, "the ultimate end" of the Sunday school was "imparting that religious knowledge, those religious impressions, and the formation of those religious habits in the minds of children, which shall be crowned with the salvation of their immortal souls."[10]

These schools also differed from the others in the concerns that moved their founders and teachers. Like the managers of the First Day Society, the evangelicals worried about children running around unsupervised on Sundays and equated proper education with the inculcation of manners, self-control, Sabbath observance, and good citizenship. Unlike them, however, they established a close link between an educated populace and the spread of evangelical Protestantism. A constant refrain in their writing—that children were growing up ignorant—referred not solely to lack of basic skills. What children lacked, they argued, was knowledge of "their duty to God and man," "the truths of religion," or "the leading doctrines of the Bible, and the duty required of them, as social, rational and accountable beings." Sunday schools would remedy this lack by teaching them the evangelical doctrines of individual accountability and the need for a personal conversion experience, while at the same time imparting cognitive skills. The secretary of a Sunday school society in upstate New York expressed it best when he stated: "Orderly lives, and minds stored with useful knowledge, will make [children] the support and ornament of civil society; but religion alone will give them a claim on the white robes and the palms of heaven."[11]

Yet another contrast between the two sets of schools lay in the backgrounds of their founders. The organizers of these schools were, first and foremost, dedicated evangelicals, many of whom had only recently experienced religious conversion during the revivals of the Second Great Awakening. They interpreted the conversion experience as a mandate not only to begin a process of personal sanctification but also to work for the salvation of others. Some formed Sunday schools as a means of carrying out that mandate; others, not yet converted themselves, formed schools as an expression of their hope of an imminent conversion. As in the revivals themselves, a majority of evangelical Sunday school founders (and later of teachers) were women, and many of the organizers (male and female) were young people in their late teens and twenties. Unlike Samuel Slater or the founders of the First Day Society, the creators of these schools were intimately involved in their operation. This personal activism facilitated the formation of Sunday school unions, all of which—from local to national unions—rested upon their members' active involvement in Sunday school teaching.[12]

But the biggest difference between evangelical Sunday schools and those with a fundamentally educational orientation was their remarkable growth and geographical dispersion. Evangelical schools spread rapidly in the 1810s and 1820s. In Phila-

Table 1

Children in Schools Affiliated with the American Sunday School Union, 1824–1832

Year	Location	Children of Sunday school age	Children in ASSU schools	Percentage of eligible children in ASSU schools
1824	United States	3,413,750	48,681	1.4
1825	United States	3,309,000	75,140	2.2
	Pennsylvania	253,000	25,365	10.0
	Philadelphia	36,452	7,435	20.0
1832	United States	3,813,405	301,358	7.9
	Pennsylvania	391,000	40,991	10.5
	Philadelphia	40,352	11,735	27.9
	Illinois	51,000	7,901	15.5

Sources: *Historical Statistics of the United States, Colonial Times to 1970* (Washington, D.C.: Government Printing Office, 1972), Series A119–134, A143–157; Philadelphia Sunday and Adult School Union, *Seventh Annual Report* (Philadelphia, 1824), pp. 68–72; American Sunday School Union, *First Annual Report* (Philadelphia, 1825), pp. 22–27, and *Eighth Annual Report* (1832), pp. 43–51.

delphia alone, where the First Day Society had operated at most three or four schools, there were 41 evangelical Sunday schools in 1818. When the American Sunday School Union was organized in 1824, it comprised 723 affiliated schools (others chose not to affiliate), including 68 in Philadelphia. By 1825 the union had affiliates in twenty-one states, two territories, and the District of Columbia; by 1832 it had expanded to all twenty-four states. The growth in enrollment was equally rapid. Whereas in Philadelphia the First Day Society had never registered more than 300 students in a given year, more than 7,400 students were enrolled in union schools there by 1825. That figure represented approximately 20 percent of the city's five-to-fourteen-year-old population. In Pennsylvania as a whole, about 10 percent of children in that age group were attending Sunday schools, compared to about 2.2 percent nationally. By 1832 the national figure had grown to nearly 8 percent, and even a relatively new state like Illinois could claim that more than 15 percent of its children were enrolled in Sunday schools (see table 1).[13]

As these contrasts demonstrate, evangelical schools were no mere variation on an eighteenth-century theme. They were very different institutions, with different origins, purposes, organization, and appeal. They grew rapidly, as their predecessors had not, largely because of specific conditions that had developed since the 1790s, notably the rise of Protestant activism during the Second Great Awakening. The years 1800 to 1830 saw the emergence of numerous Protestant voluntary associations, ranging from denominational missionary societies to interdenominational Bible and tract societies. Many of these organizations combined evangelizing efforts with charitable activities designed to meliorate the temporal condition of the poor and unfortunate. Urban missionary groups, for example, not only hired ministers to preach in poor neighborhoods but also provided clothing, fuel, food, and sometimes jobs to those in need. Tract and Bible distributors dispensed advice and aid along with spiritual information. Young seminary students spent their summers caring for the bodies as well as the souls of poor city-dwellers. Urban housewives formed societies to assist widows and orphans, and businessmen gave their time and money to charitable causes.[14]

These efforts familiarized Protestant activists with the conditions that prevailed in large urban centers and led them to experiment with a variety of palliatives. Mission chapels, asylums for the aged and orphaned, neighborhood prayer meetings, charity schools, urban revivals, missions for sailors and other groups, home visitation, and Sunday schools all found their way into the arsenal of weapons evangelical Protestants used to attack poverty and irreligion. By 1820 an intricate network of local groups was using these weapons, singly or in combination, to spread evangelical religion. Although in retrospect we can see the role each of these armaments played in the fray, it is important to stress the experimental character of the overall strategy. Early nineteenth-century evangelicals did not possess extraordinary vision or wisdom; they merely experimented with various solutions to the problems they saw and then focused their energies on those that seemed to work best. Although this process of experimentation can be shown by examples from any number of places, the experiences of one Philadelphia group have been particularly well documented.

The Evangelical Society was a group of Presbyterian laymen who began meeting around 1807 at the home of Archibald Alexander, pastor of the Third Presbyterian Church. Their stated purpose was to promote "the knowledge of and submission to the Gospel of Jesus Christ among the poor in this city and vicinity." Because of an incident in which a local artisan was accused of usurping ministerial authority through "irregular" preaching, the society's members avoided any work that might wound ministers' sensitivities. By 1808 they had settled upon a plan whereby "pious laymen might be advantageously occupied in giving religious instruction to the ignorant, without touching on the peculiar duties of the Pastoral office." The plan involved canvassing the city and suburbs for non-churchgoers and collecting "the children, and as many adults as could be persuaded to come, into little societies for instruction and for prayer."[15]

Two things made these "little societies" different from the First Day schools. To begin with, their purpose was specifically religious and evangelical; those who attended were instructed in the basic principles of evangelical Protestantism. In addition, the members did the recruiting and instructing themselves. In the words of Alexander Henry, a key organizer, "the members were not to attempt to do good merely by pecuniary contributions, but especially by personal exertions and labours. Every member of the Society was to be 'a working man.'" This emphasis on "personal exertions" heralded the new style of Protestantism that developed during the Awakening, one that stressed the need for converted individuals to work personally for the salvation of others.[16]

These little societies flourished and grew in different directions. Some became the bases for mission churches like the First African Presbyterian Church, which was erected with the Evangelical Society's aid. Others remained informal religious meetings at which Bible reading, hymn singing, catechetical instruction, and occasional preaching by ministers took place. Still others evolved into Sunday schools, the first of which dated from 1811. Its formation was sparked by the visit to Philadelphia that summer of the British Presbyterian missionary Robert May, who noted the similarities between the society's program and English Sunday schools. By October the society had built rooms to house not only the Sunday school but also a day school and occasional religious services. May himself directed the school for several months and members of the Evangelical Society taught its classes. The school soon settled into a regular routine, with prayers and hymns at the opening, followed by scripture reading, more prayers and hymns, and finally a brief sermon. By November the Sunday school had enrolled about 250 children, many of whose parents also attended. Although May left Philadelphia the following year, the Evangelical Society continued to operate the Sunday school, enrolling more than 1,800 students over a five-year period.[17] In this manner, the Sunday school found its way into the Evangelical Society's arsenal.

Other Philadelphians also included Sunday schools among their proselytizing experiments. By 1815 several evangelical Sunday schools had sprung up in the city. Each was run by a group of Protestants, drawing teachers either from one congregation or, as a "union" school, from several. Some of these societies also operated "adult schools," offering weekday-evening classes for working adults. By 1817, as the managers of the First Day Society struggled to keep their last school open, evangelical Sunday and adult schools were thriving under the guidance of about two dozen organizations. (Some, such as the Evangelical Society and the Union Society, a women's organization dating from 1804, operated both charity day schools and Sunday schools.) In May 1817, representatives of these groups met and formed the Philadelphia Sunday and Adult School Union "to cultivate unity and Christian charity" among the different denominations and to promote the establishment of more schools in the Philadelphia area. Together, the components of the Philadelphia Union operated forty-one schools, most of which were Sunday schools. Other groups that chose not to join the new union operated perhaps a dozen more schools.[18]

By 1820 the Sunday school had joined the prayer meeting, the mission chapel, and the urban missionary as a tool for combating urban problems. It became a key part of the evangelicals' expanding network of institutions and activities as city missionaries recruited scholars from among their clients, tract distributors urged parents to send their children, Bible society members promised Bibles to faithful attendees, and charity school teachers enrolled their pupils. The Protestant press played an important role in disseminating information about the schools to a recep-tive public. Religious periodicals such as the new *Religious Intelligencer* (begun in New Haven in 1817) and newspapers such as the *Boston Recorder* and *New York Observer* (both started by Sidney Morse, son of the minister-geographer-reformer Jedidiah Morse) carried frequent reports of the formation of Sunday schools and of their apparent success in "snatch[ing] from the paths of sin and wretchedness . . . thousands of ignorant beings" and guiding them to "the paths of virtue." Anniver-sary meetings held by Sunday school societies (whose proceedings were dutifully reported in the religious press), the publication of their annual reports, and word-of-mouth communication all furthered the popularity of the schools and stimulated their growth. By 1820 several magazines were devoted entirely to Sunday schools and the schools were receiving favorable attention in denominational newspapers and conferences. Although the Methodists were the earliest denomination offi-cially to urge the formation of such schools, the annual "reports on the state of religion" by local Presbyterian church organizations now spoke highly of the schools and encouraged lay people to establish more of them. Even the conservative, High Church Episcopal bishop of New York, John Henry Hobart, endorsed the formation of Episcopal Sunday schools in 1817. He cautioned, however, that they should be strictly denominational, stress "the peculiarities of our own Church," permit no input by any "foreign agency" (such as an interdenominational Sunday school union), and be under the sole superintendence of ministers.[19]

With such broad and varied support, the schools were likely to prosper. Their supporters, however, had different visions of this emerging institution. To some, such as Hobart, Sunday schools were useful primarily for denominational indoctri-nation; for others, their potential as tools of evangelization was paramount; still others saw them as purveyors of religious education in the broadest sense, produc-ing children who were both literate and religious. These varying visions stimulated the growth of the schools by enabling disparate groups to unite in their support.

A second condition that fostered the schools' growth was the changing sta-tus of children in the nineteenth century. A new approach to child psychology, combined with the growth of all types of schooling, convinced adults that children had vast untapped potential. No longer were they considered capable merely of receiving religious information; they were candidates for evangelization, perhaps even conversion. The experiences of one group of Philadelphians who switched from teaching adults to teaching children offer insights into the new focus on children.

The Male Adult Association was one of many interdenominational groups of evangelical lay people that emerged in cities like Philadelphia in the 1810s. Formed in 1815 "to teach Adult Males to read [in order] to excite them to the study of the holy Scriptures," the association also promised to teach writing and arithmetic once its original goal was achieved. Beginning in June 1816, groups of association members taught school in rotation Tuesday and Friday evenings, dividing their students (who were primarily "mechanics") into classes according to their ability to read. Once students learned basic reading from the Bible, they moved into classes where they studied and memorized the New Testament. In 1817 the members of the Male Adult Association participated enthusiastically in the formation of Philadelphia's Sunday and Adult School Union, declaring that it proved how quickly denominational barriers fell when different denominations united "for the same great object," namely, bringing religious knowledge to the ignorant. Soon after joining the new union, however, the association's members found attendance at their classes at such a low ebb that they questioned the efficacy of adult schools and began organizing Sunday schools for children, as well as any adults who wished to attend. "When the charm of novelty was gone," recalled one member, the adults "withdrew [from the school] and abandon[ed] themselves to their wonted vices." By October 1817, six months after the formation of the Sunday and Adult School Union, the Male Adult Association had decided that the "time and talents of the members could be better employed in the instruction of children" than of adults. The members then renamed their group the Auxiliary Evangelical Society (in homage to the Evangelical Society's pioneering efforts) and began sponsoring Sunday schools.[20]

The association's belief that in shifting its focus from adults to children it was moving from a "limited" to a "wide extended sphere of influence" echoed the views of other Sunday school organizers. Children, they believed, were easier to reach with the message of evangelical Christianity and offered greater chances for success. For children were, as emerging theories of child psychology posited, "pliable . . . tender, and capable of impressions." Hence, teaching children the basic doctrines of evangelical Protestantism could not help but "have a great influence in moralizing and improving their character." Furthermore, the "impressions" received in childhood could "never be entirely eradicated"; if children learned the doctrines of original sin, human depravity, inability, and the need for regeneration, they would find it difficult in later life "to stifle their consciences, throw off restraint, and pursue the ways of vanity and vice." Those who worked to evangelize adults had a much harder field to plow because adults had lifetimes of bad habits and evil ways to overcome, whereas children, still in a stage where habits were being formed, could be cultivated easily. Most important, Sunday school organizers argued that it was possible for children to experience conversion. Using examples from local school reports, they noted that children as young as seven or eight had given evidence of experiencing the change of heart associated with conversion, and some had applied for full communion in churches. Consequently, Sunday school workers argued that it made more sense to proselytize children than adults. Finally, they noted that children could be the means whereby irreligious parents were led to church. Indeed, a common theme in Sunday school reports was the story of the wicked parent (usually a father) who, as a result of his child's conversion, "forsook his vicious practices, engaged in a lucrative employment, and soon raised his family from the most abject poverty to a state of ease and respectability."[21]

The spread of these new assumptions about children paralleled the emergence of a third condition that encouraged the schools' growth: the inclusion of pupils from church-going families. During the 1820s children of Protestant, church-going families began to attend Sunday school in increasing numbers. For example, members of New York's Brick Presbyterian Church, who had formed two Sunday schools for missionary purposes in 1816, noted in 1832 that their pupils "were no longer drawn exclusively from the poor and unchurched families, but included the children of Presbyterian parents." Likewise, members of Boston's Park Street (Congregational) Church, who in 1817 had described the schools as "*missionary institutions*" for the poor, in 1829 organized a school for church members' children. In Richmond, Virginia, the Monumental (Episcopal) Church reported in 1829 that its Sunday school was "no longer confined to the poorer classes of society" but included church members' children. Other Episcopal churches expanded in similar ways. In 1830 the superintendent of St. Paul's Church Sunday school in Boston referred to it as "a parochial Sunday school" and claimed that virtually all the children of the parish, regardless of "the accidental distinctions of society," attended the school. The superintendent of Christ Church Sunday school in Philadelphia made the point explicit when he suggested in 1831: "It is indeed the glory of the Sunday School to know no distinction arising from external condition, for there, as in the sanctuary, 'the rich and the poor' meet together."[22]

Whether the rich and the poor met together in Sunday schools is questionable, but this theme became a popular refrain in Sunday school writing during the 1820s, as middle-class students entered the schools in increasing numbers. Several factors seem to have contributed to this trend. For children who attended weekly catechetical meetings, it was but a short step to attend classes on Sundays run by lay people, particularly when some ministers recommended the schools as "among the most valuable means of religious instruction." More often, parents committed their children to the schools out of a belief in their utility. Maternal associations were especially important in this regard. Begun in the 1810s by young mothers anxious to transmit their religious ideals to their children, maternal associations became very popular in the 1820s as mothers met to pray and discuss mothering techniques. When the associations recommended Sunday schools as useful adjuncts to parental religious instruction, their members took up the cause, offering themselves as teachers and enrolling their children. For other parents, the schools' curriculum was the determining factor in their decision to send their children. One speaker at a Sunday school meeting noted that Christian parents, although anxious on Sunday "to restrain and prohibit the ordinary employments and amusements of the week," neglected to "provide in their stead something that might give a profitable direction" to children's leisure activities. "Instead of being doomed to spend the day in comparative idleness," he concluded, "or to attend in the sanctuary, and hear discourses . . . not intended for them," children could spend Sunday learning Scripture "pleasantly and profitably."[23]

As these comments suggest, Sunday school workers themselves advocated broadening the schools' class base, often to skeptical audiences. In doing so, they appealed both to the new psychology of childhood and to republican ideals. They argued that it was important to "take advantage of [children's] susceptibility" to early impressions "and imbue them with the principles of religion, that the bias of their expanding minds may be brought to the side of truth!" All children, regardless of class background, "possess the same sinful nature, are exposed to the same wrath, and need the same pardoning mercy"; hence, all should have the benefits of Sunday school attendance. Having shown that children could be converted, the schools could become the locus for that experience. Furthermore, Sunday school workers suggested that "the impressive charm of novelty" made the schools especially appealing to children, as did the offer of "numerous inducements to learn and understand the scriptures," inducements such as rewards, competition for achievement, and emulation of teachers. Careful not to tread on parents' sensitivities, they depicted the schools as extensions of family religious instruction, not substitutes for it, and pressed churchgoing parents to "let others participate in [their] instructions" by teaching Sunday school themselves.[24]

Using republicanism as a touchstone, those who sought to broaden the schools' social representation argued that class-based institutions did not succeed in American society. Because of "the spirit of our *republican* institutions," suggested one writer, the American poor are independent of mind and unwilling to defer to the judgment of their "betters." Thus, attempts by middle- and upper-class people to teach religion and morality to the poor in Sunday schools frequently met with resistance or hostility. The poor, suggested another writer, "are stubborn and apt to think themselves as good as" anyone else; they would not send their children to Sunday schools if they were only for the poor. "Rich parents" had an obligation to "set a good example to the poor" by sending their own children. For if "the better classes" attended, "it would encourage the poor" and overcome their objections. This, in turn, would cultivate "republican sentiment . . . in the bosoms of the rich and poor" alike, helping minimize class distinctions.[25]

Some Sunday school promoters backed up their arguments with symbolic gestures intended to encourage middle-class attendance. The secretary of St. Andrew's (Episcopal) Sunday school in Philadelphia recorded such a gesture by the minister: "The Rev. Mr. Bedell this morning brought his son to be entered as a scholar. May the example lead others, who have heretofore felt themselves above sending their children to the Sunday-school to go and do likewise." Reports of a similar act by Lyman Beecher became commonplace in later Sunday school histories. As a result, American Sunday schools acquired a more varied clientele than British ones, which remained bastions of working-class culture for decades.[26]

Rhetorical and symbolic persuasions aside, the entry of churchgoing youngsters does not seem to have encouraged much social mixing. Instead, the schools gradually became divided into two categories: mission schools for the children of non-churchgoers (Catholics, immigrants, the unchurched poor) and church schools attached to individual congregations. To be sure, this division was partly caused by residential segregation in larger cities, where the churches tended to be located in populous downtown areas, while poorer residents lived in outlying regions. But even small towns witnessed the effects of class consciousness. Visiting a village in New York state in 1830, a missionary found that "they had a Sunday-school which met at the church, but the poor children would not attend," so he formed one for them in a joiner's shop. Rich and poor may have attended Sunday school by 1830, but it was not always the same school. Indeed, there was concern in some quarters that the entry of churchgoing children was diverting attention from the schools' original objectives. One member of the Providence, Rhode Island, Sunday School Teachers' Association argued that poor children were being "neglected" because of the rise of church-related schools. A similar comment came from the managers of a Boston organization, who noted that those who needed the schools most were the first to leave.[27]

The addition of such children went a long way toward establishing the permanency of the evangelical Sunday school. As long as the schools were primarily for the urban poor, organizers faced recurring problems with enrollments and staffing. To find pupils, they repeatedly had to canvass neighborhoods, visit families, and cajole, urge, or threaten parents to let their children attend. Teachers had to be willing to perform these tasks, while also planning and conducting weekly classes. Although a spirit of interdenominational cooperation at first propelled individuals into Sunday school teaching, it was always easier to recruit new teachers from one congregation to teach a school attached, however unofficially, to that congregation. When most of the students were children of churchgoers, it became easier to guarantee their weekly presence and to train new teachers from among their ranks.

he consolidation of free urban schooling during the 1820s and 1830s con-
tributed significantly to the growth of evangelical Sunday schools. During those
decades, educational leaders in cities like New York and Philadelphia garnered a
large percentage of public education funds and expanded the role of free schools in
educating urban children. In New York, for example, the leaders of the Free School
Society, a confederation of charity schools, called in 1825 for the admission of all
children, rich and poor, succeeded in cutting off municipal subsidies to their denominational competitors, and renamed their group the Public School Society. From
then on, most city funds for education went to the Public School Society. In Philadelphia, a state law of 1818 providing funds for monitorial schools to educate
children of indigent parents (many of whom were excluded from the city's denominational, pay, and charity schools) came under attack for "drawing an invid-
ious distinction between the wealthy and the poor." In 1827 a Society for the
Promotion of Public Schools, formed by a group of men long active in the city's
philanthropic societies, began lobbying for the establishment of a school *system* to
replace the existing maze of schooling opportunities. Charity schools and publicly
supported free schools, they argued, did not do a proper job because attendance was
not compulsory and because the poor would not send their children for fear of being
branded paupers. By 1837 Philadelphia's Controllers of the Public Schools could
report that as a result of an 1836 law, "the stigma of poverty" had been removed
from their institutions; they were now open to all children. This process of consolidation went on throughout much of the Northeast in the 1820s and 1830s. As Carl
Kaestle has pointed out, the proportion of children attending school remained
relatively stable at about 50 to 60 percent from 1800 to 1850, but the proportion
attending public rather than private schools rose dramatically. In New York, for
example, the proportion of school-attending children in public schools jumped from
38 percent between 1800 and 1825 to 82 percent between 1825 and 1850.[28]

As a result of this consolidation, the mission of urban Sunday schools changed
considerably. Whereas school advocates in the 1790s had stressed the need to
educate the poor at public expense, evangelical Sunday school promoters and common-school workers shared a republican belief that all children, regardless of background, should attend their institutions. Thus, the expansion of public schooling to
include all children paralleled and reinforced the same process in Sunday schools.
Had the latter continued to emphasize literacy training, common schools would
eventually have replaced them. But evangelicals had evolved a new definition of
their schools' purpose, a definition that made the Sunday school not a competitor
but a necessary adjunct to weekday schools. Indeed, many Sunday school workers
actively campaigned for public support of common schools, in order to relieve them

of the burden of teaching reading and enable them to concentrate on religious subjects. The New-York Sunday-School Union Society declined to teach writing and arithmetic in its schools, asserting that these subjects were "more a secular concern" and should be taught during the week. Once the new definition of Sunday schools took hold, the same child could attend both a public school and a Sunday school. As early as 1827, for example, more than 60 percent of the children in the New York Public School Society's schools also attended a Sunday school.[29]

This complementary relationship between Sunday schools and free public schools continued during the 1830s and 1840s, when universal tax-supported public education began to spread throughout the northern states. The Sunday schools provided a specifically evangelical religious education, but this is not to say that pupils in free schools and later in public schools received a purely secular education. They did not. Throughout the nineteenth century the curricula of publicly supported schools were heavily infused with Protestant precepts and assumptions, yet these represented a kind of lowest-common-denominator Protestantism, acceptable, for example, to both Unitarians and Baptists. Collected under the term "moral education," these precepts became a standard part of the school curriculum. It was precisely because public schools taught only this basic moral code that Sunday school workers deemed their schools necessary.[30]

On another level, Sunday schools complemented public schools by providing basic instruction to pupils who, for one reason or another, did not attend weekday schools. In Boston, for example, the Society for the Moral and Religious Instruction of the Poor, which had begun sponsoring Sunday schools in 1816, lobbied for public primary schools to teach children to read so that they could enter the city's grammar schools. Once they had accomplished this goal, they found a continuing demand for Sunday schools to teach reading to children who were too old to attend primary schools. (In 1820 the managers changed the society's name to the Society for the Religious and Moral Instruction of the Poor, to indicate their reordering of priorities.) The teaching of basic literacy remained an important function of Sunday schools throughout the nineteenth century, where other opportunities were absent.[31]

By 1830 the Sunday school was well on its way to becoming a permanent fixture in American life. Although one experiment with schools on Sundays had failed, a second had proven a resounding success, largely because it combined several factors necessary for launching a new institution at a time when Americans were increasingly committed to institution building as a means of handling a variety of social tasks. First of all, the evangelical schools had a dedicated corps of young workers, new converts whose personal involvement in the cause helped insure its success. Second, as institutions for children, they had a potentially large clientele, ranging from the poor, unchurched children whom they enrolled at first to the middle-class, churchgoing youngsters who joined later. By encouraging youngsters from all social classes to attend, Sunday school workers helped transform the schools from a temporary expedient for teaching the poor reading and religion to a permanent means of religious training for all Protestant children. Finally, because they focused on religious education, Sunday schools developed in tandem with weekday schools—both private and public—serving the same students instead of competing for them. The convergence of all these factors in the 1820s guaranteed the institution's growth and permanence.

Chapter Two

SUNDAY SCHOOLS
& AMERICAN EDUCATION

Sunday schools and common schools complemented each other in the nineteenth century, but their functions often overlapped. Although primarily religious institutions, Sunday schools provided some Americans, particularly those excluded from common schools, with opportunities to achieve literacy. They were more important, however, as sources of Protestant values and ideals to children who received training in the fundamentals of literacy elsewhere. Unlike British Sunday schools, which were responsible for the basic education of many working-class children, American Sunday schools divested themselves of that responsibility as much as possible by cultivating their early partnership with common schools. This relationship had its share of difficulties, especially when the partners disagreed over what the "moral education" taught in common schools should encompass. Still, few Protestant Americans ever seriously considered any alternative ideas (denominational schools, for example) for the religious education of their children.[1]

As sources of basic literacy, Sunday schools were especially important to individuals and groups excluded from public or tax-supported schools in the early nineteenth century. In Boston during the 1820s, for example, children who were required to be able to read before attending city schools turned to Sunday schools for training, as did those deemed too old for public schools. In New York in 1817, the Sunday-School Union Society distributed handbills advertising "education free of expense" and promised that "those boys and girls able to read the Testament, who *attend regularly and behave well,* may be recommended for further instruction, to the Trustees of the Free-School." In such cases, Sunday school instruction was a stepping-stone to more advanced schooling.

For girls, who were often discouraged from attending or denied admission to publicly funded schools in the 1810s and 1820s, Sunday schools provided a chance to learn reading and writing. Six out of seven city schools in Boston in the 1819–1820 school year, for example, had large majorities of male pupils. By contrast, girls generally outnumbered boys as Sunday scholars in evangelical schools. (This had not been true in earlier Sunday schools: between 1797 and 1800, girls had constituted only about 42 percent of the pupils of Philadelphia's First Day schools.) Sunday schools also attracted a contingent of adults eager to learn to read, a majority of whom were women.[2]

But it was among blacks, both adults and children, that the schools found their most eager clients. Excluded from most sources of free schooling, blacks responded so quickly to the formation of Sunday schools that in New York, for example, they constituted 25 percent of the pupils in the Sunday-School Union Society's schools by 1817. In some cities, such as Utica, New York, it was the plight of free blacks that initially led whites to form the schools. Throughout the South, as well, reports from cities like Charleston, Nashville, and St. Louis frequently mentioned schools that included blacks, usually in separate classes and at different hours from whites.

Adult blacks in particular sought out Sunday schooling opportunities and exhibited a "disposition for receiving instruction and an intenseness of application" that often astonished whites. In 1819 about two-thirds of the almost eleven hundred adults in Philadelphia Sunday and Adult School Union schools were black; within the affiliated Union Adult Society, which supported four schools, 57 percent were black (see table 2). Here, too, women outnumbered men. In New York's two evangelical Sunday school unions, nearly half of the 1,372 black students in 1821 were adults; of these, almost 70 percent were women. In Philadelphia's Northern Liberties district, a Sunday school begun in 1815 for black adults reported in 1818 that its students were mostly women, ranging in age from forty to ninety.[3]

Among other groups, it was not exclusion from formal schooling that prompted an interest in Sunday schools, but rather the lack of alternatives. In many factory towns, Sunday schools offered a curriculum that was primarily religious in content but included instruction in the fundamentals of reading and writing (see figure 1). At the Brandywine Manufacturers' Sunday School in Delaware, for example, children of du Pont company employees and nearby farmers could start in the alphabet class, proceed through the one- and two-syllable word classes, and finish their educations with Bible reading and lessons in the catechism of their choice. Children who already knew how to read were placed in the appropriate class. From approximately 1816 until 1856, this Sunday school taught reading, writing, and spelling, as well as religion, to an average of 150 to 230 students, and received a share of the state's school fund to help pay expenses. The story was similar in other factory

Table 2

Adult Sunday Scholars in New York and Philadelphia, by Race, 1818–1821

Year	Organization	Black adults	White adults	Total (N)	Blacks as percentage of N
1818	Philadelphia Sunday and Adult School Union	155	157	312	49.6
1819	Philadelphia Sunday and Adult School Union	716	377	1,093	65.5
1819	Union Adult Society (Philadelphia)	258	191	449	57.6
1821	Female Union Society for the Promotion of Sabbath Schools (New York)	447	22	469	95.5
1821	New-York Sunday-School Union Society (male)	216	2	218	98.6

Sources: Philadelphia Sunday and Adult School Union, *First Annual Report* (Philadelphia, 1818), p. 9, and *Second Annual Report* (1819), pp. 4, 29–31; *Sunday-School Facts, Collected by a Member of the General Association of Teachers* (New York: D. H. Wickham, 1821), pp. 10–11.

locales and in newly settled areas where public schooling was not readily available, or where working children could not attend weekday schools.

For all these groups—girls, adults, blacks, factory children, frontier residents—Sunday schools assumed special importance in the absence of publicly funded or weekday schooling opportunities. With the spread of tax-supported public schools during the 1820s and 1830s, particularly in the North, Sunday schools eventually relinquished their function as purveyors of basic literacy. Far from decrying this shift, Sunday school workers heralded it, arguing that it enabled their institutions to concentrate on religious subjects. By the late 1830s the various Sunday school unions had virtually ceased discussing the teaching of reading in their annual reports. A seven-page questionnaire that the American Sunday School Union sent to its affiliated schools in 1832 requested information on their pedagogical content and techniques, but touched only perfunctorily on the issue of literacy training. Two questions out of seventy-eight dealt with reading; of these, one asked whether teachers saw to it that children who could not read were placed "in public school or otherwise instructed." In compiling the questionnaire, the union's managers clearly assumed that most Sunday scholars learned to read elsewhere. Ten years later, the corresponding secretary disclaimed "every thing of a mere secular character" for union schools, explaining: "If we find a child who does not know how to read, we ascertain what means of instruction are within his reach, and endeavour to per-

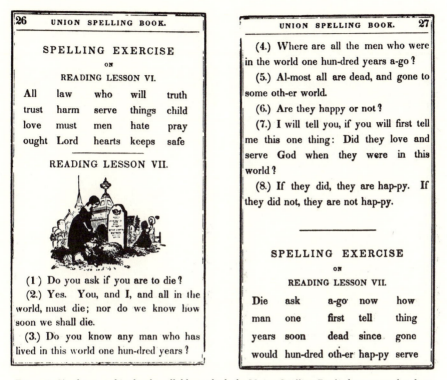

26   UNION SPELLING BOOK.

SPELLING EXERCISE
ON
READING LESSON VI.

All	law	who	will	truth
trust	harm	serve	things	child
love	must	men	hate	pray
ought	Lord	hearts	keeps	safe

READING LESSON VII.

(1) Do you ask if you are to die?

(2.) Yes. You, and I, and all in the world, must die; nor do we know how soon we shall die.

(3.) Do you know any man who has lived in this world one hun-dred years?

UNION SPELLING BOOK.   27

(4.) Where are all the men who were in the world one hun-dred years a-go?

(5.) Al-most all are dead, and gone to some oth-er world.

(6.) Are they happy or not?

(7.) I will tell you, if you will first tell me this one thing: Did they love and serve God when they were in this world?

(8.) If they did, they are hap-py. If they did not, they are not hap-py.

SPELLING EXERCISE
ON
READING LESSON VII.

Die	ask	a-go	now	how
man	one	first	tell	thing
years	soon	dead	since	gone
would	hun-dred	oth-er	hap-py	serve

Figure 1. Teaching reading by the syllable method, the Union Spelling Book *also imparted a clear religious message*

suade him or his parents to avail themselves of such means." Failing this, "we will . . . draw him into the Sunday-school, and there teach him to read and understand the Scriptures." Thus, although many rural and frontier schools continued to teach reading—and even writing and spelling—after the 1830s, these were seen as incidental, not essential, aspects of their mission.[4]

The most immediate impact of this diminished focus on literacy training was felt by adult Sunday schools. As early as 1824, Philadelphia's Union Adult Society—which taught adults of both races, but especially blacks, basic reading skills—abolished two of its four schools for want of funds and teachers. By 1830 the society had disappeared from Sunday school reports entirely. Despite the continued need for adult literacy training, in 1860 only one of Philadelphia's 124 non-church-affiliated schools—the Bethany Colored Mission—was teaching reading to adults. A similar trend was evident in New York, where by 1831 the Sunday School Union had simply stopped counting the number of adults in its schools. Because so many of the union's black students had been adults, their withdrawal contributed heavily to the overall shrinkage of black enrollments in the 1830s and 1840s (see table 3). As

Table 3

Adult and Child Sunday Scholars in New York, by Race, 1821–1847

Year	Organization	White scholars	Black scholars	Total (N)	Blacks as percentage of N
1821	Female Union Society for the Promotion of Sabbath Schools	2,021	764	5,579	24.6
1821	New-York Sunday-School Union Society (male)	2,186	608		
1831	New-York Sunday School Union (male and female)	9,937	1,336	11,273	11.8
1834	New-York Sunday School Union	11,696	1,355	13,051	10.3
1847	New-York Sunday School Union	15,414	938	16,352	5.7

Sources: *Sunday-School Facts, Collected by a Member of the General Association of Teachers* (New York: D. H. Wickham, 1821), pp. 10–11; New-York Sunday School Union, *Fifteenth Annual Report* (New York, 1831), appendix; *Eighteenth Annual Report* (1834), appendix; *Thirty-First Annual Report* (1847), appendix.

Note: The Sunday-School Union Society was all-male in 1821; later membership figures include both males and females.

Sunday schools increasingly emphasized religion and focused teachers' energies on children, illiterate adults—both black and white—no longer felt at home in them. To be sure, other groups took up the flagging cause of adult literacy by sponsoring evening classes or informal tutoring, but such efforts were no longer pursued through Sunday schools. And although church-related Sunday schools of some denominations—especially Baptists—continued to encourage adult attendance (as they still do), it was for prayer and Bible lessons, not for basic reading.[5]

Black children, too, were hard hit by the diminished emphasis on reading and writing in the 1820s and 1830s. Racial prejudice, combined with the repercussions from Nat Turner's 1831 slave revolt in Virginia, took a further toll on black Sunday scholars' aspirations. When white parents in Baltimore objected to the presence of black children in one of the Asbury [Methodist] Sunday School Society's schools, (even though they were restricted to separate classes), the blacks were dismissed. After forming schools strictly for black children, the Asbury Society found them difficult to sustain because of "the want of effective teachers willing to labour in them." White Sunday schools in Washington, D.C., turned black children out

Table 4

Racial Makeup of New York Sunday Schools, 1821–1847

Year	Organization	Schools reporting both black and white scholars	Percentage of all schools	Schools reporting whites only	Schools reporting blacks only
1821	Female Union Society for the Promotion of Sabbath Schools	24	70.5 ⎫	9	1
1821	New-York Sunday-School Union Society (male)	20	54.0 ⎬ 61.1	15	3
1831	New-York Sunday School Union (male and female)	32	55.1	22	4
1834	New-York Sunday School Union	37	55.2	26	4
1847	New-York Sunday School Union	39	35.7	63	7

Sources: See table 3.

after the Turner revolt. Black students in New York, who had constituted almost 25 percent of union Sunday scholars in 1821, made up only 11.8 percent of the total in 1831 and 5.7 percent in 1847. During the same period, the proportion of schools that reported having both white and black students dropped from 61.1 percent in 1821 to 35.7 percent in 1847 (see tables 3 and 4).[6] As noted above, much of this slippage can be attributed to the withdrawal of black adults from the schools.

Diminishing white interest, however, did not bring about the disappearance of black schools; some of the slack was taken up by black-run schools. Black Washingtonians organized their own schools when their children were expelled from white Sunday schools. According to one historian, these schools allowed "the great mass of the free people of color [to learn] about all the school knowledge that was allowed them in those days." After the members of Baltimore's African Methodist Episcopal Church took over the job of running black Sunday schools from the Asbury Sunday School Society in 1824, they experienced few of the difficulties the Asbury society had complained of; indeed, the schools reportedly flourished and had plenty of teachers. In Elizabeth, New Jersey, where the First Presbyterian Church Sunday School Teachers' Association had operated a "colored school" for years, the formation of an African church in 1838 led to a wholesale withdrawal of black students from the Presbyterian Sunday schools. There is no way to know how many black children in other cities may have acquired basic literacy at Sunday schools in black churches. Because black-run schools were seldom affiliated with the national (white) Sunday school organizations, their work was not reported; it was not until the establishment of regular reporting procedures by black denominations after the Civil War that any remotely reliable statistics were collected.[7]

Most black Sunday scholars were free persons, of course, but slaves attended some Sunday schools during the 1820s, especially in cities. Nevertheless, their presence was controversial, especially after Turner's rebellion. The Baptist missionary John Mason Peck, after visiting a school in St. Charles, Missouri, noted in his journal for 1825: "I am happy to find among the slaveholders in Missouri a growing disposition to have the blacks educated, and to patronize Sunday-schools for the purpose." Despite such examples, masters often strongly opposed schooling for slaves. Peck later recalled incidents where slaves were forbidden to attend Sunday school when the extent of their learning became clear. After 1831, as many Southern states established prohibitions on teaching slaves to read and enacted statutory limitations on the liberty of free blacks, black attendance at white Sunday schools became virtually impossible. At the same time, the rise of militant abolitionism in the North made Southern whites wary of Sunday schools, which they associated with Northern schemes to reform the South and its institutions.

Because the most threatening aspect of the schools was their potential to make slaves literate, white Sunday schools for slaves provided exclusively oral instruction after 1831. Charles Colcock Jones, the Presbyterian minister who made a career of preaching to masters on the duty of religiously instructing their slaves, suggested that Sunday schools supervised by ministers be established on plantations to supplement the schools connected with white churches. "The most honest, faithful and well behaved servants," argued the Baptist writer E. T. Winkler, "are those who have the greatest amount of religious intelligence," though that "intelligence" should be communicated only orally. Similarly, the Alabama Baptist Convention approved an instruction book "designed for the use of families, Sabbath Schools, and Bible classes, and especially for the oral instruction of the colored population." Not surprisingly, such books emphasized certain aspects of Christianity, reminding slaves of their duty to be submissive and loyal. Still, many whites remained suspicious of anything resembling a "school" for blacks. A white woman who established a Sunday school on her Louisiana plantation in the 1840s found that although it "was always well attended" by slave children, teaching a Sunday school "was at that time not a very popular thing to do." She persisted, however. "I could afford to do so," she explained, "as I had influential friends to defend my course." On occasion, there were reports of schools where slaves learned to read. Writing in 1856 for a Northern audience, a Southern correspondent for the (Old School) Presbyterian New York *Observer* reported that his unnamed city contained eight Sunday schools for blacks, each of which had slave members. "*In all of these schools,*" he contended, "*the scholars are taught to read.*" If true, this report suggests that at least a few slaves had access to literacy through Sunday schools.[8]

Despite the efforts of whites to limit their knowledge, slaves occasionally formed Sunday schools for their own benefit, just as they sponsored their own preachers, expressed their theological understanding in spirituals, and held clandestine church services. Frederick Douglass, for example, helped teach a Sunday school in Baltimore "at the house of a free colored man named James Mitchell." It was eventually broken up by angry whites who accused Douglass of wanting "to be another Nat Turner." The revolutionary potential of black literacy was not lost on Douglass. Later, while serving on a rural Maryland plantation, he started his own school, where he taught "twenty or thirty young men" to read the Bible. Douglass derived all the more satisfaction from these activities because he understood the importance of literacy as a weapon against white control.[9]

When the end of slavery brought an overwhelming demand for education from the newly freed people, blacks and their white allies turned once again to Sunday schools for basic instruction. Missionaries of the (Congregational) American Missionary Association, the Methodist Freedman's Aid Society, the American Sunday School Union, and various home mission societies started both day and Sunday schools wherever they could, reporting back to their superiors on the extraordinary eagerness of blacks—adults as well as children—to learn to read the Bible. "*They ask us to give them instruction,*" wrote a Sunday school missionary from North Carolina in 1865, "and manifest great anxiety to learn." To many whites, the schools were not merely a means of teaching reading; they were also a way "to elevate the moral character of the freedmen" and "restore quiet to the people." At least one missionary claimed that it was possible to recruit Sunday school teachers among Southern whites who refused to teach in regular black schools. "The aversion to negro equality is so strong," he explained, that "no [white] person could be found here to teach a school where blacks were allowed to attend[.] Yet these very same people feel it no disgrace to teach them in the Sabbath School." As under slavery, some whites may have hoped to use the schools to teach the freed people a submissive version of Christianity. Blacks themselves, however, asserted their desire to run their own schools, and by 1870 most Southern black Sunday schools were probably in black hands. Despite white complaints that black schools were unsophisticated, poorly run, and too much given to singing rather than studying, blacks persevered in establishing schools. In 1882 members of the African Methodist Episcopal Church formed a Sunday School Union, which was adopted two years later as a permanent institution by the church's General Conference. By 1884 the church estimated that its Sunday schools enrolled 178,000 scholars—about one-quarter of the denomination's children. Many of them used spelling books as well as religious literature.[10]

There is little question, then, that Sunday schools ought to be included in any assessment of educational resources in the nineteenth century. Still, the schools' contribution to the rise in American literacy in the nineteenth century should not be exaggerated. It was made in conjunction with, not in place of, other free schooling opportunities. It is clear, for example, that Sunday schools flourished in precisely the same locales where common schools were prevalent. Especially numerous in East Coast cities during the 1810s and 1820s, they spread in the ensuing decades to new population centers in the Midwest as well as to rural areas of the Northeast and Midwest. A survey by the American Sunday School Union in 1832 estimated that more than half of its 8,268 affiliated schools were in six states: Massachusetts, Connecticut, Rhode Island, New York, New Jersey, and Pennsylvania (see table 5).

A very different pattern emerged in the Deep South slave states, where the union counted 499 schools (approximately 6 percent of the total). Thus, while Illinois, for example, had one Sunday school for every 750 whites, Georgia had one for every 5,000 whites. These figures are, of course, very approximate and underestimate somewhat the number of schools, since not all were auxiliaries of the American Sunday School Union, but they do help pinpoint the geographical distribution of the schools.

Regional differences in school formation persisted throughout the antebellum years. In the South, several factors—the sparseness of population in rural areas, a tradition of private schooling in cities and towns, and a slavery-bred wariness of things Northern—hampered the success of both public and Sunday schools. Moreover, the lower rate of literacy among Southern whites limited the number of potential teachers. By 1875, however, when the International Sunday School Convention collected reliable statistics on all Protestant schools, this regional imbalance had virtually disappeared. Although midwestern states continued to have a better school/population ratio than the southern states, the growth of church schools in the South, combined with heavy non-Protestant immigration to other regions, had largely erased the disparity (see table 6).[11]

In the Northeast and Midwest, common and Sunday schools were often founded by the same individuals. Several missionaries and agents of the American Sunday School Union, for example, were active in creating or promoting tax-supported state school systems. The Presbyterian minister Robert Baird helped promote tax-supported schools as an agent of the New Jersey Missionary Society before joining the union as its general agent from 1829 to 1834. In Illinois, the Baptist minister John Mason Peck—who toured that state and Missouri in the 1820s as an agent for several Eastern denominational and benevolent societies, including the American Sunday School Union—expended his considerable energies in behalf of Bible societies, Sunday schools and tax-supported public schools. And John McCullagh, the Scotch-born Presbyterian missionary who served the union for more than three decades, was common-school commissioner of Henderson County, Kentucky, for twenty-two years. Even more important were the common-school teachers who did double duty in the Sunday school. As early as 1830, the American Sunday School Union published an appeal to educated Christians, particularly "pious females in single life," to move to the Midwest in order to teach both weekday and Sunday schools. Asa Bullard, who toured Maine in the early 1830s as an agent of the Massachusetts Sabbath School Society, recalled attempts to hire female district

Table 5
Geographical Distribution of Schools Affiliated with the American
Sunday School Union, 1832

Regions and states	Number of schools	White population in 1830	White population: school ratio
New England:			
Maine	249	398,000	1,598
New Hampshire	374	269,000	719
Vermont	427	280,000	655
Massachusetts	578	603,000	1,043
Connecticut	237	290,000	1,223
Rhode Island	118	94,000	794
Mid-Atlantic:			
New York	2,708	1,868,000	690
New Jersey	441	300,000	680
Pennsylvania	679	1,310,000	1,929
Midwest:			
Ohio	669	928,000	1,387
Illinois	207	155,000	750
Indiana	276	338,000	1,224
Michigan	41	31,000	756
Border states:			
Delaware	38	58,000	1,526
Maryland	243	291,000	1,197
Kentucky	200	519,000	2,595
Tennessee	224	536,000	2,392
Missouri	58	115,000	1,983
South:			
North Carolina	90	473,000	5,256
South Carolina	30	258,000	8,600
Virginia	157	701,000	4,465
Georgia	59	297,000	5,030
Louisiana	12	89,000	7,417
Mississippi	41	70,000	1,707
Alabama	76	190,000	2,500
Florida	2	18,000	9,000
Arkansas	3	26,000	8,667
Washington, D.C.	29	21,000	724
Total schools:	8,268		

Sources: *Historical Statistics of the United States, Colonial Times to 1970* (Washington, D.C.: Government Printing Office, 1972), Series A 195–209; American Sunday School Union, *Eighth Annual Report* (Philadelphia, 1832), pp. 43–55.

Table 6
Sunday School Statistics Collected by the National Convention, 1875

Regions and states	Number of schools	White and black population in 1875	Population: school ratio
New England:			
Connecticut	944	537,417	569
Maine	1,000	628,719	629
Massachusetts	1,738[b]	1,457,351	839
New Hampshire	703[b]	317,710	452
Rhode Island	401[a]	217,356	542
Vermont	708	330,582	467
Mid-Atlantic:			
New Jersey	1,714	903,044	527
New York	6,000	4,382,759	730
Pennsylvania	7,660[b]	3,502,311	457
Midwest:			
Illinois	5,968	2,141,510	359
Indiana	3,161	1,655,675	524
Iowa	2,659[b]	1,026,750	386
Kansas	908[b]	379,497	418
Michigan	1,998[a]	749,113	375
Minnesota	805[b]	500,000	621
Nebraska	729	222,392	305
Ohio	5,545	2,665,260	481
Wisconsin	2,454[b]	1,055,501	430
Border states:			
Delaware	200[a]	125,015	625
Kentucky	2,376[b]	1,320,407	556
Maryland	1,656	790,095	477
Missouri	2,834[b]	1,182,612	417
Tennessee	2,451[b]	1,225,937	500
West Virginia	1,021[b]	441,094	432
South:			
Alabama	1,000	1,002,000	1,002
Arkansas	505[a]	473,174	937
Florida	247[a]	189,995	769
Georgia	2,323[b]	1,174,832	506
Louisiana	1,377[a]	743,420	533
Mississippi	1,583[a]	791,305	500

(continued)

Table 6   (Continued)

Regions and states	Number of schools	White and black population in 1875	Population: school ratio
North Carolina	1,985[a]	992,622	500
South Carolina	1,412[a]	705,789	500
Texas	320[a]	800,000	2,500
Virginia	2,423[a]	1,211,442	500
West:			
California	633[b]	549,808	869
Nevada	67[a]	42,456	634

Source: *First International (Sixth National) Sunday-School Convention, Baltimore, May 11–13, 1875* (Newark, N.J.: W. F. Sherwin, 1875), pp. 134–35.

[a]Figure estimated but based on a school census carried out by the convention's statistician

[b]Figure estimated by the convention's statistician

school teachers who could also run a Sunday school. The success of such efforts is reflected in the parallel growth of the two institutions.[12]

To argue that Sunday schools played a relatively small role in literacy training is not to suggest, however, that their overall educational contribution should be minimized. Education consists of more than learning to read; it encompasses all the means through which a culture transmits its standards and values, including families, newspapers, and churches. From this perspective, the impact of nineteenth-century Sunday schools was dramatic. For through them passed millions of children who came into contact, briefly or for an extended period, with the tenets and world view of evangelical Protestantism. As an agency of cultural transmission, the Sunday school almost rivaled in importance the nineteenth-century public school.

In urban areas, Sunday schools often served as nuclei around which more permanent chapels or churches grew up. Typically, members of a church school sponsored a mission school in a "destitute" urban area, collecting potential students from the neighborhood, finding (or in some cases building) a room in which to meet, and staffing the school with teachers from the original school. Over time the mission school might merge with the church school, become a chapel with regular preaching, or divide into a series of churches, each with its own congregation. A few schools simply died out. The original Sunday school of the First Presbyterian Church in Newark, New Jersey, for example, was started in 1814 by the pastor's daughter, who collected poor neighborhood girls as students. After this school evolved into a church-sponsored Sunday school for the children of the congregation, a group of teachers and students decided to form "a Mission School in some needy section of the city." Held above a shop, this new school was filled through a canvass of the neighborhood by the women teachers. The mission school met in the same building as the church school, though at a different hour, and eventually merged with it. In Utica, New York, a "Union Sunday School" begun in 1816 by five teenage girls drew scholars "of all ages and without distinction of color" from "the lowest dregs of society"; its teachers belonged to several denominations. As the town grew and each denomination built its own church, the Sunday school, which now included middle-class children, was divided into a series of church schools. The Meridian Street Methodist Episcopal Sunday school was established in a city wardroom in East Boston in 1839 by members of the more established Bennett Street Church. A mission station was soon founded at the site and in 1842 a new church emerged, calling itself the First Methodist Episcopal Church of East Boston. And so it went in towns and cities across the country, as the schools proved highly successful in reaching children and adults who did not attend regular church services (see figure 2).[13]

In rural and frontier areas, too, the Sunday school often served as a vehicle for introducing religious services in places destitute of religious institutions. Missionaries for agencies like the American Sunday School Union and the American Home Missionary Society, realizing the impossibility of establishing regular Sunday services in newly settled or remote areas, used the school as an interim institution. Thus, one missionary of the American Sunday School Union claimed in 1859 that "most, if not all, the Churches of the West of recent formation, have grown out of Sunday-schools previously existing." No doubt he exaggerated, but the schools often were the first religious institutions in a newly settled area. If the experience of the missionary J. W. Vail in Wisconsin is any indication, Sunday schools may have preceded churches in more than two-thirds of Northern frontier settlements. According to Vail's detailed records, he established 759 Sunday schools and assisted in establishing 355 more between 1843 and 1857. About 72 percent of these schools preceded churches in their communities. Another missionary, Abijah W. Corey, claimed to have established, alone and with others, more than 25,000 schools in the lower Mississippi Valley between 1845 and 1872.[14]

In frontier communities, as well as in some rural and urban areas, the Sunday school was not just for children. It served, as one missionary noted, as a "central point, where all in the neighborhood meet to teach or be taught." In the absence of regular preaching, the school became a place for Sunday prayers and lessons; when a minister happened to be present, a full church service could be held. John Mason Peck described the situation in the 1820s and 1830s:

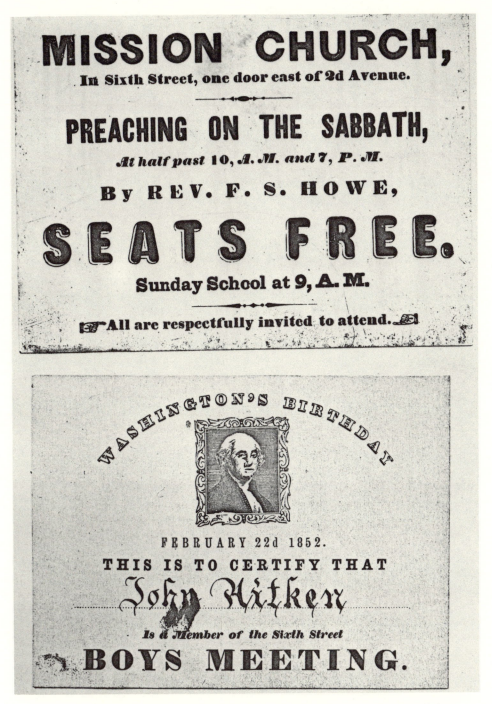

Figure 2. Cards like these advertised mission churches and gave Sunday scholars a feeling of belonging

*I never saw a village, or a farming settlement of any importance, in the West, but
what is visited once in two, three or four weeks by an itinerant methodist or
baptist minister, and occasionally a presbyterian. . . . Those preachers usually
looked into the Sabbath school, and by their presence and a word of exhortation,
encouraged the teachers in their work. . . . I have known Sabbath schools established . . . in settlements where no preacher visited, and prove instrumental of
introducing regular preaching and even be the precursor of a revival of religion.* [15]

As the forerunner of other Protestant institutions, the Sunday school brought to
both city-dwellers and rural people the standards that evangelicals believed essential to right living, chief among which was keeping the Protestant Sabbath. Orderly
public behavior on Sundays was essential, in the minds of evangelicals, in order for
religious activity to take place. Reflecting this view were the published reports of
Sunday school workers. A typical report from Nantucket, Massachusetts, claimed
that before the schools' founding "our wharfs and streets on [Sunday] exhibited
groups of riotous children, and even the yards and porches of our sanctuaries were
profaned by their clamours, and that too, in time of Divine service. The friends of
decency and religious order, could scarcely restrain *their* children from a shameful
profanation of holy time. The condition of our youth was alarming; and the enquiry
arose, what can be done?" The answer, of course, was to form a Sunday school.

Scarcely less typical, if more colorfully expressed, was the report of the missionary Stephen Paxson of "3 Christian famalies" whom he met in 1859. Recent migrants to a remote area of Illinois, they "comenced to tell me what wild People lived
thare no preeching no S[unday] S[chool] no religious society of enny kind But
Sunday was a Day for hunting and fishing and hors rasing Drinking and gambling."
To both Paxson and the three families, forming a Sunday school offered an alternative way of spending the day. Equally important, the school's existence established an evangelical standard of public order and stood as a silent rebuke to those
who viewed Sabbath observance differently. In Marietta, Ohio, reported a correspondent of the *Religious Intelligencer,* the formation of a Sunday school led to an
immediate diminution in the number of people who spent their Sundays "in noisy
gangs." Moreover, even those who did not attend the school "retreated from public
view, to escape the disgrace which they seemed conscious would attach to them, for
neglecting the benefit offered." If the Sunday school could wrest from the Sabbath-
breakers and "noisy gangs" the determining role in shaping public behavior on
Sundays, then the way was open for communicating other Protestant values and
ideals. [16]

Beyond promoting Sunday observance, their supporters believed, Sunday
schools enhanced social order generally. New York's Episcopal bishop, John Henry
Hobart, summed up the common view when he referred to religious education as
"the engine that is to preserve and advance social order, peace and happiness." To
Hobart, Sunday school attendance did more than keep children off the streets

during church services; it changed their behavior fundamentally. One writer professed to discern "a marked distinction between Sunday school boys and those who do not attend." While the latter displayed "levity of manner and a turbulent temper and impudent demeanor," the former were characterized by "[a] serious deportment and mildness of temper and meek and modest manners." Another report told of "an obstinately disobedient daughter" who was transformed into "a useful and obedient child" at Sunday school. Statements like these—repeated throughout the nineteenth century, but especially in the early decades when enthusiasm had yet to be tempered by experience—led to the ultimate claim for the schools: that they prevented or reduced crime. Arguments that there had never been "a child belonging to a Sunday-school who has been confined by public authority," or that in an area where all children attend Sunday school "the prison doors stand open," drove home the notion that the schools could work radical changes. "Seven years' good schooling," declared the secretary of the American Sunday School Union, in a logical extension of this argument, "will cost less than the sheriff's bill for hanging a man."[17]

Sunday school workers were not alone, of course, in making such exaggerated claims. Supporters of free public schooling were equally willing to extol its ability to deter crime. Both groups saw agencies like theirs as powerful tools for improving social order, not by coercion but through the regulation of behavior. Thus, in suggesting that Sunday schools enhanced "the peace and order of society" and that teachers were "a sort of moral police . . . [who] give themselves to the great work of ferreting out and correcting moral evils by moral means," advocates envisioned the schools as sources of values rooted in self-discipline, not external discipline. Insofar as either school produced a person who had, in Daniel Walker Howe's words, "internalized a powerful sense of obligation and could then safely be left to his own volition," it fulfilled its ordering function.[18]

It would be easy to portray the Sunday school as an alien institution imposed upon unwilling populations by outside organizations, a middle-class project designed to control the surly lower classes. And certainly the rhetoric of some Sunday school promoters, who spoke of promoting orderly and docile behavior, lends credence to such an interpretation. Indeed, historians of both British and American Sunday schools have accepted this view as canonical ever since E. P. Thompson, in his book *The Making of the English Working Class,* singled out Methodist Sunday schools as agents through which British industrialists created a tractable labor force. Although Thomas Laqueur effectively challenged Thompson's argument, many American historians have adopted it as an explanation for how rural migrants and European immigrants were transformed into factory laborers in early industrial America.[19]

However accessible and readily quoted, the promoters' rhetoric does not explain the Sunday school's very real appeal to groups outside the urban middle class. Factory Sunday schools, for example, flourished not merely because mill owners thought them important and provided meeting space but also because factory workers sent their children and participated in the schools themselves as teachers. The Brandywine Manufacturers' Sunday School, which was built with contributions from Eleuthère Irénée du Pont and neighboring mill owners and superintended by du Pont's daughters, nevertheless received most of its financial support from the voluntary contributions of workers, managers, and superintendents. Moreover, workers and mill superintendents served side by side as school trustees and teachers. A similar mixing of social classes was evident in the company town of Webster, Massachusetts, and at John P. Crozer's Baptist Sunday school in Rockdale, Pennsylvania.[20]

It is possible, of course, that workers who taught in factory schools, dropped their annual sums into the collective hat, and sent their children off to classes every week did so because of thinly disguised coercion or sycophancy. Employers surely let it be known that they valued such employees more highly than those who spent their Sundays in grog-shops, and employers' daughters, whether surnamed du Pont or Smith, could be very useful as sources of jobs, references, or gifts. Still, coercion—whether disguised or open—is not an adequate explanation for the workers' behavior. Employees with ties to the Brandywine Sunday school seem to have done no better, and no worse, than those who never patronized it. And the du Pont daughters (who were themselves Episcopalians) were extraordinarily careful to avoid offending their students' religious beliefs. In this they were unusual. Most Sunday school workers envisioned the schools as vehicles for protestantizing pupils. Not only were a quarter of the Brandywine school's students Catholic, but the teachers routinely instructed Catholic students in their own catechism and accepted prizes from a local priest for bestowal upon "the most attentive Catholic scholar" of the year. At least one pupil, Ann McGran, went on to enter a convent and continued to correspond with the du Pont sisters after taking her vows. Had the du Pont sisters wanted to impose their religious beliefs on their scholars, they hardly chose the most effective method. Moreover, the behavior of Catholic parents in sending their children suggests that this school's teachings were consonant with parental values.

To be sure, Sunday school lessons in all localities placed a heavy emphasis on punctuality, obedience, self-discipline, and order, all values consistent with the requirements of an industrial age. But there is no reason to suppose that the urban middle class had a monopoly on those values. Although some working-class Americans may have preferred the local pub to the local church, the lessons of the Sunday school were hardly alien to people whose religious traditions had stressed order and self-discipline long before factories appeared on the landscape. When they participated in churches and Sunday schools, working-class evangelicals were just as likely to be expressing their own religious principles as they were to be reflecting the views of their employers.[21]

Rather than viewing Sunday schools as impositions, communities often sought them out for the same broad educational purposes that writers in Sunday school magazines advocated. Frontier settlers, for example, were often eager to have schools as both symbols and agents of order. Quoting a national Sunday school magazine, the *Texas Banner* referred to the school as "an organizer of society" which "introduce[s] the elements of a wholesome social organization" by providing an order similar to that existing in older settlements. Echoing this view was the Mississippian who complained that many of his neighbors "violate[d] the Sabbath continually" and were "ignorant of the God who made them." Feeling it his "duty to do Something for my Blessed master," he decided to "prepare and arrange Several addresses on the Subject of Sundy Schools" in order to "Show them their duties and obligations and Influence on there childern and thos around them." Like the Illinois residents who were shocked that their new neighbors spent Sunday "hors rasing Drinking and gambling," this man believed that Sunday schools fostered old verities in new settings.

Direct involvement with the schools often evoked passionate commitment. Consider, for instance, the experience of Stephen Paxson, a semiliterate Illinois farmer with little formal schooling who began attending his daughter's Sunday school when he was thirty. After undergoing a religious conversion, Paxson began to organize Sunday schools on his own in his spare time. Eight years later, in 1846, he became a missionary of the American Sunday School Union. Traveling six months a year as a preacher, exhorter, and educator, Paxson occasionally lived on corn bread because, as he wrote, "i hav not the meenes to By flower." Nevertheless, he rejoiced that he was "counted worthy to suffer for they gospel sake."[22]

Urban dwellers, too, found mission schools appealing for their own reasons. For many, the prospect of entering a fashionable congregation on a Sunday was daunting. "A vast majority of the very poor classes will not go to our large elegant churches," commented an urban missionary in the 1850s; "you cannot make them believe they are welcome, in truth their dress is an objection." A similar comment by a church school superintendent that poor children "contrast their personal appearance with the well-dressed children around them, and through pride will not attend" underscored the social unease some church schools engendered in children whose clothing was a badge of their poverty. Sunday school organizers were often well aware of the need to employ "aggressive" means "for reaching the masses" who did not attend regular churches. They designed programs to attract children who, initially drawn by a mission school's novelty or preferred rewards, stayed on to take advantage of its social services and recreational opportunities. Free clothing and books were the first attractions, but by mid-century many mission schools offered an ambitious list of services to poor students in their own neighborhoods. The Benton Street Mission Sunday school in St. Louis, for example, sponsored free Saturday sewing classes for its female students, held a free annual picnic and excursion, gave out prizes "for Scripture recitations, attendance and good conduct," and promised students free magazines "with beautiful pictures and many excellent stories" (see figure 3). The fruits of such programs were seen in this Baptist school's rapid growth from two hundred students in 1861 to more than a thousand in 1867. During the 1860s and 1870s, almost every large city in the country had its counterpart to the Benton Street Mission: a large, service-oriented Sunday school, located in a poor neighborhood and often operated in connection with a city mission. Chicago had its Railroad Mission School, founded in 1857 in two railroad cars, and Dwight L. Moody's school, whose students were recruited by the evangelist from among tough street youths. Boston had its North End Mission, a city mission that started in 1867 as a Sunday school and soon grew into a neighborhood institution. It comprised a restaurant providing cheap meals; an industrial school where women and girls could learn "sewing, and the duties of industry, cleanliness, morality, and religion"; a work room to provide them with temporary employment; and an industrial home for reformed prostitutes. And in Philadelphia, the Bethany Mission Sabbath School, superintended by the wealthy entrepreneur John Wanamaker, included among its programs a literary society, an employment agency, a relief committee providing food and clothing, and a periodical called the Bethany Voice (see figure 4).[23]

Because their constituents expected Sunday schools to promote discipline, order, and stability, as well as imparting information, the lessons children learned in evangelical schools were not all contained in a catechism or question book. To be sure, the schools' textbooks, chief among which was the Bible, contained a wealth of information, and a common cultural heritage passed from generation to generation as children learned the stories of Adam and Eve, Noah and the ark, and Moses and the Exodus, along with the outlines of Jesus' life. A child who had spent any appreciable time in a Sunday school would be well equipped to participate in American public life, where references to Biblical characters and events were commonplace. Similarly, catechisms and question books taught pupils the basic doctrines of evangelical Christianity, including original sin, redemption, and the need for a personal experience of regeneration. Teachers in church schools supplemented this instruction with denominational theology and training in their sect's history and rituals, including preparation for baptism (in the case of Baptists) or confirmation (in the case of Episcopalians). Moreover, children learned subtler lessons through the organization and curriculum of the schools and their teachers' expectations.

Memorization was the central pedagogical technique employed in nineteenth-century Sunday schools (as it was in common schools). Particularly in the early decades, Sunday school organizers encouraged students to commit to memory vast quantities of Bible verses, catechism answers, and hymn stanzas, then proudly

BENTON STREET

Mission Sunday School,

SAINT LOUIS.

Corner Twelfth and North Market Sts.

WHAT OUR SUNDAY SCHOOL DOES.

It employs the best men and women it can get for teachers.

It gives a hearty welcome to all who desire to learn the truths of the Bible.

It gives papers every Sunday to the pupils, with beautiful pictures and many excellent little stories.

It teaches the young people to sing the beautiful songs of Zion.

It gives, once a year, a delightful pic-nic excursion or celebration to the Sunday-school scholars.

It offers prizes in the shape of Bibles, Testaments, books, medals, or picture cards, for Scripture recitations, attendance and good conduct.

If the pupils are sick, the good Sunday-school teacher or Superintendent visits them.

It gives fifty lessons a year in that best of books—the Bible.

It trains the children in the practice of benevolence, love, obedience to parents, truthfulness, kindness to one another, and purity of language.

It seeks to lead them to love Jesus, and to walk in the path of wisdom, and the way of everlasting life.

CAN PARENTS AFFORD TO HAVE THEIR CHILDREN OUT OF THE SABBATH SCHOOL?

A. C. OSBORN, D. D.,   E. D. JONES,
Pastor.   Superintendent.

Figure 3. A card advertising the Benton Street Mission Sunday school in St. Louis, emphasizing the benefits to scholars

Admission Certificate

Bethany Sabbath School,

22D & SHIPPEN STS., PHILADA.

LOAG PR GRISON S HALL

DO GOOD AS YE HAVE OPPORTUNITY.

GO YE INTO THE HIGHWAYS AND COMPEL THEM TO COME IN.

My Duties as a Sabbath Scholar.

1. I must remember the Sabbath day, to keep it holy at home, and by the way, in the House of God, and in the School.

2. I must be at School in good time every Sabbath.

3. When I reach the School, I must go directly in, and walk softly to my seat.

4. During prayer, I must reverently bow my head, close my eyes, and be perfectly still.

5. I must bring my Hymn Book, and take part in the opening and closing exercises of the School, especially the reading of the Scripture.

6. I must learn my lessons perfectly, repeat them softly, yet distinctly, and improve all my time to the best possible advantage.

7. I must be orderly in all my behavior, and strictly observant of the Rules of the School.

8. I must never quit my seat without the permission of my Teacher or Superintendent.

9. I must not loiter by the door at the close of the School.

10. I must attend the regular Sunday School meetings, especially on Sabbath evenings.

11. I must try to persuade all Children, who do not go to Sabbath School, to attend and unite with our School.

12. If I know of any of my Schoolmates that are sick or in destitute circumstances, I must at once inform my Teacher or the Superintendent.

13. I must try and persuade my Parents and Friends to accompany me to Church and to the Sabbath Evening meetings.

14. I must give my heart wholly to God.

Love One Another.

Entered the Bethany Sabbath School on

the _____ 18 ____

_____ Secretary.

Figure 4. The Bethany Sabbath School in Philadelphia had more than a thousand scholars in the 1870s, thanks in part to the social services it offered. Admission certificates like these were popular with students.

reported their accomplishments in school records. Typical was the notation in the records of the McKendrean Sabbath School Society of Baltimore that its scholars, averaging forty in number every Sunday, had recited exactly 18,038 verses, answers, and stanzas in 1821. Individual students at times astounded their teachers by reciting close to three thousand Scripture verses in six months, or one hundred on a given Sunday. Although this practice might seem extreme to modern educators, nineteenth-century teachers believed that it imparted incomparable mental discipline. Since the child's mind, in their view, was an empty receptacle in need of filling, memorization "stor[ed] a vacant mind with fertile sources of reflection in riper years." Through memorization, it was said, "their minds are led to reflection on [the Bible], while they commit the precious truths to their tenacious memories." In theory, then, the child whose mind was "stored" with Bible verses would have something to think about in idle moments, as well as a source of elegant language for verbal and written expression. (One wonders what these theorists would make of modern children, whose memories presumably are "stored" with popular song lyrics and jingles from television commercials.) Memorization not only disciplined the child's mind, encouraging traits like concentration and self-discipline, it also instilled information and might reform behavior. After all, argued one teacher, God "will own his word. Fixed in the memory, it must find its way to the heart; then will the fruit appear in holy obedience to his commands."[24]

In order to spur students to prodigious feats of recitation, teachers offered rewards, most commonly in the form of tickets that could be collected and traded in for book prizes (see figure 5). As a superintendent explained the system: "One white ticket . . . is the reward for reciting 10 verses of Scriptures or Watts Divine Songs or 2 Lessons of . . . Catechism. Five white tickets are redeemed by one red ticket which in awarding premiums . . . are considered worth 2½ cts." As a scholar who had often recited a hundred verses of Scripture every Sunday during the 1820s later recalled, "We were stimulated by promises of reward to increase the number of verses to the greatest possible extent, and [our] ambition . . . was greatly excited to excel."[25]

Even after the reward system fell into disfavor in the late 1820s, memorization remained a popular fixture in Sunday and common schools. Critics of reward tickets disliked the envy and competition they encouraged; more important, they believed that offering rewards for random memorization discouraged students from understanding what they had learned. "The heart is left unimproved by moral truth," commented a typical critic (who perhaps had had to listen while an eager student recited the "begats"). To get around this difficulty, Sunday school workers advised teachers to channel student memorization toward selected portions of the Bible, through lessons containing ten to twenty verses apiece. Continuity and uniformity, rather than random selection, were the new watchwords. Students still memorized and recited every Sunday, but now they did so in response to teachers' questions, ostensibly revealing their understanding of what they had learned. "My first re-

REWARDS, TICKETS, &c.

———

Series.	No.		
XLI.	4101	**SMALL REWARD TICKETS ON BLUE PASTE BOARD.** With a passage from the New Testament on each, and a reference to chapter and verse.	By 1000 56 cents.
"	4102	**SAME ON RED PASTE BOARD.** A different value is attached to these two colours, when they are used as rewards, and they are very useful also to give as a lesson for each day, &c.	By 1000 75 cents.
"	4103	**SMALL REWARD TICKETS ON VARIOUS FANCY COLOURED PAPER.** In large type, and a new selection of scripture, both from the Old and New Testament; with references to chapter and verse.	By 1000 62½ cts.
"	4104	**PICTURE REWARD TICKETS WITH A HYMN.** These are printed on stiff fancy coloured paper. Each ticket contains a picture; a passage of the Bible, with a reference to chapter and verse; and one or two appropriate verses of a hymn.	By 100 50 cents.
"	4105	**HYMNS ON PASTEBOARD, WITH A PICTURE.** These are the simplest hymns that could be selected from various sources, and on various subjects.	By 100 75 cents.

Figure 5. An advertisement from an 1835 catalog describing the tickets and rewards sold by the American Sunday School Union

membrance of the Sunday school," recalled one scholar, "was standing up in a row, with many other children, to say our catechism, and sing one of Watts' children's hymns. . . . It was a point of emulation to answer each question instantly, and to repeat the verses of the lesson perfectly."[26] Evident in this student's recollection is the sense of discipline that religious educators sought.

Other pedagogical techniques reinforced this lesson. Schools put great emphasis, for example, on regular attendance and punctuality by both teachers and students, often keeping detailed attendance records and attempting to impose sanctions for tardiness. Sunday school writers advised teachers to visit children who missed two

Sundays and to conduct their classes using the same sequence of activities every week. "Let every minute thing be done with method," suggested one advisor, and "thus teach them by example." Real classes did not often measure up to the ideal standards of Sunday school magazines, but teachers' efforts to conduct orderly and disciplined classes conveyed these values to students. Over the decades, schools became more efficient and sophisticated at encouraging order and punctuality. Some installed bells in imitation of public schools in an effort to make both students and teachers time-conscious.[27]

The schools' rules and rituals also taught subtexts that students quickly imbibed. By requiring that pupils "come clean, washed and combed," schools stressed that cleanliness in itself was a virtue. Many teachers went further, providing clothing to needy children in order to spread the message that "neatness and decency of dress and personal appearance" were marks of self-respect. The First Presbyterian Church Sunday school of Elizabeth, New Jersey, maintained a "fragment society" that provided clothing to needy scholars. Other schools followed suit with "Dorcas societies" or clothing banks that loaned garments out for the school session. A former student recalled the practice at his school in the 1820s: "I used to see the little vagabonds led up the stairs in all the rags of their forlorn condition, and into a room adjoining the Hall, whence they were brought out neatly and comfortably clothed." From the recipients' standpoint, the offer of new clothing was often a major incentive to begin attending Sunday school. In the 1850s Dwight L. Moody enticed Chicago youngsters into his school with sweets and kept them there with promises of new suits in exchange for regular attendance.[28]

Clothing poor children taught not only the importance of cleanliness but also the value that teachers placed on benevolence. Benevolence was demonstrated in other ways, too, most commonly through the practice of collecting money for missions at home and abroad. The Framingham, Massachusetts, Congregational Sunday school began taking regular collections in 1831. The money was sent to the Massachusetts Sabbath School Society or the American Sunday School Union, either to buy "life memberships" for teachers (see figure 6) or to purchase books for frontier schools. By 1868 the average monthly collection was $65. More ambitious still were the teachers of the Fourteenth Street Presbyterian Church school in New York, who formed a "Sabbath School Missionary Association" to interest students in missions and "form them in liberal habits" of benevolence. After collecting $669 over nine months, the association donated $400 to support a Sunday school missionary in Ohio, $200 to the building fund of a foreign mission ship, and the rest to send libraries to schools in the West. At St. George's Episcopal Sunday school, students and teachers collected enough money to build two mission chapels, one of which opened in 1861, the other in 1872. By the 1850s, particularly in church schools, collections for missions had become routine, and even in the poorest mission schools teachers encouraged students to donate their pennies to missionary causes. Although occasionally criticized for inciting competition and envy among students of

"SPREAD THE GOSPEL"

"GIVE, AND IT SHALL BE GIVEN UNTO YOU."
LUKE. VI. 38.

"SAY AMONG THE HEATHEN THAT THE LORD REIGNETH"
PS. XCVI. 10.

THIS CERTIFIES

THAT

Sophie Brinckerhoff

By a contribution of three Dollars from Rev. Dr. Burchard's Bible Class

IS CONSTITUTED

LIFE MEMBER OF THE

Sabbath School Missionary Society

OF THE

THIRTEENTH STREET PRESBYTERIAN CHURCH.

New York, January 1869.

E. C. Jenkins
Sec'y.

W. H. Christie
Pres't.

Figure 6. This elaborate certificate of life membership, inscribed on parchment, acknowledged Sophie Brinckerhoff's donations to Sunday school missions

the same social class and between affluent and poor students, the practice of holding collections became a fixture in nineteenth-century Sunday schools as teachers, parents, and superintendents lauded its value in teaching habits of self-denial and concern for others.[29]

An even subtler lesson in benevolence emerged from the schools' prohibition of corporal punishment. "Persuasion forms the only weapon of the Sunday School Teacher," organizers insisted; "*kindness alone*" would discipline the children. Unlike common schools, where children might be "punctually coaxed or whipped into submission" through the use of the rod, Sunday schools sought to achieve their goals through "the kind influence of a teacher over a child." The Sunday school, which maintained an average class size of about ten pupils to a teacher, encouraged teachers to become personally involved in their students' lives, and placed disciplinary stress on rewards rather than punishments, often constituted a world apart from the weekday lives of many of its constituents.[30]

To reinforce the ideas and values taught at school, religious educators formed libraries which disseminated evangelical children's literature. These libraries grew out of the schools' early role in literacy training. To encourage students' reading efforts, teachers gave away tracts and little moral tales published by Sunday school organizations (see figure 7). With the introduction of reward tickets for attendance, punctuality, and memorization came the practice of giving books as premiums. In return for a designated number of tickets, a student could receive his or her own copy of a book such as *The Dairyman's Daughter* or *Little Henry and His Bearer*. As schools began to discourage random memorization in the late 1820s, many switched from giving books as premiums to awarding library privileges instead. In 1829 the Methodist Episcopal Sunday School Union recommended the establishment of a library in each of its member schools and the abolition of reward tickets for memorization. Instead of rewarding children with individual books, the union suggested that library privileges be extended to well-behaved and punctual scholars. The American Sunday School Union made a similar recommendation that library privileges be given "as a reward for regular and punctual attendance at school, for devout and orderly conduct in church, for attention to the Scripture lessons during the week, for obedience to parents, and kindness and affectionate conduct to brothers and sisters at home." Although the Methodist Union later revised its recommendations on rewards, its support of Sunday school libraries reflected a growing trend (see table 7). In 1826, when the American Sunday School Union began to collect statistics on libraries, 395 (17 percent) of its 2,321 affiliated schools reported having libraries, with an average of 32 books in each. By 1832 more than three-quarters of affiliated schools had libraries and the average size had grown to approximately 91 books. There were, of course, great variations among schools. The New-York Sunday School Union counted 15,162 volumes in the libraries of 53 of its schools in 1831, or 292 volumes in each school, whereas some frontier school libraries consisted of little more than a Bible and a hymnbook. Generally, urban schools had larger

THE
CONVERTED CHILD.

Mrs. Manly had one little son, and his name was Arthur. She took notice that he often went into the room by himself, and came out again with his eyes red, as if he had been crying.

2

3

One day she said to him, "My dear Arthur, what is the matter with you? Does any thing distress you?"

Arthur threw himself into his mother's arms, and began to weep. "O, mother," said he, "I am afraid I shall lose my soul."

"What is it that troubles you, my son?"

"O, mother, I am afraid I shall not be saved. I want to love the Lord Jesus Christ, and to be his servant; but I feel very badly, because I am not sure that my sins are pardoned."

Figure 7. Tiny paperbound books like The Converted Child *were commonly given as rewards to outstanding Sunday scholars*

libraries than rural schools and church schools were more likely to have libraries than mission schools. In Chicago, for example, 77 percent of church schools but only 42 percent of mission schools had libraries in 1864. The number of schools boasting libraries increased as the American Sunday School Union and its competitors packaged their publications into "Sunday School Libraries" and sold them for five or ten dollars (see figure 8). Such practices had the advantage not only of spreading "wholesome" children's literature and evangelical beliefs but also of helping large and small communities to acquire libraries at a time when few public facilities were available.[31]

As the schools' promoters recognized, libraries did more than provide reading material; their very presence attracted students and their parents. "[F]amilies of children would come cheerfully a very great distance, and learn their lessons promptly," observed an organizer in rural New York, "if they could carry home with them a good library-book." Drawn by the presence of books, the students would stay to imbibe the schools' other lessons. Thus did libraries "foster . . . a taste for reading among the rising youth," according to Sunday school promoters. Even more important, good library books nourished "those habits of domestic

Table 7
Sunday School Libraries

Year	Total number of schools	Schools with libraries	Number of books	Books per library
	American Sunday School Union			
1826	2,321	395 (17%)	12,493	32
1832	4,258	3,360 (79%)	335,427	91
	New-York Sunday School Union			
1831	62	53 (85%)	15,162	292
1834	67	59 (88%)	21,673	367
1847	109	88 (81%)	33,870	385
	Chicago Sunday School Union			
1864	98 (church schools)	68 (77%)	24,762	364
	26 (mission schools)	11 (42%)	2,709	246

Sources: American Sunday School Union, *Second Annual Report* (Philadelphia, 1826), pp. xxv–xxxii, and *Eighth Annual Report* (1832), appendix; New-York Sunday School Union, *Fifteenth Annual Report* (New York, 1831), appendix; *Eighteenth Annual Report* (1834), appendix; *Thirty-First Annual Report* (1847), appendix; "Tabular Statement," Cook County Sabbath School Convention, *Proceedings* (Chicago: Church, Goodman and Donnelley, 1864), unpaginated.

retirement which contribute so largely to the happiness of real life." In the minds of Sunday school workers, providing appropriate reading material was a good way subtly to reinforce the schools' lessons of order, discipline, and respectability.[32]

Determining what constituted appropriate material for the libraries involved a certain amount of give-and-take between students and Sunday school workers. Superintendents and teachers agreed on the inclusion of question books, catechisms, Bible concordances and dictionaries, Scripture biographies, and inspiring life stories, but they also recognized that children seldom checked out such books voluntarily. The librarian at the Seventh Presbyterian Church Sunday school in New York summed up the situation at her library: "There is a class of Books continually in use; and of this class the number is wholly insufficient to meet the demand, while those of a more solid religious character are almost wholly unasked for; some, probably, have never been taken from the shelves for the purpose of reading." In order to provide "such books as are within the compass of these youthful minds, and thereby encourage their taste for reading," teachers turned to the ever-growing number of entertaining tales with moral messages that emerged from the Sunday school presses, particularly after mid-century. Titles such as *The Cabin Boy; or the Fruits of Sabbath-School Instruction* and *Gold Bought Too Dear; or the Selfish Boy* rolled off the presses every year, along with illustrated magazines designed for children. (In 1847, for example, the Beneficent Congregational Sunday

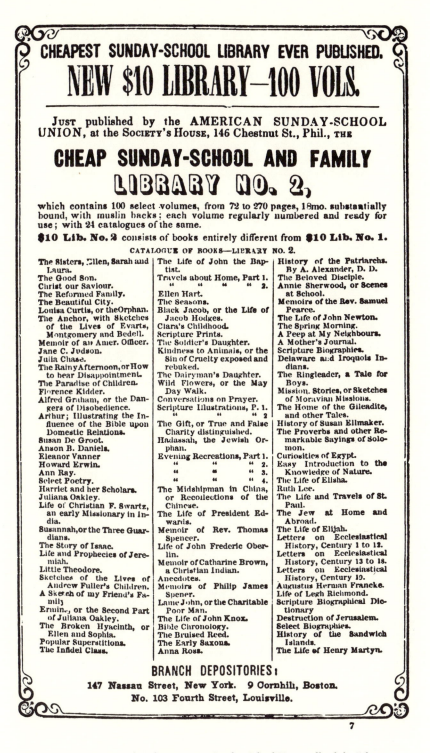

CHEAPEST SUNDAY-SCHOOL LIBRARY EVER PUBLISHED.

NEW $10 LIBRARY—100 VOLS.

JUST published by the AMERICAN SUNDAY-SCHOOL UNION, at the SOCIETY'S HOUSE, 146 Chestnut St., Phil., THE

CHEAP SUNDAY-SCHOOL AND FAMILY LIBRARY NO. 2,

which contains 100 select volumes, from 72 to 270 pages, 18mo. substantially bound, with muslin backs; each volume regularly numbered and ready for use; with 24 catalogues of the same.

$10 Lib. No. 2 consists of books entirely different from **$10 Lib. No. 1.**

CATALOGUE OF BOOKS—LIBRARY NO. 2.

The Sisters, Ellen, Sarah and Laura.
The Good Son.
Christ our Saviour.
The Reformed Family.
The Beautiful City.
Louisa Curtis, or the Orphan.
The Anchor, with Sketches of the Lives of Evarts, Montgomery and Bedell.
Memoir of an Amer. Officer.
Jane C. Judson.
Julia Chase.
The Rainy Afternoon, or How to bear Disappointment.
The Paradise of Children.
Florence Kidder.
Alfred Graham, or the Dangers of Disobedience.
Arthur; Illustrating the Influence of the Bible upon Domestic Relations.
Susan De Groot.
Anson B. Daniels.
Eleanor Vanner
Howard Erwin.
Ann Ray.
Select Poetry.
Harriet and her Scholars.
Juliana Oakley.
Life of Christian F. Swartz, an early Missionary in India.
Susannah, or the Three Guardians.
The Story of Isaac.
Life and Prophecies of Jeremiah.
Little Theodore.
Sketches of the Lives of Andrew Fuller's Children.
A Sketch of my Friend's Family
Ermina, or the Second Part of Juliana Oakley.
The Broken Hyacinth, or Ellen and Sophia.
Popular Superstitions.
The Infidel Class.

The Life of John the Baptist.
Travels about Home, Part 1.
"   "   "   " 2.
Ellen Hart.
The Seasons.
Black Jacob, or the Life of Jacob Hodges.
Clara's Childhood.
Scripture Prints.
The Soldier's Daughter.
Kindness to Animals, or the Sin of Cruelty exposed and rebuked.
The Dairyman's Daughter.
Wild Flowers, or the May Day Walk.
Conversations on Prayer.
Scripture Illustrations, P. 1.
"   "   "   " 2
The Gift, or True and False Charity distinguished.
Hadassah, the Jewish Orphan.
Evening Recreations, Part 1.
"   "   "   " 2.
"   "   "   " 3.
"   "   "   " 4.
The Midshipman in China, or Recollections of the Chinese.
The Life of President Edwards.
Memoir of Rev. Thomas Spencer.
Life of John Frederic Oberlin.
Memoir of Catharine Brown, a Christian Indian.
Anecdotes.
Memoirs of Philip James Spener.
Lame John, or the Charitable Poor Man.
The Life of John Knox.
Bible Chronology.
The Bruised Reed.
The Early Saxons.
Anna Ross.

History of the Patriarchs. By A. Alexander, D. D.
The Beloved Disciple.
Annie Sherwood, or Scenes at School.
Memoirs of the Rev. Samuel Pearce.
The Life of John Newton.
The Spring Morning.
A Peep at My Neighbours.
A Mother's Journal.
Scripture Biographies.
Delaware and Iroquois Indians.
The Ringleader, a Tale for Boys.
Mission Stories, or Sketches of Moravian Missions.
The Home of the Gileadite, and other Tales.
History of Susan Ellmaker.
The Proverbs and other Remarkable Sayings of Solomon.
Curiosities of Egypt.
Easy Introduction to the Knowledge of Nature.
The Life of Elisha.
Ruth Lee.
The Life and Travels of St. Paul.
The Jew at Home and Abroad.
The Life of Elijah.
Letters on Ecclesiastical History, Century 1 to 12.
Letters on Ecclesiastical History, Century 13 to 18.
Letters on Ecclesiastical History, Century 19.
Augustus Herman Francke.
Life of Legh Richmond.
Scripture Biographical Dictionary
Destruction of Jerusalem.
Select Biographies.
History of the Sandwich Islands.
The Life of Henry Martyn.

BRANCH DEPOSITORIES:

147 Nassau Street, New York.   9 Cornhill, Boston.
No. 103 Fourth Street, Louisville.

7

Figure 8. *In its 1851 catalog, the American Sunday School Union offered the "cheapest Sunday-school library ever published"—one hundred volumes for ten dollars*

school in Providence, Rhode Island, had 127 subscriptions to eight magazines.) As might be expected, the stories in Sunday school books and magazines reinforced the schools' teachings on the importance of cleanliness, order, self-control, and delayed gratification. Although students reading the publications of the Massachusetts Sabbath School Society might get a different picture of slavery from the one painted in *The Sunday-School Visitor* (a periodical published by the Methodist Episcopal Church, South), the overall message of the books and magazines did not vary much from publisher to publisher, and teachers could, and often did, buy books from a variety of sources.[33]

Like the common school, the Sunday school educated in many ways. As missionaries and lay people planted it on frontiers both rural and urban, the school itself became the advance guard for the introduction of other "civilizing" institutions, especially the church and the common school. Its very presence in a community stood as a reminder of the evangelical Protestant world view it sought to transmit. Similarly, as congregations adopted it for the religious education of members' children, it perpetuated denominational theology and rituals. Within its walls, library books and libraries, school rules and rituals took their place alongside lessons and catechisms as didactic tools for achieving the school's ends. Here children (and occasionally adults) learned not only the basic tenets of evangelical Protestantism or the doctrines of a specific sect but also the central values of Protestant culture, including self-discipline, benevolence, orderliness, and self-improvement. Seen in the broad context of cultural extension, the schools' educational importance can hardly be overstated.

Sunday schools made their mark in yet another way, as their promoters and spokesmen participated in the wide-ranging public discussion about the nature and goals of American education in the nineteenth century. In this discussion, Sunday school workers were often allied with common school promoters (some individuals, of course, wore both hats), especially in their shared republican ideology. As Carl Kaestle delineates it, this "common school ideology" included a belief in the fragility of the republican experiment and the superiority of American Protestant culture, as well as an emphasis on the importance of individual morality as the underpinning of social virtue. Sunday school spokesmen often echoed these ideological tenets in their statements on the value of their schools to society. "It is a truth established by uniform experience," declared the secretary of the Massachusetts Sabbath School Union in 1826, "that a people in order, for any length of time, to enjoy civil liberty, and the blessings of self-government, must be virtuous. The foundation of the liberty and happiness of this nation was laid in the piety of our ancestors; and the most effectual steps we can take to transmit, unimpaired, to succeeding generations, the rights and immunities, civil and religious, which we enjoy, is by instilling into the minds of our children and youth the principles of virtue and religion." Another Sunday school spokesman concluded, "Our institution illustrates the republican principles of our government while, at the same time, it inculcates obedience . . . and submission" to God.[34] Indeed, Sunday school workers attempted to turn the Fourth of July into a celebration of their view of republicanism, holding mass assemblies of students for rallies and prayers and sponsoring Fourth of July orations. In 1833 the managers of the American Sunday School Union proposed that its members "show how closely the knowledge we propose to furnish in Sunday-schools is allied to the preservation of the liberty and intelligent exercise of the rights of an American citizen" by using the holiday to explore "every neigh-bourhood in our land" and invite "every suitable subject of Sunday-school instruc-tion" to join one. (Spokesmen later claimed that Sunday school celebrations had done a great deal to improve the tone of Fourth of July observances in general.)[35]

Despite their common ideology, Sunday school workers and common school promoters nevertheless sought to delimit the particular responsibilities of each institution. Setting limits was hardly an issue during the 1800s and 1810s, when Sunday schools were few in number, many weekday schools were run by members of individual congregations, and there was general agreement that religion should be taught in all schools as the foundation of individual morality (and hence of social virtue). Children in day schools might need supplementary instruction in specific denominational principles, but their basic religious education was taken care of. Thus, the students in the New York Free School Society's schools received religious training but were also released on Tuesdays for denominational instruction. Very quickly, however, this pattern changed. With the proliferation of free schools in the 1820s and the entry of churchgoing children into Sunday schools, weekday schools and their Sunday counterparts developed the coordinate relationship discussed in chapter 1. Increasingly, Sunday school proponents described their institution as auxiliary to the common school, designed "to make the young thoroughly ac-quainted with the word of God." Perhaps to justify their schools' expansion, Sun-day school workers often argued that weekday school teachers were so busy they gave short shrift to religious instruction, or even that "the sacred Scriptures . . . had almost been banished from the common schools" until Sunday schools were established. By the mid-1820s the two institutions had achieved a modus vivendi: Sunday schools filled in gaps in schooling opportunities where no common schools yet existed and provided religious teaching that ranged from rudimentary common-denominator Protestantism to full-scale denominational instruction. For their part, common schools provided what was termed "moral education"—that is, character training, based on Protestant principles in such virtues as obedience, self-discipline, truthfulness, and honesty.[36]

During the late 1820s and 1830s, however, the passage of state laws restricting the content of moral teaching in common schools created unease among some

Sunday schoolmen over what they saw as an effort to water down basic Protestant principles. The Massachusetts textbook law of 1827, which became a focus of their concern, prohibited the use of schoolbooks favoring "any particular sect or tenet," though it did nothing to restrict the inculcation of general moral education. Still, Sunday school spokesmen, worried that the law was being interpreted so as to exclude the Bible as a text, began publicly to criticize the common school curriculum. "Projects without number are in a course of experiment for the general education of the people," noted the author of the American Sunday School Union's 1830 *Annual Report*, adding that these projects were designed "TO DIFFUSE KNOWLEDGE WITHOUT RELIGION." His theme was taken up by other Sunday school workers, who advanced the notion that common schools trained only children's intellects, not their characters. Knowledge alone, suggested one writer, "is not, in itself, a blessing to the individual or to society. If the love and fear of God is not the all-controlling, all-pervading, all-absorbing principle, it is very problematical whether knowledge tends either to individual or national happiness." Underlying this view was the fear, expressed by Thomas Grimké at the 1831 meeting of the American Sunday School Union, that "heathen classics" rather than the Bible would serve as the basis of common school teaching and thus destroy "the inseparable connexion between the mind, the conscience, and the heart."[37]

The remedy proposed for this perceived deficiency in common school education was "introducing religious instruction" and "moral education" into the common schools. As the Princeton theologian Charles Hodge put it in 1828:

> *Unless some plan can be adopted of introducing religious instruction into the common schools, we must consent to see a large portion of our population growing up in ignorance of the first principles of moral and religious truth. . . . If public virtue be necessary to the existence of free institutions, if reason and experience teach, that religious knowledge and culture are essential to virtue, to leave the people destitute of this knowledge and this culture, is to secure the destruction of our civil liberty.*[38]

To the modern ear, such complaints sound quixotic, as they must have to nineteenth-century schoolmen, who stressed moral education over intellectual training as the foundation of the school curriculum. Moreover, the ministers and devout laymen who constituted nineteenth-century school committees undoubtedly thought it odd to find themselves accused of draining religious content from school texts and courses. Yet Sunday school spokesmen were not merely tilting at windmills. They and their allies were convinced that individuals like Horace Mann, secretary to the Massachusetts Board of Education, were using the state law to exclude not just "sectarian" books but books with any religious content whatever. Moreover, the two sides had substantially different views on what constituted "moral education."[39]

The precise nature of their complaint was most clearly revealed in an 1838 exchange of letters between Mann and Frederick A. Packard, corresponding secretary of the American Sunday School Union. Early that year the union's managers had begun "offering a select library of our books to the common schools of the country"—some 121 volumes for thirty-three dollars—including "biography, travels, natural history, and striking narratives" (see figure 9). When the Massachusetts Board of Education apparently rejected the purchase of the libraries, deeming union books "sectarian" under the 1827 law, Packard took it upon himself to defend the union from charges of sectarianism and to address the broader issue of what constituted acceptable religious teaching in Massachusetts schools. In March 1838 he sought Mann's opinion on the suitability not of a union publication, which he knew Mann would reject, but of John F. C. Abbott's popular book *The Child at Home*. Mann responded that Abbott's book was unacceptable for Massachusetts schools because it "would be in the highest degree offensive to the Universalists" and "would ill accord with the views of Unitarians." Over the following six months, the two men conducted an increasingly rancorous correspondence. Packard accused Mann of recommending antireligious books for Massachusetts schools and generally attempting to strip the curriculum of any religious content whatever. Mann, for his part, held firm to his position.[40]

In their letters, Mann and Packard articulated different definitions of "sectarian" teaching. To Mann, books like Abbott's *Child at Home* and the publications of the American Sunday School Union were "sectarian" not because they promulgated the views of one religious denomination but because they espoused doctrines held in common by orthodox Protestants (such as Congregationalists) but unacceptable to liberal Protestants (such as Universalists and Unitarians). The two doctrines that Mann singled out for comment were future punishment (the belief that God would not only reward the good but also punish the wicked in some future state) and special providence (the notion that ordinary events of life could be interpreted as part of God's action in the world). Packard, on the other hand, asserted that Mann favored the "sectarian" views of Universalists and Unitarians by refusing to sanction books that taught orthodox Protestant doctrines. The effect, he believed, would be to make *only* Universalist-Unitarian books acceptable in Massachusetts schools, a policy that he denounced as "anti-evangelical."[41]

Underlying their dispute was a more fundamental issue: how to teach children to behave morally. On this question, as well, Packard served as a spokesman for the views of orthodox Protestants, who believed that one could not teach morality through intellectual training alone. Such an approach artifically separated the "faculties" through which children learned, whereas true moral education engaged both "the intellect" and "the affections." Children would behave morally only when they understood, both intellectually and emotionally, the orthodox beliefs that they possessed a fallen nature (because of Adam's sin), that Jesus had atoned for that sin, and that each individual needed to undergo regeneration (that is, conversion) before he or she could be worthy of heaven. The unregenerate would

LIBRARIES
FOR SUNDAY-SCHOOLS, FAMILIES, &c.

THE AMERICAN SUNDAY-SCHOOL UNION is prepared to furnish Libraries of the following descriptions, suited for Sunday-schools, public and private schools, families, manufactories, steamboats, &c.

No. I.—**712** volumes, being a full set of the Society's publications, exclusive of Maps and Question Books, &c., each book numbered on the back, with 100 catalogues of the same, without a case, $125 00; including maps of the Ancient World and Palestine, $127 50; and the whole in a neat case, $133 00.

No. II.—THE CHILD'S CABINET LIBRARY, containing seventy-five books, bound in fifty volumes 32mo size, from the fourth and fifth series; morocco backs, lettered and numbered, only $2 50 for the Library, being at the rate of 5 cents per volume. *See page 9.*

No. III.—THE VILLAGE AND FAMILY LIBRARY, No. 1, containing the monthly volumes published concurrently with the London Religious Tract Society, 192 pages 18mo; paper covers, 12½ cents; bound, 21 cents each. *See page 11.*

No. IV.—THE VILLAGE FAMILY LIBRARY, No. 2; 24 volumes for $3 00. *See page 11.*

Cheap Library, No. 1.

No. V.—THE SUNDAY-SCHOOL AND FAMILY LIBRARY, No. 1, consists of 100 select volumes, from 72 to 252 pages 18mo, substantially bound, with muslin backs and marbled paper sides; each volume regularly numbered and ready for use, with 24 catalogues of the same.

This Library will be found useful not only for Sunday-schools, but for Families and Public Schools; the 100 volumes contain 11,628 pages, and are illustrated by more than 400 wood engravings. Only **$10** for the Library, at the rate of ten cents per volume. *See page 6.*

Cheap Library, No. 2.

No. VI.—THE SUNDAY-SCHOOL AND FAMILY LIBRARY, No. 2, which contains 100 select volumes, from 72 to 270 pages 18mo, substantially bound, with muslin backs; each volume regularly numbered and ready for use; with 24 catalogues of the same. Only $10.

New Cheap Library, No. 3.

No. VII.—THE SUNDAY-SCHOOL AND FAMILY LIBRARY, No. 3, contains 100 select volumes, from 72 to 288 pages 18mo, substantially bound, with muslin backs; each volume regularly numbered and ready for use, with 24 catalogues of the same. Only $10.

Cheapest Sunday-school Library ever Published.
75 Vols. for $5.

No. VIII.—THE JUVENILE LIBRARY, containing 100 books, bound in 75 volumes, from 52 to 162 pages 18mo, with muslin backs and marbled paper sides; each volume regularly numbered, with 12 catalogues of the same. ONLY FIVE DOLLARS. *See page 10.*

Figure 9. This advertisement from the American Sunday School Union's 1851 catalog specifically recommended the use of Sunday school libraries in public schools

suffer future punishment in hell. True morality could not be taught through "the beggarly elements of ethics and natural philosophy," as Packard contemptuously termed Mann's approach, but only through "the doctrines of revealed religion." Orthodox Protestants like Packard wanted children to be taught the doctrines of future punishment and special providence not because they enjoyed scaring children with visions of hell but because they believed it was the only way fully to engage the child's "affections." In speeches at meetings and in school minutes, other Sunday school workers echoed Packard's view, downplaying mere "human learning" as a source of moral conduct and stressing the need to teach children evangelical Protestant theology. In Mann's opinion, such doctrines—human depravity, atonement, regeneration—had no place in a common school because they belonged to "the creeds of men" and "divide[d] one set of Christians from another." Instead, he favored encouraging moral behavior by teaching children God's essential goodness and mercy ("the Religion of Heaven") and "the immediate & instantaneous effects of bad conduct," not the threat of future retribution. Union books, he felt, portrayed God and religion in too unpleasant a light, using illustrations that "inspire[d] fear instead of admiration."[42]

Orthodox Protestants believed that Mann was bent on excising "*all religious teaching*" from the schools, a policy that would make them "radically defective" in teaching morality. Indeed, Packard claimed that the logical extension of Mann's position would be to exclude the Bible entirely from the school curriculum and no longer recognize "the Christian religion . . . as the basis of public instruction in Massachusetts." All that would remain in the curriculum would be such doctrines as the existence of God, general providence, and the need to emulate Jesus' good deeds—principles acceptable to the broadest spectrum of Christians, including even Catholics. One of Packard's supporters urged Mann to restore "the kernel, not the shell—the substance, not the shadow" of Christianity.[43]

In the wake of this confrontation, those who hewed the orthodox line faced the problem of devising a plan of action. (Packard's views were widely shared, despite accusations that his primary interest was in hawking his employers' books.) Some supported a move in 1840 to abolish the Massachusetts Board of Education and return control of educational policy to local school boards. Although this initiative had a religious dimension, supporters and opponents did not generally divide along religious lines; even Packard himself opposed the proposal. However much he disliked Mann's policies, he did not translate his dislike into a desire to decentralize the Board of Education. He believed that a central board was necessary for efficiency, but hoped that someone of orthodox views could command its "invisible, all-controlling influence" over "the remotest district and the lowliest schoolhouse in the commonwealth."[44]

Others in the orthodox camp took their position to its logical conclusion, advocating the complete abandonment of common schools in favor of denominational parochial schools. The Old School Presbyterian theologian Charles Hodge addressed the issue of whether Catholic schools in New York should receive a share of public school funds. "I have all along thought the Papists right in the New York controversy," he wrote in 1841. "The State must do one or the other of two things. She must make her schools accessible to all classes of people, by excluding religion from them entirely; or she must let every denomination, or the people in every district, regulate the schools as they please." The decision of the New York legisla-ture to create a statewide school system and forbid the teaching of "religious sectarian doctrine" in state-supported schools led Hodge and others to conclude that denominational schools were their only alternative. In 1844 the Old School Presbyterian General Assembly established a committee, headed by Princeton's James W. Alexander (an American Sunday School Union author and friend of Packard), to study the possibility of establishing Presbyterian parochial schools. By 1847 the assembly had voted an initial sum of three thousand dollars for such schools, beginning an experiment that lasted until the 1870s.[45]

For most Protestants, however, religious weekday schools were hardly a feasible solution to the apparent defects of the common schools. Instead, most orthodox critics continued to press for changes in the schools' curricula and texts. Many advocated the use of the Bible as the basis for courses in literature, science, and history, as well as ethics and morality. As Alexander put it before he became disillusioned with the prospects for reshaping the public school curriculum: "*The Bible is the book to educate the age.* Why not have it the *chief* thing in the family, in the school, in the academy, in the university?" Others, such as Theodore Dwight, Jr., advocated efforts "to train as many pious persons for teachers as possible." Let us, he suggested to Packard, "send them to take public schools of different orders in the most influential situations, privately making up any deficiency of salary out of a fund" collected for that purpose from supporters.[46]

In the end, the critics settled for something less than infiltrating the schools with orthodox teachers or using the Bible as a text. Indeed, the kind of Bible-based curriculum that many of them sought became increasingly elusive, simply because common schools served so diverse a clientele. Instead, Bible reading and Protestant prayers became fixed parts of the school day, a compromise that fully satisfied neither the orthodox, who wanted more, nor the non-Protestants, who wanted less. Within this context, the Sunday school assumed increasing importance as the only institution that could correct the "unavoidable deficiencies" of common-school education. Although often very critical of common schools for abandoning true "moral education" in favor of mere "mental culture," advocates of the Sunday school generally came to agree that their institution could be "the evangelist of the common school," providing a specifically religious education to the youth of the nation. Even Packard, who remained throughout his life a critic of the common schools as providing "an exclusively *secular* and intellectual education," became reconciled to the position that Sunday schools, combined with family teaching and ministerial preaching, helped make common schools "tolerable" to devout Protestants. In a book published in 1865, *The Daily Public School in the United States,* Packard once again criticized the common-school curriculum for failing to train children's characters properly, but did not repeat his lengthy harangues of a quarter century earlier. Although still convinced that common schools needed a firm grounding in Protestant theology, Packard, along with other Sunday school spokesmen, had come to accept their supposed defects, as long as students received supplementary Sunday training.[47]

The partnership that evolved between the common school and the Sunday school over the course of the nineteenth century, although prickly at times, served the needs of both. Where possible, Sunday school workers handed over the job of teaching basic reading and writing to whatever free schools were locally available. In return, common school advocates were happy to assign to Sunday schools the teaching of basic religious doctrine, confining themselves to imparting more general "moral education." If this arrangement enabled Sunday schools to prosper by taking them out of competition with their weekday counterparts, it was no less important to the triumph of common schooling as the American ideal. Without Sunday schools, "the common school ideal" (with all its racial and religious blind spots) would never have worked. Sunday schools enabled Americans to reject denominational schooling and class-oriented public education in favor of the ideal—if not the reality—of free public schooling for all.

Chapter Three

SUNDAY SCHOOL ORGANIZATIONS

Throughout the nineteenth century, Sunday school organizations did more than publish books, sponsor missionaries, gather statistics, and disseminate information to teachers. They embodied the collective dreams of Sunday school workers and formed institutional networks through which those dreams could be realized. Although the organizations' functions did not change greatly over the course of the century, the visions of their creators did. As the largest such organization of the antebellum era, the American Sunday School Union embodied the millennial expectations of a group of influential Protestants who sought, in essence, to remake society along evangelical lines. In later years, the leadership torch passed to state and national teachers' conventions that stressed church extension and teacher training, and whose organizers' hearts burned less with millennial fire than with the steady glow of practicality.

As experiments in evangelical institution building, the American Sunday School Union and the convention movement reflected different approaches to cross-denominational cooperation. Adopting a sweepingly optimistic stance in the antebellum years, the men of the American Sunday School Union sought to embed their schools permanently into the fabric of American life and mold them into vehicles of unprecedented cultural influence. In an era when few national institutions existed and even a system of state-wide common schools seemed a distant dream, they envisioned a far-flung enterprise bringing religion, education, and general enlightenment to the masses. They believed that networks of evangelical institutions, built through cross-denominational cooperation, would not only fill churches but also cushion the excesses of a dynamic and democratic society. Only the realities of denominational opposition and sectional conflict showed how difficult it was to speak for all Protestants in a rapidly changing society.

By contrast, the conventions' leaders eschewed millennial pan-Protestant dreams and judged interdenominational efforts primarily by their ability to strengthen individual sects. Devoting their energies to improving the Sunday school curriculum and professionalizing teaching, they focused on internal organizational concerns and gave only scant attention to the kind of evangelization favored by their predecessors. If the American Union's plans reflected an era of seemingly boundless expansion, the conventions' plans were more in keeping with the inward-looking, consolidating tendencies of the late nineteenth century.

The formation of the American Sunday School Union in 1824 was both an end and a beginning. On the one hand, it culminated the eight-year process whereby Sunday school teachers had formed local unions, in part to supply textbooks and curricular materials.[1] On the other hand, it represented a departure for the Philadelphia Sunday and Adult School Union, which sought, by rechristening itself the American Sunday School Union, to certify its position as a national organization. Although their prospects were uncertain, the men who founded the new union were convinced that the name change was completely warranted. After all, in the space of a few years they had turned the Philadelphia group from a small teachers' union into an enterprise with three traveling missionaries, auxiliaries in nineteen states and the District of Columbia, and a publishing operation with its own book depository. They saw no reason their successes should not continue. Their counterparts in New York, Baltimore, and other cities concurred, approving a constitution for the new organization in December 1823 and applauding the change at the seventh and final anniversary meeting of the Philadelphia Union in May 1824.[2]

The architects of the new organization's ambitious programs were Alexander Henry (its president until his death in 1847) and a group of managers with similar social backgrounds, common interests, and a shared social vision. Like other nineteenth-century city-dwellers, many of these men had come to Philadelphia from rural and farm families to seek their fortunes in the burgeoning commercial economy of post-Revolutionary America. Henry had a thriving import business, Thomas Latimer was a flour merchant, and W. H. Richards sold china in his Third Street shop. Others were connected to Philadelphia's small publishing trade: the engraver James B. Longacre, the printer William Bradford, and his protégé Isaac Ashmead (who became the union's official printer). Also among their number were Frederick Erringer, a shoemaker who by 1833 was designated a "gentleman" in the city directory; Abraham Martin, an accountant; and John C. Pechin, one of the city's tax collectors and guardians of the poor. Over the years, as old managers left and new ones arrived, the union retained its connections to Philadelphia's commercial and financial networks. During the 1830s, 1840s, and 1850s, merchants like Lewis Ashhurst and Levi Knowles, Jr., became managers, as did the financiers Benjamin

Bartis Comegys, G. W. Fahnestock, and Jay Cooke. Despite the growth of manufacturing during those decades, however, only a few factory owners (such as the brush manufacturer George W. Morris and the textile magnate John P. Crozer, who became a manager in 1868) entered the ranks of union officials.[3]

The individuals hired to run the organization came from the same social backgrounds as the managers. From the 1820s until about 1860, two men—Frederick W. Porter and Frederick A. Packard—did most of the day-to-day work, serving as the managers' aides and policy executors, handling the business affairs of the Philadelphia office and book depository, and editing union publications. Both were originally from Massachusetts and both had had experience in publishing before joining the union, Packard as owner and editor of the *Hampshire Federalist,* Porter as editor of New York's *Christian Herald.* Of the two, Packard had perhaps the better pedigree, with a Harvard degree and a law practice behind him, whereas Porter had been a New York merchant before becoming an editor. But in terms of their commitment to the union and their influence within it, they were equals. None of the other men who occasionally assumed full-time positions within the union could rival them in power and influence. Although taking orders from the managers (who met monthly), they had by far the best attendance records at meetings and participated fully in decision making, developing close personal friendships with some managers and effectively running the American Sunday School Union in its early decades. And unlike the managers, who as volunteers could choose their level of commitment to the organization, Porter and Packard invested their professional capital in the business of benevolence, taking incalculable risks with their careers and their families' security when they joined the fledgling organization.[4]

As these brief descriptions indicate, few union officials started out without some advantages in life. Henry arrived in Philadelphia from his native Ulster with letters of introduction to local merchants and enough dry goods in his baggage to turn a tidy profit; Latimer's flour business was a far-flung family affair, encompassing mills in Maryland and Delaware. Although few were extraordinarily well-off financially at the time of their initial involvement with the society, most could be termed comfortable, some even wealthy, at their deaths.[5]

Family and marital connections cemented the ties that bound these men to each other and to their organization. During the 1820s, several managers were relatives of Alexander Henry: his son John; his brother-in-law, John Claxton; and his son-in-law, Silas E. Weir. Managers John Welsh and Joseph Dulles were father- and son-in-law (as well as business partners), and in time Dulles's son, John Welsh Dulles, became a manager, too. Among later generations, the union could count another Henry son-in-law, Samuel Austin Allibone; Packard's son-in-law, Samuel C. Perkins; and the sibling or father-son teams of Lewis and Samuel Ashhurst, Isaac and Samuel Ashmead, Cornelius and Benjamin Comegys, and Benjamin and G. W. Fahnestock.[6]

Religious affiliations formed yet another bond among these men. Most early managers were Presbyterians and Episcopalians who attended the same Philadelphia churches. And although the union frequently tried to broaden its management to encompass the range of Protestant denominations, it had small success. Of the managers in 1824 whose religious affiliations can be determined, 50 percent were Presbyterians and 43.75 percent Episcopalians; most attended the Second and Fifth Presbyterian Churches or Old St. Paul's Episcopal Church. Frederick Porter was an Episcopalian, Packard a Congregationalist who attended Presbyterian churches (more numerous than Congregationalist in Philadelphia) and later became an Episcopalian. Beyond broad denominational associations, the men of the American Sunday School Union shared deeper religious connections. Almost all of the Episcopalians, for instance, came from their denomination's Low Church faction, a segment that encouraged the introduction of evangelical elements into church liturgy and theology. Unlike High Church Episcopalians, Low Churchmen actively participated in benevolent organizations and revivals. Among the Presbyterians, a majority may have allied with the New School branch when their denomination split in the 1830s, but some were Old School Presbyterians.[7]

Common interests contributed additional filaments to the web that connected these men to each other. As might be expected, many of them were active in the city's Sunday school associations. The Philadelphia Association of Male Sunday School Teachers, founded in 1824 at the suggestion of Frederick Porter in the interests of improving teaching methods, was sustained for seven years by a core of American Union managers and employees, who contributed numerous articles detailing its activities to the *American Sunday-School Magazine*. Similarly, the Philadelphia City Sunday School Union, which existed from 1826 to 1829, met at the American Union's bookstore and was led by Thomas Latimer and Frederick Porter. When a new Philadelphia Sunday School Union emerged in 1840, its central board included Porter, Frederick Packard, and two other American Union managers; five of its twenty officers were also connected with the larger body, at whose headquarters meetings were held. The two groups cooperated closely in fundraising, holding anniversary celebrations, and hiring missionaries until the late 1840s, when the Philadelphia Sunday School Union fell into decline; it ceased to exist in 1851. Members of the American Sunday School Union also served as managers of the old First Day Society during the 1820s, disbursing funds to local Sunday schools. By 1830 they had for all intents and purposes amalgamated the two organizations.[8]

Beyond their obvious interest in local Sunday schools, union officials shared an involvement in other benevolent activities in Philadelphia. Among the early managers, Alexander Henry, Thomas Latimer, and John Claxton were active in relief societies for the poor, such as the Philadelphia Society for the Promotion of Public Economy (founded in 1817), which drafted and successfully lobbied for Pennsylvania's 1818 law providing for the public education of indigent children. These men also served on the boards of two societies designed to provide jobs for indigent

Philadelphians: the Society for Bettering the Condition of the Poor (1820) and the Provident Society for Employing the Poor (1824). Henry, Packard, and four other managers were involved in the Philadelphia House of Refuge, an institution for juvenile delinquents. Packard carried this interest further, joining the Prison Discipline Society and later becoming editor of the *Journal of Prison Discipline.* Educational and religious institutions also drew the interest of the group's managers; at various times, several were members of the Philadelphia Society for the Establishment and Support of Charity Schools (later the Ludwick Institute), the Philadelphia Infant School Society, and local Bible and tract societies. Finally, some of the younger managers belonged to the Young Men's Colonization Society of Pennsylvania in the 1830s and 1840s. But, with the exception of George Hay Stuart, who became a manager in 1851, none joined any abolitionist society. Indeed, several had close business ties to the slave-holding South and one, Joseph H. Dulles, became the absentee owner of a South Carolina plantation when he inherited it from an aunt in 1834.[9]

Neither abolitionists, Jacobins, nor Paineite rebels, the managers of the American Sunday School Union exhibited a common interest in meliorist, gradual approaches to the problems of urban society. They were sure that most types of poverty could be solved by conversion to evangelical religion and to the values they associated with it, not by fundamental changes in the economic and social order. Thus, the programs to which they devoted their energies invariably included as key elements character training and inculcation of the virtues of hard work, sobriety, and self-discipline. At times they sounded like moral autocrats, recommending Sunday schools because they would encourage neatness and decency among the poor and save the public money by reducing the populations of jails and poorhouses. They likened the Sunday school to "a mighty moral engine" or "a piece of moral machinery," implying that it had the capacity to process its clients into new products. Carrying this favorite metaphor one step further, they occasionally indulged the secret hope that men like themselves would "take hold of every crank" to run the "gigantic machine" of "our growing but unformed chaotic tumultuating society." But equally often they spoke in moderate and optimistic tones, distancing themselves from those "who would look for popular order and security in the ignorance of the multitude" and proposing the Sunday school as a means to "improve the moral condition of the people" through knowledge and general enlightenment.[10]

In this they sounded like the Whigs that most of them were, using the metaphors of a machine age yet rejecting the implication that they wanted to control all the switches or return to a preindustrial era. Although active as individuals in the political arena, collectively they eschewed any direct political role for the Sunday school or the union. And even if they had fantasized about the possibilities of overt power, a jarring experience with political activity convinced them early on that it was neither a popular nor a profitable route to achieving their goals.[11]

That experience arose out of their decision to seek an act of incorporation from the state of Pennsylvania to replace the one that had lapsed when the Philadelphia Sunday and Adult School Union became the American Sunday School Union. Not only was their first application rejected in 1826 (legislators accused the union of being an arm of the Presbyterian Church) but their second application, in 1827, elicited a furious, year-long debate over whether the organization sought "union of Church and State." Adding fuel to the fire was a sermon delivered on July 4, 1827 by the Presbyterian clergyman Ezra Stiles Ely, who had written the union's 1827 annual report. Ely spoke of "the duty of Christian freemen to elect Christian rulers," proposed that voters form "a Christian party in politics" in order to elect an orthodox Protestant to the presidency, and suggested that the votes of "true Christians" could "govern every public election in our country." Opponents seized upon Ely's sermon as proof that the American Sunday School Union planned to subvert religious freedom in the name of Calvinism. Although the sermon had no union support or sponsorship, it was not difficult for the opposition to quote statements from union literature about the power of Sunday schools to control children's minds, suppress books of a non-evangelical character, and eventually influence a majority of voters.

The charter controversy was not simply sparked by the rhetoric of sermons or annual reports. It was part of a much larger argument that raged during the 1820s between evangelicals and their opponents, a loose coalition that included Quakers and Unitarians, freethinkers and religious skeptics. As evangelicals lobbied for a ban on Sunday mail deliveries in order to impose their conception of proper Sabbath observance, or worked to influence the content of common-school textbooks, the advocates of "rational religion" discerned an evangelical conspiracy to undermine separation of church and state. In their minds, stopping the union's bid for a charter was necessary to slow that conspiracy. Moreover, the charter fight highlighted the ongoing contest between evangelicalism and radical free thought for the loyalty of working-class Philadelphians. The union's chief opponent in the Pennsylvania legislature was Jesse Burden, a representative of Philadelphia's working-class Northern Liberties region and an artisan by trade. "I can find no one who knows Burden," commented the union manager John Atwood. "He is a hatter in N[orthern] Liberties & of low esteem." Indeed, one of the managers' tactics in the case was to circulate petitions among Burden's constituents in support of a charter for the union. The tactic failed. The charter request was denied and the union did not receive an act of incorporation until 1845.[12]

The 1838 controversy between Packard and Mann over the kinds of books assigned in Massachusetts public schools brought further confirmation that political controversy—or indeed any public controversy, as we shall see below—was detrimental to the union's interests. The union's managers also agreed on the futility of other mechanisms of overt control. American society, as they observed it, was changing so rapidly that older forms of social discipline, based on deference and visible, external controls (the church, neighbors, the community), were quickly becoming obsolete. In their minds, social order could be guaranteed only through individual regeneration in a conventional conversion experience. Only by knowing, believing, and experiencing the doctrine of individual accountability would citizens in a republic behave in socially constructive ways. Once individuals knew, and came to recognize in their hearts, that God would judge and punish them for sinful behavior, they would act properly and ensure social order. "Every form of sin is a social poison," declared the American Sunday School Union author James W. Alexander, reflecting the managers' belief that social problems had their roots in individual sins. Similarly, the manager Joseph H. Dulles decried what he saw as a "growing spirit of libertinism" among the young, asserting that it was "destructive of good order in society and good morals in individuals." The Sunday school would achieve the goals of "preserv[ing] and advanc[ing] social order, peace and happiness," not by policing the young but by giving them the internal regulator—a conscience—by which to police themselves.[13]

The managers' faith in the efficacy of orthodox religion was not merely theoretical; it emerged out of personal experience. They had found evangelical religion and its institutions to be powerful sources of self-discipline in their own lives. In a journal he kept from the time he was twenty-seven, Lewis Ashhurst described both his struggle to live what he considered an orderly and useful life and the role of evangelical institutions in helping him to do so. Like many another evangelical Christian in the nineteenth century, Ashhurst maintained a weekly round of religious observances and meetings that structured his days, offered sociability and entertainment, and provided alternatives to the "sinful" pleasures of mid-nineteenth-century Philadelphia. His journal records weekly or monthly attendance at meetings of the Episcopal Education Society, the Missionary Society, the American Sunday School Union, and the Young Men's Colonization Society, as well as two sermons and Sunday school on Sundays and religious lectures on Wednesdays. In addition, he had frequent conversations with his minister, spent many evenings with friends collecting money for the Education and Missionary societies, and attended special meetings for such causes as building an Episcopal college. His journal reveals a life that revolved around his work as a merchant, his family, and his religious activities.[14]

For Ashhurst, who became an American Sunday School Union manager in 1839, institutional affiliations structured daily life and enabled him to avoid the "sins" associated with urban existence: idleness and excess. Thus, records of religious meetings are interspersed in his journal with frequent criticisms of "my evil tempers and lusts, and my coldness and deadness in spiritual things." Passion was to be channeled into religious conduits, where it could flow safely and avoid diversion into more dangerous streams. Similarly, he worried that there was too "much of self in all my exertions, every act of duty polluted by it." "Self-seeking" and "the desire of worldly applause" seemed to taint his activities. He should, he felt, "do every thing with a single eye to the glory of God," not worldly success. Ashhurst's ambivalence about his work was shared by many of his contemporaries. Work (whether remunerative or religious) was innately valuable, particularly as a means of self-discipline, yet it also brought "worldly applause" and the danger of self-aggrandizement. Although this introspection waned and his benevolent interests narrowed somewhat, with advancing age, Ashhurst throughout his life viewed benevolent employments as his personal bulwark against chaos.

For other union officials, as for Ashhurst, faith in the ordering functions of evangelical religion was deeply felt and personally experienced. Only once was that collective faith shaken, when it was revealed in 1857 that Frederick Porter had embezzled $88,000 from the union. Caught up in the speculative mania that swept Philadelphia in the mid-1850s, Porter had succumbed to the temptation of making money for himself and a friend by issuing a series of unauthorized union bonds. (The managers had routinely approved his issuance of limited-term bonds as a means of raising capital.) Although the primary beneficiary of Porter's sin was the Philadelphia businessman Joseph McDowell—Porter's own total assets, turned over to the union in settlement of a lawsuit, amounted to $10,000—the revelation profoundly shocked his associates. Ashhurst became physically ill at the news. "I am *completely overwhelmed*," cried the veteran missionary John McCullagh; "how could any man so rob God!" Commented another missionary: "I should hardly have been more surprised by the discovery of faithlessness on the part of my own father."[15]

Lurking beneath their horror and disbelief lay a deeper fear. Suppose they were wrong? Suppose even a carefully constructed associational network could not protect them from worldly seductions? Porter had been one of their own for more than thirty years. Like them, he had built a life bounded by family, church, Sunday school, benevolent work, and the American Sunday School Union, yet it had not been enough to save him from falling. As men who had devoted themselves to work while resisting the temptations that success inevitably brought, they needed to find some explanation for Porter's betrayal. In the end, they closed ranks to heal the gaping wound he had inflicted, dismissing his behavior as an aberration committed by someone who had never "really" been one of them. They excised his contributions from the union's history and sought to dismiss him from their collective memory. As late as 1917 Edwin W. Rice, who had been a student missionary in Wisconsin during the scandal, continued the tradition by barely mentioning Porter in his history of the union.

Like many nineteenth-century Americans, the American Sunday School Union's managers at times looked nostalgically back to the simpler society of the eighteenth-century village, but they were not simply attempting to revive the past. Instead, they shared an emerging "evangelical conception of social order" (as Donald Scott has termed it), in which discipline was essential but hierarchy was not. Their attempt to substitute internal self-control for the external mechanisms of social deference that had regulated eighteenth-century society represented an effort to find techniques of social discipline appropriate to the dynamic, democratic society in which they lived. They might not like the changes they saw; indeed, they were often highly critical of the excesses spawned by democratic politics and unlimited immigration. Still, they knew that the old ways could not persist.[16]

As upwardly mobile, middle-class businessmen and financiers, these men had cast their lots with the city and its expanding market economy. If evangelical institutions had been important sources of self-discipline in their struggle upward, then there was no reason they could not serve the same functions for others. Self-control, instilled on a mass basis by participation in evangelical institutions, would lead both to worldly success and to social harmony. Projecting personal experience onto a national screen, they saw the Sunday school as an anchor and the American Sunday School Union as a lifeboat in the volatile seas of antebellum urban life. Only through such institutional bulwarks could personal happiness and community harmony be achieved.[17]

Having rejected politics as a means to control the lives of others, the men of the American Sunday School Union pursued a more elusive goal: influence. To wield that influence, they chose two channels, the press and the voluntary society, both uniquely adapted to the needs of a rapidly growing yet decentralized country. The Sunday school, while coercing no one, held up standards of conduct to which members could voluntarily submit. As part of a national network of institutions, it offered individuals a source of guidance and direction in a highly mobile society. The American Sunday School Union took advantage of the ongoing revolution in printing to publish affordable books, tracts, texts, and magazines reflecting the managers' views. As one of the union's most prolific writers put it: "My aim is to do something . . . to reach the millions of youth in our land . . . [and] make an impression on the children. This I wish to do by writing." The union's managers recognized that the printed word gave them an unprecedented opportunity to influence the lives of children, and they aimed to use that opportunity to full advantage.[18]

In addition to issuing books, magazines, and texts for use in Sunday schools, the union's directors inaugurated a missionary project designed to increase the number of schools. Together, these two programs offered the potential to affect large numbers of Americans. For as Sunday schools grew and prospered, they served as markets for union publications; the publications, in turn, provided opportunities to reach a broad audience of Sunday school teachers as well as students, their parents, and their friends. Thus the Union's missionary and publication activities, although separate on paper, were intertwined in the pursuit of evangelical influence. Picturing themselves at the top of a national hierarchy of Sunday school management, union officers hoped to centralize such functions as fund-raising, missionary activity, and publication at their Philadelphia headquarters. Likewise, they expected the union to serve as the supplier of publications to all the nation's Sunday schools, which would join together under its banner.[19]

The missionary program represented the managers' response to the atomization of American society. By forming local auxiliaries and encouraging individual schools to affiliate with Philadelphia either directly or through the auxiliaries, the managers envisioned the American Union as the symbolic apex of a pyramid. Americans around the country would be tied together by their connections to the union, their involvement in the Sunday school cause, and their use of union publications. When they sent periodic reports to Philadelphia and received in return the union's annual report, members of local schools and auxiliaries would mentally place themselves in a web emanating from Philadelphia and encompassing all Sunday school workers.[20]

The key to this web was the missionary. In its first few years the union relied heavily on volunteer or part-time workers (usually theological students) to travel in Pennsylvania and nearby states establishing schools. In more remote states and territories, the union had the occasional help of workers from the American Home Missionary Society, the Presbyterian Board of Missions, and the Baptist Home Missionary Society, many of whom founded Sunday schools while also engaging in home mission work. The Baptist missionary John Mason Peck, for example, served not only his own denomination but also the American Sunday School Union and the American Bible Society in Illinois and Missouri in the 1820s. By the latter part of that decade, however, the union's managers had decided to employ some thirty full-time missionaries and sought out ministers and theological students for the task. Soon thereafter, they immersed the union in two highly ambitious missionary projects, the Mississippi Valley Enterprise and the Southern Enterprise.[21]

These two undertakings drew their inspiration and energy from the postmillennial thinking that had captivated evangelical Protestants in the 1820s. Convinced that America lay on the brink of the millennium, Protestants around the nation sought to hasten its arrival by making converts. As missionary projects multiplied, their scope expanded. In 1830 the postmillennial vision became focused on a plan devised by the New York merchant-philanthropist Arthur Tappan to bombard the frontier region loosely termed "the Valley of the Mississippi" with Bibles, tracts, missions, and Sunday schools. By giving individual grants as seed money to the American Bible Society, the American Tract Society, the American Home Missionary Society, and the American Sunday School Union, Tappan challenged them to raise funds to attack the problem of "infidelity" in the western states. Prompted by a $2,000 grant and additional pledges, the American Sunday School Union passed its own "Mississippi Valley resolution" at its 1830 annual meeting, pledging "within two years, [to] establish a Sunday school in every destitute place . . . throughout the Valley of the Mississippi." This resolution led to an outpouring of fund-raising zeal at missionary meetings held in major cities up and down the East Coast and convinced the managers that the goal was achievable. Within two years the group had collected more than $60,000 for the cause, of which two-thirds came from New York, Pennsylvania, Connecticut, and Massachusetts. A second project, the Southern Enterprise, launched in 1833, sought to plant Sunday schools in seven southern states and the District of Columbia. In this way the union committed itself to creating and sustaining a network of Sunday schools across the nation.[22]

Although neither project fulfilled the grandiose claims made for it, the Mississippi Valley and Southern enterprises revealed the union leadership's understanding of how a missionary program could shape the future of American society. They saw their missionaries as links in a chain of evangelical influence, extending from Philadelphia to each school and back again. The missionary, going into an area to establish a school and returning periodically to check on it, became a dispenser of evangelical culture and a bearer of news about the entire Sunday school cause. To the people in his territory, his commission from a national society symbolized their ties with other parts of the country, while the services he performed drew them into a wider institutional and intellectual orbit. Above all, through the sale of union books and periodicals, he offered his constituents access to the mental universe that the organization's writers, editors, and supporters inhabited. Faithful union customers entered that universe, absorbed its tenets, and joined its community of believers, without ever leaving home.[23]

The missionary helped ensure that the connection with the national union was reciprocal. His letters and reports, as well as occasional visits to Philadelphia, gave his superiors and supporters in the union a first-hand view of Sunday school work on the local level. Depending on the volume of his sales, the missionary wrote weekly or monthly letters to Frederick Porter, the corresponding secretary, who, in turn, acknowledged receipt of orders and donations, discussed the union's work and prospects, and informed the missionary of any important news from Philadelphia. Thus, the missionary program promoted communication among Sunday school workers and established a national network of like-minded people who could share ideas and resources despite never having met.[24]

Some of these functions were also performed by itinerant agents who visited churches in established communities to solicit donations for the cause. The agent's yearly visit to a church and Sunday school offered him the opportunity to relay the "short, pointed, racy, effective" and "thrilling" stories of missionary work conveniently supplied by the missionaries in their reports. Agents encouraged Sunday school students to "adopt" a missionary or a rural or frontier school as the recipients of their donations. In this way, Sunday school pupils gained a personal interest in promoting the institution and often received letters of gratitude from the sponsored missionary. No doubt the recipients of this benevolence at times felt condescended to—one such individual sarcastically referred to "the East" as "the land of Books and plenty"—but the technique was often very effective in establishing ties among Sunday school pupils across the nation.[25]

Like the missionary program, the publications of the American Sunday School Union were designed to enhance its role as a nationalizing agency and as a disseminator of evangelical values. The publications editor maintained a stable of freelance writers who contributed articles to its magazines and wrote books for its lists. Although generally free to choose topics and modes of expression, these writers were constrained to abide by the union's nondenominational code and to include "nothing to which Christians of any evangelical denomination would object." More important, the moral values inscribed by their pens were to fit snugly into the union groove. Not that they merely parroted ideas handed out from Philadelphia; the union's writers belonged to an evangelical community whose members shared a mind-set and a vocabulary that made parroting unnecessary. Writers for the magazines in particular were often ministers or teachers whose articles were based on internal discussions within their own schools. Thus, union publications reflected the thinking and concerns of active Sunday school workers as well as the ideas of the Philadelphia management. Here again, union practices encouraged reciprocity, its publications permitting the exchange of ideas among far-flung subscribers.[26]

The union's management adapted their publications to meet the changing needs of their constituency (see figure 10). In the early years, when many schools were concerned with basic literacy, they published a great deal of material designed for teaching reading and spelling, such as the widely used *Union Primer* and *Union Spelling Book*. As time went on, however, the emphasis in union publications shifted towards children's books and religious texts. The 1825 catalog listed textbooks first and children's books last, but the 1840 catalog reversed the order. Similarly, whereas the 1825 catalog contained 75 children's books, many of them English, the 1863 catalog listed 953 such books for sale, almost all by American authors. Periodicals were similarly geared to different constituencies. The union published not only a general magazine for adults and Sunday school workers but also two special-interest magazines for students, one for older children and another for younger. The *American Sunday-School Magazine,* issued from 1824 to 1830, offered a medium of communication to Sunday school workers by reporting on their work, giving information and advice on organizing and conducting schools, and promoting the cause of Sunday school missions. Its successors, the *Sunday-School Journal, Sunday-School Times,* and *Sunday-School World,* served similar functions, although their emphases gradually shifted toward lesson preparation as time went on. At a time when magazines for children were relatively new, the union also began publishing *Youth's Friend* (1824), designed for older students and teachers, and *Infants' Magazine* (1826), for students aged seven and older. Although to modern sensibilities they seem rather rigid and charmless, these periodicals and their successors—*Youth's Penny Gazette, Youth's Sunday-School Gazette, Sunday-School Banner,* and *Child's World*—enabled the union's officers to harness the developing potential of the press in order to have some direct influence on Sunday school pupils.[27]

DESCRIPTIVE CATALOGUE

OF

BOOKS,

AND

OTHER PUBLICATIONS,

OF

THE AMERICAN SUNDAY SCHOOL UNION;

DESIGNED FOR

SUNDAY SCHOOLS,

JUVENILE, FAMILY, AND PARISH LIBRARIES,

AND

FOR GENERAL READING.

———

PHILADELPHIA.

1835.

CATALOGUE OF BOOKS

PUBLISHED BY

THE AMERICAN SUNDAY SCHOOL UNION.

NOTE.—The first seven series are books in paper covers, generally designed for the younger classes of children. The eighth series commences the catalogue of bound volumes, and the size of them increases through the succeeding series, from 24 to 324 pages.

Series.	Size.	Pages.	No.		Price by 100
1.	48mo	8	101	JANE AND HER BROTHER WILLIAM:	45 cents.
				Stories from Scripture, read and conversed about by two little children.	
"	"	"	102	RAINY SUNDAY.	
				How a sabbath at home may be profitably and pleasantly spent.	
"	"	"	103	BOOK FOR YOUNG CHILDREN.	
				Six cuts, with eight rhyming lines under each.	
"	"	"	104*	THE DISOBEDIENT BOY.	
				Account of a little boy that disobeyed his mother and was lost in the woods.	
"	"	"	105	THE AFRICAN WOMAN.	
				Story of little Mary, showing the piety and benevolence of a poor African; and how we should regard our fellow creatures of every colour and condition.	

* The twenty-four little books from 104 to 128 inclusive, are of uniform style and character. They are put up with picture covers, and form a complete set by themselves.

B

SPELLING AND READING BOOKS.

———

Series.	No.		
XL.	4001	THE ALPHABET.	12 cents each.
		Containing the large and small letters, with vowels, large and small, and the common points, on a large card of stiff binder's board, for the reading of a whole class, or school.	
"	4002	SAME.	4 cents each.
		Large and small letters, with five plain reading lines, and the figures 1 to 9, on binder's board, 9 by 12 inches; designed for the use of a class or single scholar.	
"	4003	SAME, on a card, 7 by 9 inches.	3 cts. ea.
"	4004	SAME, on still smaller cards, with reading lessons, designed for the use of a single scholar.	By 100 75 cents
"	4005	THE UNION PRIMER.	By 100 $3 00
		Containing alphabets, spelling lessons, picture alphabet; points or stops; the Lord's prayer and ten commandments; a table of figures and numbers; with a variety of reading lessons, engravings and directions to teachers.	
"	4006	THE UNION SPELLING AND READING BOOK.	9 cents each or by 100 $9 00
		Reading lessons, in double columns, consisting of passages of scripture, selected and arranged, with references to chapter and verse.	
"	4007	THE FIRST READING BOOK.	By 100 $3 00
		Prepared with great care, and designed for the youngest reading classes in Sunday and daily schools. It contains simple and useful lessons, illustrated with engravings.	

Series.	No.		
XL.	4008	QUESTIONS ON THE FIRST READING BOOK.	By 100 $3 00
		This is a volume for the use of the teacher or pupil; containing questions on each sentence of the First Reading Book, designed to analyze and apply the sentiments it contains. There are also directions to the teacher, and prayers and graces, with explanations of the same.	
"	4009	THE SECOND READING BOOK.	By 100 $3 75 cts.
		Designed for spelling as well as reading exercises, and the lessons so prepared as to be capable of catechetical examination. Illustrated with fine wood engravings.	
"	4010	QUESTIONS ON THE SECOND READING BOOK.	By 100 $3 75 cts.
		Same plan, design and use as Nos. 4008 and 4012.	
"	4011	THE THIRD READING BOOK.	By 100 $4 50 cts.
		Containing lessons, in reading and spelling, suited to the more advanced reading classes; and prepared with a view to catechetical instruction. Illustrated with fine engravings.	
"	4012	QUESTIONS ON THE THIRD READING BOOK.	By 100 $4 50 cts.
		Same plan, design and use as Nos. 4008 and 4010.	
		☞ These three reading books have been used with great approbation in many infant and primary schools, and are now used in the public infant schools in the city of Philadelphia, and are exceedingly well adapted to their purpose.	

Figure 10. These pages from the American Sunday School Union's 1835 catalog reflect the variety of its publications: a, title page; b, description of books for children; c, description of spelling and reading books

In marketing and distributing their publications, union officials devised methods that took into account the diversity and decentralization of American society. Both the auxiliary system and the use of missionaries were tailor-made to facilitate the sale of union materials. The managers hoped the auxiliaries would buy the parent society's publications—and most did. Missionaries functioned as booksellers and distributors, taking and filling book orders on their circuits. Early in its history, the union established a series of depositories, or bookstores, in strategically located towns and cities, especially where there were large or active auxiliary societies. Thus, the depository at Utica, New York, not only supplied books to the vigorous Western Sunday School Union but also served as a distribution point for missionaries in western New York and Ohio. The union made its books still more attractive to auxiliaries by enabling them to purchase books at a discount. The officers were not shy about advertising their publications on the flyleaves of newly issued books and in children's magazines, which often contained articles on the importance of reading good books. The five- and ten-dollar "Sunday School Libraries" developed in the 1830s also did their part to boost sales of union books.[28]

The managers of the American Sunday School Union thus shared not only a vision of their organization's role in American society but also an ability to devise the missionary and publication programs necessary to implement their collective vision. At a time when the United States had few national institutions, virtually no national communications network (except the United States mail, which these men molded to their needs), and no national corporations, the management of the American Sunday School Union established the framework for what was, in effect, a national evangelical corporation. In their mind's eye, the union was the center of an evangelical community whose members, though widely scattered, were bound together by participation in a common institution and use of a common literature. Through the union, the small islands that were local Sunday schools would become part of a national archipelago, where individuals could always find refuge and strength.[29]

It would be a mistake, however, to confuse frameworks with structures, plans with actualities. While recognizing union officials' achievements, it is important also to acknowledge the obstacles they confronted, obstacles that frequently limited the realization of their plans. Although contemporary observers (and some later historians) have been beguiled by the verbal edifices erected in the union's annual reports, the structure of the organization was actually quite simple, with few of the trappings of a modern bureaucracy. Until the mid-1850s, the union had a permanent managerial staff of two—Porter and Packard—plus a few office clerks and copyists. Much of the work, including keeping the union's financial records and approving new manuscripts for publication, was done by the volunteer managers. And although the managers shared the same basic values and goals as their counterparts in other national benevolent societies (such as the American Bible Society), collaboration was very limited, both because no other group had its headquarters in Philadelphia and because all were competing for the donations and labors of "the Christian public."[30]

Two types of obstacles limited the union's influence. One involved practical problems with carrying out plans made in Philadelphia; the other was more fundamental, arising from deep fissures in American society as a whole. These obstacles forced the union to contract its operations in the 1830s and 1840s and undermined its ability to achieve the ambitious goals of its early days. They also illustrated the difficulties faced by any group that attempted to offer central direction in a society as decentralized as antebellum America.

Recurring logistical difficulties with their missionary and publication programs beset the group's officers throughout the antebellum years. Relations with auxiliaries were never as smooth as the managers envisioned. Because auxiliary schools had no real obligations beyond sending an annual report (the requirement that they pay a small fee was dropped in 1832), the union had no mechanism for assuring the schools' loyalty or their continued willingness to purchase union books. As a result, statistical tables in the union's annual reports frequently contained large gaps when data from local auxiliaries failed to materialize. Moreover, in the early decades at least, the American Union tended to have its strongest ties with healthy schools and local unions that were self-sustaining anyway; its ability to maintain small or weak schools was limited. The large auxiliaries tended to be strongest in areas such as New York and Massachusetts, where the schools were well established and supported. Hence, as a missionary organization in the pre–Civil War years, the union was most active in large cities and towns—in other words, in precisely the same locations that were likely to have schools, libraries, and churches already. Even the placement of missionaries reflected this imbalance, older states like Pennsylvania receiving more workers than newer areas like Illinois.[31]

Nor did the union's managers ever control the auxiliary societies as effectively as they had planned. Relations with groups like the New York Sunday School Union, the Western [New York] Sunday School Union, or the Rhode Island Sunday School Union (which were, after all, completely independent organizations) were frequently disturbed by disagreements over fund-raising, allocation of resources, book orders, appointment of missionaries, and a variety of other issues that frustrated the Philadelphia officials' hopes for a smooth-running "engine." Because local unions were particularly adamant about retaining control over funds raised in their localities, delicate negotiations were often necessary to determine what percentage of local collections should be forwarded to Philadelphia. Agents of the parent society, by collecting in local churches, were often seen as competing unfairly with the auxiliary group. Disputes also arose about who should run the book depositories and how large a discount the auxiliaries were entitled to receive from Philadelphia. Members of local societies complained that the American Union was too remote to understand their problems and that its managers were too eager to centralize decision making and fund-raising. For their part, the managers, who believed the auxiliaries should be subordinate to their direction, felt frustrated by their inability to exercise more control. Relations with local unions thus varied considerably, the Philadelphians having the most cordial ties with the New York Sunday School Union.[32]

By far the greatest difficulty with the missionary program was that of hiring missionaries and agents and ensuring some permanence in their endeavors. Because their posts were temporary and often seasonal (winter weather made it nearly impossible to form schools), missionaries were usually theological students or minis- ters who needed short-term or transitional work. "I need more exercise in the open air," explained a former pastor applying for a job; "I think the confinement requisite to a proper discharge of my [pastoral] duties is unfavorable to health." Theological students sought work as missionaries or agents to earn summer money, to prepare for the pastorate, and to gain first-hand experience at public speaking. The "oppor- tunity of travelling about" while getting paid enabled them to scout around before deciding where to settle in a pastorate. The prevalence of this practice among Andover Seminary students prompted Frederick Packard's sarcastic suggestion that the union "could easily raise a fund for the support of candidates for the ministry while [they are] exploring the country with a view to settlement."[33]

Missionaries varied in their qualifications and devotion to duty. Areas visited by a gifted missionary one summer might see none for several seasons thereafter. And, of course, each new missionary had to relearn the territory another had traversed. As a result, promising schools in remote regions often fell by the wayside for lack of continued encouragement. Likewise, agents were often inept at the delicate task of separating Christians from their money. As early as 1827 the managers complained about the unsatisfactory performance of its agents, most of whom were "young persons, students in different Theological Seminaries, or those who have just been licensed to preach." Using their posts to hone their preaching skills, these men might neglect their real business of soliciting donations. Finding agents with the right combination of "prudence, meekness, ardour, suavity, simplicity and elo- quence" was difficult, and when the union sought to hire "clergymen of eminent standing and influence" to solicit in churches of their own denominations, it found them in short supply. Consequently, the managers were often unable to follow up on promising contributors from year to year or even to take up regular annual collections in churches.[34] By the 1840s a few permanent missionaries were sta- tioned in places like western New York, Ohio, Kentucky, and Missouri, some hired directly by the union, others by its auxiliaries. However, it was not until the late nineteenth century that the potential for systematic coverage of mission areas was realized.

The union's frequently uncertain financial condition exacerbated these problems. (Only in the 1870s did the organization acquire a permanent fund and place its finances on a sound footing.) Depending as it did on contributions to pay missionary salaries, the union could not promise permanent employment. During the Mississippi Valley campaign in the 1830s, for example, the union fielded seventy-nine missionaries; a few years later, their number had shrunk to thirty-five. Indeed, for a society run by merchants, the American Sunday School Union often adopted rather unusual business practices. It permitted individual missionaries to extend credit at their discretion to communities where schools were being established, aware that the debt might never be repaid. It shipped books to missionaries without first receiving payment and often let them build up large outstanding debts. The managers reasoned, in the words of Joseph H. Dulles, that because "our object is to do good," it was too important "to be controlled by those considerations which govern a mercantile establishment." As a result, when depressions occurred in the national economy, as in 1837 and 1857, the union found itself in serious financial straits and had to cut back its programs drastically. In fact, the 1837 panic dealt a virtual death blow to the union's ambitious missionary plans, forcing a five-year contraction. The 1857 depression threatened the existence of the organization itself, not only because of its effect on sales and donations but also because it brought to light Frederick Porter's issuance of fraudulent bonds. That a trusted employee of long standing was able to embezzle union funds undetected for several years offers further testimony to the managers' often haphazard oversight of its finances.[35]

By contrast, the society's publication division was generally successful. Sales of union books were high from the very start, when the organization published primarily texts and reference works. They remained strong as the society moved, in the 1840s and 1850s, into heavier emphasis on general works for children. Only minor problems arose, concerning such matters as disputes over copyrights, complaints from authors about editorial changes, and the distribution or delivery of periodicals. Publishers who offered larger discounts than the American Sunday School Union, or whose books were perceived as livelier or more appealing, presented serious competition. Perhaps because of their determination to publish only "moral and religious" books, the managers had difficulty deciding whether to publish fiction. Like many evangelicals, they denounced "that unhealthful taste for novel-reading" so common in their society, yet they believed that some forms of fiction (for example, Bunyan's *Pilgrim's Progress*) could be highly instructive. Although they got around the dilemma by agreeing to publish "wholesome reading matter . . . by the use of all lawful methods, to impress and improve morals and manners," as the years went by they found their books pronounced "dull" in comparison to the increasingly vivid fiction issued by nonreligious, commercial publishers. Nevertheless, the American Sunday School Union remained a major publisher of children's literature throughout the nineteenth century.[36]

Because of these logistical and organizational problems, the union's achievements often fell short of its managers' aspirations. A recurrent theme in the minutes of their meetings is the need for "system" and "order" in the conduct of the group's business. Continually frustrated by bungled book orders, inept agents, temporary missionaries, recalcitrant auxiliaries, and cash shortages, the managers had to settle for an influence which, however great, was never as widespread as they envisioned.[37]

Intertwined with these internal obstacles to implementing their ideas, the managers faced problems arising from their attempt to speak for all evangelical Protestants in a society divided by denominational and sectional loyalties. If in the fervor of the 1820s it appeared possible to form a "union" of Christians devoted to the cause of Sunday schools, that dream quickly faded as sectarian groups began their own publishing operations. As a result, the union increasingly had to compete with denominational organizations for book and magazine customers, donations, and auxiliaries. Nor were these simply rivalries over esoteric issues in Protestantism. The competition between the American Sunday School Union and the various denominational societies highlighted fundamental differences among Protestants both over the best means to reach the unchurched masses and over proper approaches to the major social issues of the day.

Denominational challenges to the union's plan to concentrate Sunday school work in its hands emerged first in the form of rival publishing groups. New York's High Church Episcopalians formed the General Protestant Episcopal Sunday School Union in 1826, and Methodists created their own Sunday School Union the following year. Baptist and Presbyterian groups set up publishing and tract societies to print Sunday school materials. In organization and program, these groups were almost exact copies of the American Sunday School Union.[38]

Initially, the denominational challenge was more philosophical than material. Until the 1840s these organizations remained small, weak, and lacking in the resources necessary to compete with the Philadelphia group. Their very existence, however, raised the question of whether it was possible for any group to do what the American Sunday School Union proposed: to unite evangelicals in promoting a kind of common-denominator Protestantism. Whereas the union's officials argued that the ties that bound Protestants together were more important than the doctrines that divided them, those who formed denominational unions felt that the doctrines of their individual churches were incompatible with the theological orientation of the American Union. This was particularly true of the Methodists and High Church Episcopalians, who believed it would be impossible to retain their doctrinal integrity within a group dominated by Presbyterians and Low Church Episcopalians. "Our own publications," stated the founder of the Methodist Episcopal Sunday School Union, should be used "exclusively . . . in all our schools" to teach the doctrines and practices of Methodism. Similarly, the organizers of the General Protestant Episcopal Sunday School Union appealed to members of their church for support, citing their "duty . . . to instruct her younger members in the nature of her own peculiar character and claims." The "primitive and evangelical principles of the Protestant Episcopal Church," they declared, "admit of no compro-mise with other views on the same subjects."[39]

In claiming the right to speak for all evangelical Protestants, the American Sun-day School Union's officers championed the "union principle," arguing that their organization could achieve more than any sectarian group and urging church bodies in the name of "Christian brotherhood" to "express [their] approbation of the principles" the union espoused. They seemed genuinely puzzled that some of their coreligionists could not accept their definition of a common denominator. Yet the continuing growth of church schools and denominational unions forced the union's leaders to redefine the scope of their work. By 1838 they had begun to articulate a position that accommodated both "union" and sectarian views. "It is no part of our principles," they asserted, "to discountenance the action of denominational schools or societies. . . . We only profess to cover more ground than they can occupy, and much that can be reached in no other way than by union." Increasingly, they defined their role as forming schools in "villages and neighborhoods where there [were] no churches or schools" in order to teach the unreligious "their duties to God and man" and to urge them to seek "repentance and faith." In other words, the managers began to limit their operations to what they called "mission" areas.[40]

These areas remained quite large in the antebellum years. Only the Methodists, with their circuit-riding preachers and class-meeting system, challenged the Ameri-can Sunday School Union's missionary program, particularly after 1840. Members of most evangelical denominations found it easiest simply to split their allegiances, sending their missionary dollars to the union as well as to denominational associa-tions and purchasing Sunday school books from both denominational and union sources.[41]

Even within the union itself, the reality of sectarian loyalties often shattered the smooth facade of interdenominational harmony. In the appointment of missionaries and agents, for example, American Sunday School Union officials had to worry continually about matching the individual to the population with whom he would work. In Kentucky and Tennessee, Methodist, Baptist, and Cumberland Pres-byterian missionaries were required, whereas New England called for Congrega-tionalists and Northern Baptists. Both the board of managers' minutes and the union's correspondence files reveal how important this matching was. "My collec-tions are mostly from Presbyterian and Congregat churches," went a typical com-ment from a Presbyterian agent in upstate New York; "I am with very few excep-tions shut out from the churches of other denominations." Similarly, a New England minister had his job offer from the union revoked because "our Board [wishes] to secure the services of some *Baptist* brother in that field." The managers had to consider other qualities in choosing missionaries, too—men who were seen as too "eastern," for example, would not do well out west—but a candidate's denominational affiliation often headed the list of desirable qualifications.[42]

Even the managers' choice of administrators for the Philadelphia office drew denominational fire at times. A Baptist agent, for example, complained in 1851 about the rumored appointment of an Episcopalian clergyman to an administrative post on the grounds that the two secretaries (Porter and Packard) were also Episcopalians. Did members of that church, he wondered, have "some very preeminent and almost exclusive superiority of qualification?" He claimed that the managers ignored the candidates of "several denominations, far more numerous and in the country at large, more influential, and more generally disposed to cooperate with our Union." Such sectarian jealousies required delicate handling from Philadelphia.[43]

When denominational loyalties warred with "the union principle" within auxiliary organizations, the principle often had to be abandoned. At the state and city levels, Sunday school unions were coalitions of evangelical groups, the composition of which varied depending on the relative strength of the denominations. Hence, in New England, the Rhode Island Sunday School Union (based in Providence since its founding in 1825) and the Massachusetts Sabbath School Union (organized the same year in Boston) were coalitions of Baptists and Congregationalists, while in New York the Female Union Society for the Promotion of Sabbath-Schools and the Sunday-School Union Society were heavily Presbyterian (or Reformed Dutch) and Episcopal. The perennial squabbles within the Rhode Island and Massachusetts unions centered primarily on the denominational affiliation of local missionaries and agents. The Rhode Island group settled the issue by permitting the Congregationalists and Baptists to make appointments in alternate years—a compromise that lasted from the 1840s until 1862, when the society dissolved. The Massachusetts group, after seven years of fragile unity, decided in 1832 to let each denomination go its separate way.[44]

One of the offshoots produced by this decision was the Massachusetts Sabbath School Society, a strictly Congregationalist group whose relationship with the American Sunday School Union shows how difficult it often was to make interdenominationalism work. Practical issues, such as appointing missionaries and agents, supervising depositories, and publishing books, became intertwined with sectarian concerns. The Massachusetts men believed that they could (and should) promote the cause of Congregational Sunday schools better than the American Sunday School Union. When the parent society and the auxiliary argued over who should collect money for the cause in Massachusetts, which books should be stocked in Massachusetts depositories, and how missionary collections should be allocated, they were really arguing over whether the "union principle" or denominationalism should prevail. Against objections from Philadelphia, the Massachusetts union insisted upon publishing its own books, collecting money exclusively for its operations, and sending missionaries to the Mississippi Valley. By 1839 the impossibility of compromise on these questions led the Massachusetts organization to sever its ties with the Philadelphia union. It became, in effect, a competing Congregationalist society. "As sons of New England . . . —sons of the Puritans,—and as Congregationalists," declared the Massachusetts managers, "we are unwilling to confine our children wholly to a course of religious instruction, in which some of the most precious doctrines and practical truths of the Bible are not recognised."[45]

To be sure, the denominations often disagreed on questions of theology and practice. Baptists held very different views on baptism from Congregationalists, and Episcopal church ritual differed substantially from that of other evangelical bodies. Methodists objected to reading the books of the American Sunday School Union because they did not teach "the doctrine of *general redemption*," while Congregationalists found them wanting because they did not teach the opposing doctrine of election. Yet apart from catechisms and lesson books, the children's literature published by the various denominational societies was hardly sectarian in content. Aside from occasional references to infant baptism in Congregationalist and Presbyterian publications, and to adult baptism in Baptist books and periodicals (see figure 11), the "moral and religious" works turned out by the denominational publishing houses were hardly distinguishable from those of the American Sunday School Union.[46]

The issue of denominationalism, however, had still deeper implications. The real differences between the union's publications and those of the denominations emerged in the area of moral teaching. This had always been a province of the churches, which often policed their members' behavior through disciplinary procedures, and the American Sunday School Union had no difficulty promulgating in its literature a set of generally accepted moral principles. During the 1830s, however, as abolitionists began to argue that slaveholding was a sin, the union confronted a moral issue about which Protestants were deeply divided. In that decade and the next, denominational groups such as the Massachusetts Sabbath School Society and the Methodist Episcopal Sunday School Union began to take clear-cut stands on the slavery question in their children's books and magazines. The union's unwillingness to do the same prompted strong sectarian criticisms of its publications. Slavery, more than any other issue, undermined union officials' visions of creating a national society that would transcend sectarian loyalties. As in so many areas of American life—government, politics, the churches—slavery became the single issue that undermined claims to national influence.[47]

Slavery posed no problem for the union in its early years. Union officials actively supported schools for blacks—slave and free—through their publications and auxiliaries. Indeed, one of the strong selling points for early schools was their ability to reach free blacks, who were often excluded from other schooling opportunities.

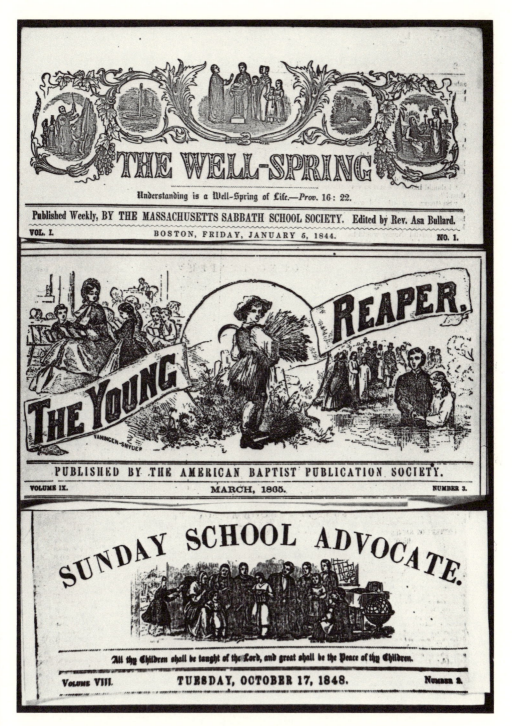

Figure 11. The Well-Spring, *published by a Congregationalist group, emphasized infant baptism on its* masthead, while the Young Reaper, *a Baptist publication, depicted adult baptism. The Methodist* Sunday School Advocate *showed individuals of all ages studying together.*

Union reports referred frequently to the virtues of Sunday schools for blacks, particularly slaves. "If our slaves were all instructed in the Bible," argued one speaker at the union's 1825 annual meeting, "the ties which bind them to God and their masters, would be made more strong, and tender, and holy. Thus they would gradually prepare for freedom, and their masters gradually be prepared to give it to them." Although missionaries occasionally reported objections to the schools among slaveholders who feared that learning might lead to dissatisfaction and flight, relatively few objections to Sunday schools were raised in the South.[48]

With the launching of the Mississippi Valley Enterprise, the union's managers found themselves the targets of criticism for attempting to over-centralize Sunday school work and usurp local initiatives. Such criticisms were especially strong in the slaveholding states, where fear of outside interference and especially of "Northern domination" was increasingly marked. The tariff fights of the 1820s, the nullification controversy, and especially Nat Turner's 1831 revolt all contributed to this growing suspicion of outsiders and Northern institutions. The veteran missionary James E. Welch, who had been promoting Sunday schools in the slaveholding states for years, reported in 1834 that a Georgia Presbyterian congregation regarded the schools as "a Northern scheme," and refused to listen to his sermon. He observed that the nullification issue had called into question the motives of any representative of a Northern benevolent society, even Southern men like himself. "Let the subject entirely alone," advised another missionary, speaking of the slavery question; it was, he felt, "the only safe course."[49]

The managers' response to this opposition in the South was to develop a policy toward such issues. "Avoid all unnecessary controversy and vain disputations," they advised their agents. Questions of social policy, like those of denominational theology, should be left alone or the union would lose its claim to being a national society. In 1833 the managers' missions committee explicitly directed missionaries to avoid "*studiously* and *constantly* . . . the subject of *slavery*, abolition, and every other irritating topic" in order to prevent harm to "this noble enterprise." The entire board of managers then made it union policy to avoid forming Sunday schools for blacks if the local white population objected. Simultaneously, they censored union publications to eliminate references to slavery.[50]

Yet in that same year the managers launched a campaign specifically to evangelize the South, the Southern Enterprise. The passage of stringent slave codes in the aftermath of Nat Turner's rebellion, combined with the union's new policy on blacks, meant that this was almost entirely a white undertaking. Still, union missionaries encountered white resistance and reported that white Southerners who supported Sunday schools were forming their own without union involvement. When the financial panic of 1837 caused the union to retrench on all fronts, the managers cut the greatest number of missionaries from the Southern campaign. By 1840 only two were working full-time in the South. Although other factors— antimissionism, anti-Yankeeism, denominational strife—exacerbated resistance to the work of the union and groups like it, the slavery issue emerged in the 1830s as the focus of Southern opposition. As one missionary summarized the problem, Southerners' "inventive imaginations associate Northern influence—a rupture of our civil compact—dissolution of all social order—an armed host of incendiary *abolitionists*—blood and murder—and a thousand other hydra-headed gorgons dire, with the establishment of a Sabbath School." Leaving the slavery issue alone, as the managers wanted, was not enough to defuse Southern white opposition.[51]

Nor was that course especially popular in the North. Arthur and Lewis Tappan, who had previously contributed to the union and other national benevolent societies, withdrew their support when they joined the ranks of immediatist abolitionists in the 1830s. Although several of the union's managers supported the American Colonization Society's efforts to purchase slaves and repatriate them to the West African colony of Liberia, they all agreed that taking a stand against slavery (even a mildly colonizationist one) would jeopardize the organization's claim to national status. By avoiding slavery "as a subject foreign from the purposes of the Society," the managers hoped "to avoid plunging the Society into a controversy which would necessarily direct its influence and its energies" away from Sunday schools. To the abolitionists, however, taking no position on slavery was tantamount to supporting it, and so the American Sunday School Union increasingly became a target of their criticism.[52]

One incident clearly illustrates both the abolitionists' tactics and the union's dilemma. In 1847 the managers withdrew from publication a book entitled *Jacob and His Sons,* which contained a reference mildly critical of slavery. Although the book had been in circulation since 1832, the offensive passage supposedly "escaped observation" until a Southern reader pointed it out to several Southern newspapers, which then called upon Southern whites to withhold donations from the union. After praying for direction, the managers decided to discontinue the book, explaining that while their action involved no judgment on "the exciting subject of slavery," the passage gave "a wrong impression" of the American variety. The desire of union officials to remain neutral on the slavery issue outraged the ever-vigilant Lewis Tappan, who saw their decision as "evidence of the control this 'institution' exercises over the literature and religion of the Northern states." By dropping the book, he argued, the managers "forget their impartiality and become apologists, if not defenders, of the atrocious system." Thus, an attempt to avoid antagonizing Southern white supporters succeeded in antagonizing Northern ones.[53]

Slavery presented a dilemma for the union in the 1830s and 1840s, as it had not in the 1820s, because it was increasingly defined as *the* moral issue of the day. The abolitionists succeeded in forcing Protestants to decide whether slaveholding was a sin. If it was, then the churches were obligated to include it among the moral evils against which they preached and to judge members' conduct accordingly. As the question of denying membership to slaveholders gained center stage, the issue became so divisive that it rent three major denominations—the Presbyterians in 1837, the Methodists in 1844, and the Baptists in 1845. Given the bitterness of these intradenominational disputes, it is not surprising that in the 1840s denominational positions on slavery became a kind of litmus test for antislavery and proslavery Americans alike. Nor is it surprising that in this atmosphere the American Sunday School Union's official position of neutrality should cost it supporters on all sides. In Wisconsin, for example, the Congregational Association censured the union for the book-dropping incident and urged conscientious Congregationalists to buy their books elsewhere.[54]

Although it is difficult to chart the precise impact of the slavery controversy on the American Sunday School Union, either in terms of books not sold or of schools not established, at the very least the controversy undermined the union's attempts to be truly national and interdenominational. For every Southerner who remained willing to buy union books "so long as they continue, as now, strictly evangelical and *conservative,*" there were many others who shunned the union because they associated all Northern benevolent societies with abolitionism. "There are fanatical sentiments dominant in . . . all churches against the North and her institutions," noted a missionary in Mississippi. A Kentucky worker found that his Northern origins made him an abolitionist in the eyes of many who "would have nothing to do with my books, because they were published in the North." Opposition to the union made his work so "exceedingly unpleasant" that he asked for a change of assignment. "I pity a poor Northerner down South in the book business," he sighed.[55] As the dominant issue of American public life in the 1840s and 1850s, slavery helped to destroy the American Sunday School Union's claims to national influence in much the same way that it divided denominations and tore at the fabric of national life.

Internal problems further eroded the union's base of support. In 1857 a financial panic and the revelation of Frederick Porter's fraud rocked the organization, sending it into a tailspin that lasted almost five years. During that period, a new group of managers and employees embarked upon an aggressively expansionist policy, firing all collecting agents, requiring union depositories to become self-supporting or close, terminating all existing union periodicals and launching several new ones, publishing a new children's book every Saturday, and sponsoring an unprecedented national convention of Sunday school workers. Although this policy briefly met with success, it precipitated a power struggle within the union between supporters of expansion and advocates of a more conservative publishing and financing program, a struggle that culminated in the firing of Frederick Packard in 1860. A second financial downturn in 1860, combined with the political excitement surrounding the election that year, precipitated another crisis. Soon Packard was back and most of the new men were gone. By March 1861 the union had only forty full-time missionaries (compared with almost three hundred full- and part-time in 1855) and its finances were once again in disarray. "Certain laymen," wrote James Alexander to Packard in the midst of the crisis, "every where use a new language," one that "discriminate[s] between Sunday Schools & *the Society.*" Although the union's managers regrouped their forces once again, placing their organization back on track by the mid-1860s, the society's troubles had long-term consequences.[56]

Whatever problems they faced in 1861, the managers could look back over an impressive organizational history. The institution to which they had devoted so much energy had become firmly embedded in American culture. Their publications were widely disseminated, sales having grown from $10,000 in 1826 to $185,000 in 1855. (They reached $235,000 in 1860 before dropping off sharply during the war.) Like modern-day evangelists who computerize their fund-raising lists and employ television talk shows to reach a mass audience, the union's officials had harnessed newly available means, particularly the press and the voluntary society, to spread their group's influence. And because they so often equated the influence they sought with the spread of their schools and publications, they could derive some comfort from the statistics they were so fond of collecting. Still, those among them who had been present during the heady early years could see how much the decades had changed the group's expectations. Denominational and sectional tensions, combined with internal problems not of their making, had made their dream of providing centralized national direction for the Sunday school movement an elusive one.

By the late 1860s, other men were dreaming a similar dream and beginning to believe that they had found the key to its realization. The Methodist educator Edward Eggleston summed up their perspective in 1869, when he reviewed recent changes in Sunday school work and pronounced them nothing less than "a revolution." During the brief space of a decade, between the 1859 national convention sponsored by the American Sunday School Union and a similar event in 1869, Eggleston contended that Sunday school workers had seen the emergence of new leaders, new forms of organization, new programs, and new periodicals, all of which had reinvigorated and transformed their work.[57] The occasion that elicited this pronouncement—the 1869 convention—was also a symbol of the changes he chronicled. For at that convention, more than five hundred Sunday school editors, publishers, missionaries, pastors, superintendents, and teachers put aside their denominational differences and came together to discuss common problems and goals. One of the new organizational forms of which Eggleston wrote, the convention completely bypassed the American Sunday School Union. Through such national gatherings, as well as hundreds of local, state, and county conventions, Eggleston and others proposed a new style of interdenominational cooperation that owed no debts to the union or its auxiliaries.

Sunday school conventions were not entirely new in the 1860s. They had originated on the local level with the effort of teachers in the 1850s to borrow a leaf from the notebook of their public school counterparts. To encourage mutual self-improvement, they held city- and county-wide training classes and institutes that disseminated new methods adopted from common school teaching. Perhaps hoping to capitalize on the popularity of such meetings, six officers and managers of the American Sunday School Union issued a call for a national teachers' convention to be held in Philadelphia in February 1859. At that time a committee was appointed to organize another convention, but the union's internal problems, combined with the outbreak of civil war, derailed plans for the gathering. The second national convention eventually met in 1869; thereafter, they convened every three years.[58]

The ten-year hiatus between the first two conventions brought the "revolution" of which Eggleston wrote. The 1859 convention had been dominated by the American Sunday School Union: its publications editor served as temporary chairman and several of its managers, missionaries, or agents acted as convention officers. By contrast, the 1869 convention in Newark, New Jersey, was called by a group of state Sunday school workers who had met at a Young Men's Christian Association convention the previous year. They relegated most union participants to honorary positions. No union personnel served on the convention's powerful executive committee and only one union official had a major role (as one of the convention's three secretaries). Perhaps the most notable change in leadership between 1859 and 1869 was the prominent role taken by the Methodists, who had previously been unwilling to participate actively in interdenominational Sunday school work and were frequently hostile to American Union activities.

The programs of the two meetings also formed a sharp contrast. In 1859 the participants had listened to three days of reports from American Sunday School Union–affiliated schools and supporters, discussed prearranged questions, then passed resolutions offered by the speakers. In 1869 the delegates heard reports from a variety of national and state Sunday school associations, then met in small groups for open discussions from which emerged resolutions that were proposed to the entire body. The format of the 1869 convention was much more decentralized and provided a larger role for the teachers, superintendents, and pastors who came as delegates.[59]

The contrasting resolutions adopted by the two conventions hinted at broad changes in the emphasis of Sunday school work in the intervening decade. The twenty-seven resolutions adopted at the 1859 meeting addressed issues that had been current among teachers for years: the need for punctuality and order in schools, the importance of visiting students and encouraging their early conversion, the difficulty of keeping older students in school, and the necessity of getting congregational support for the schools. The 1869 convention adopted only eleven resolutions, three of which dealt with teacher-training institutes and conventions. Sunday school leadership had passed to individuals whose primary interest was to promote system, method, and order in their work and who used convention-style meetings to achieve those goals.

By 1869 regular state conventions were being held (in some cases annually) in such places as New York, Kentucky, Illinois, Massachusetts, New Jersey, and Missouri. In many states the conventions led to the formation of teachers' associations which were almost invariably separate from existing Sunday school unions and exhibited no interest in affiliating with the American Sunday School Union. Unlike the union, the conventions were organized from the bottom up and run by volunteer executive committees that maintained continuity from year to year and planned successive meetings. Thus, the national conventions that met in 1869, 1872, 1875, 1878, and 1881 were essentially gatherings of delegates from local conventions. Moreover, Methodists, who had usually remained aloof from interdenominational causes, were especially active in both state and national meetings. Forty-one percent of the 341 delegates to the 1857 Indiana Sunday School Convention, for example, were Methodists.[60]

This system of local, state, and national conventions fostered a new type of interdenominational cooperation by ignoring doctrinal issues and bringing workers together on the basis of a common interest in teaching. By focusing on teaching techniques, conventions handily sidestepped any doctrinal differences among participants and encouraged them to come together as teachers. Although participants shared an evangelical orientation (Unitarians and Quakers would have felt out of place), the existence of denominational loyalties was taken for granted. Unlike the American Sunday School Union, which in the past had criticized "narrow sectarianism" and tried to promulgate common Protestant doctrines, the delegates to the conventions avoided doctrine as much as possible.

The heart of the convention system, indeed the very basis for its continuance, was the teachers' institute. Popularized in the early 1860s by the Methodist minister John H. Vincent, the institutes were a conscious adaptation of techniques used in public school teaching. Aimed at professionalizing Sunday school teaching, they were designed to banish, in Vincent's words, "the false and injurious notion that *anybody* is competent to teach in a Sabbath school." Instead, like common schools, Sunday schools should employ "a regular system of teacher training." Institutes quickly became a regular part of teachers' meetings on both the county and state levels. Indeed, teacher training, along with sessions on missionary work and school extension, formed a large segment of convention agendas. By the late 1860s, teachers in Illinois, New York, and Pennsylvania had created an efficient system of local institutes, county associations, and state conventions.[61]

Although their format changed over the years, the institutes and conventions drew heavily on the work of state normal schools. Initially, the convention programs reflected the normal schools' interest in sharing new pedagogical ideas and making teaching more of a profession. Thus, the delegates to an 1867 New York institute conducted by Vincent listened to lectures on such topics as "The Model Superintendent Described," "Defects in Sunday-School Teaching," "Teachers' Meetings," and "Bible Illustrations" (see figure 12). As time went on, however, convention planners introduced sessions on "Blackboard Illustration," "Object Teaching," and other practical subjects, as well as demonstration classes. Thus, the institutes and conventions were important in making teachers aware of the variety of secular teaching techniques available for adaptation in religious education.[62]

Another means of disseminating such information were periodicals for teachers. Although the American Sunday School Union had published one since the 1820s, these periodicals proliferated and took on a new look in the 1860s. Particularly popular and influential were the new, nominally pan-denominational journals such as the *National Sunday School Teacher* and the *Sunday School Times*. (In practice, the *Teacher* had strong Methodist leanings, while the *Times* was Con-gregationalist.) Emphasizing teaching techniques over religious content, these periodicals reflected in their pages a new emphasis on system, order, teacher training, and pedagogy, offering detailed instructions on how to teach Sunday school classes using the techniques employed in normal schools. In addition, they supported the convention movement by providing information about local and national meetings.[63]

Both conventions and magazines succeeded largely by avoiding the theological and denominational battles that had bedeviled the American Sunday School Union during the prewar years. To be sure, convention prayer meetings were rousing cross-denominational affairs, with plenty of inspiring preaching and lusty singing, but theological themes were deliberately muted in the interests of overall harmony. And although the strong participation of Methodists contributed to the conventions' success (the denomination had grown phenomenally in the course of the century), it also helped that the theological lines between Methodism and orthodox Calvinism had become considerably blurred. For these and other reasons, the conventions seemed able to animate and realize the old goal of interdenominational cooperation.

In reality, however, the goal itself had changed, and nothing reflected that change so much as the leadership of the conventions. Here was a new generation of workers, with their own goals and aspirations. The path they chose diverged from the broadly millennialist road favored by their predecessors. Its signposts directed them not toward the reformation of all American society but toward efficiency and professionalism in the one area where they labored. These men—for as yet few women took leading positions—generally eschewed the utopian visions of the 1820s and 1830s, when American Sunday School Union officials had dreamed of a

PROGRAMME.

Sunday Evening, March 17th, at 7½ o'clock.

Preliminary Sermon,

By Rev. T. E. VERMILYE, D.D., LL.D.

First Session, Monday Evening.

7 o'clock, DEVOTIONAL EXERCISES, conducted by Rev. J. H. VINCENT. Subject, "Our Homes."

7.30 " INTRODUCTORY ADDRESS. "The Object of Sunday-School Teaching," . . . . Rev. S. H. TYNG, D.D.

8 " EXERCISE IN SACRED TOPOGRAPHY, . . Rev. J. H. VINCENT.

8.15 " SERIAL QUESTIONS:
1. "What are the Objects of the Mission Sunday-School?"
2. "What are the Objects of the Church Sunday-School?"
[Brief written answers to the above questions are requested from the audience. They will then be referred to a committee, and reported at the second session.]

8.30 " "THE RELATION OF THE PASTOR AND THE CHURCH TO THE SUNDAY-SCHOOL," . . Rev. HOWARD CROSBY, D.D.

Second Session, Tuesday Evening.

7 o'clock, DEVOTIONAL EXERCISES, conducted by Rev. WM. M. PAXTON. Subject, "Our Unconverted Scholars."

7.20 " REPORT OF COMMITTEE, on "The Objects of the Sunday-School."

7.30 " THE MODEL SUPERINTENDENT DESCRIBED. R. G. PARDEE, Esq.

7.55 " THE DUTIES OF SUNDAY-SCHOOL TEACHERS TO THE SUPERINTENDENT, ... ANDREW A. SMITH, Esq.

8.20 " DEFECTS IN SUNDAY-SCHOOL TEACHING, . Rev. H. D. GANSE.

8.50 " ORDER OF EXERCISES IN SUNDAY-SCHOOL.
[Reports will be made from four Schools.]

Third Session, Wednesday Evening.

7 o'clock, DEVOTIONAL EXERCISES, conducted by Rev. Dr. ANDERSON. Subject, "Sunday-School Teachers."

7.30 " BIBLE ILLUSTRATIONS, . . . Rev. S. H. TYNG, JR.

8 " INFANT CLASS LESSON, conducted by RALPH WELLS, Esq.

8.50 " BLACKBOARD, PICTURE AND OBJECT TEACHING. R. G. PARDEE, Esq.

Fourth Session, Thursday Evening.

7 o'clock, DEVOTIONAL EXERCISES, conducted by Rev. W. T. SABINE. Subject, "Mission Sunday-Schools."

7.20 " SACRED GEOGRAPHY.

7.45 " BIBLE CLASS LESSON, conducted by Rev. C. S. ROBINSON, D.D.

8.30 " SERIAL QUESTIONS:
1. "Why should our Sunday-School Teachers receive some Preparatory Training for their Work?"
2. "What should this Training Comprise?"

8.45 " ADDRESS TO SUNDAY-SCHOOL TEACHERS. JOHN S. HART, LL.D.

Fifth Session, Friday Evening.

7 o'clock, DEVOTIONAL EXERCISES, conducted by Rev. E. P. ROGERS, D.D. Subject, "Educational Institutions."

7.20 " REPORT OF COMMITTEE, on "The Training of Sunday-School Teachers."

7.35 " ADDRESS on "Teacher-Training," . Rev. J. H. VINCENT.

8.05 " ADDRESS on "The Secular School and the Sunday-School." N. A. CALKINS, Esq.

8.35 " ADDRESS on "Teachers' Meetings," . R. G. PARDEE, Esq.

9 " CLOSING ADDRESS, . . . Rev. R. J. W. BUCKLAND.

Figure 12. This program from a New York teachers' institute in 1867 reflects the growing interest in "object teaching" and other new techniques. Note that all the speakers at this institute were men.

perfected world run on Christian principles. Instead, they aimed to establish Sunday schools, staff them with trained teachers, provide them with systematic lesson plans, and encourage the religious development of each individual student. Although they agreed that "Christian character, earnestness and love for souls" were "essential" in their work, they believed that these attributes did not "do away with the necessity for practical efficiency among practical men." In stressing practicality and efficiency, these men symbolized the emerging tendency towards consolidation in American culture as a whole, as well as the increasingly inward focus of the Protestant denominations.[64]

Three of their number illustrate some of the contrasts between the prewar and postwar generations. Perhaps the most typical of the new men, certainly the best known, was John H. Vincent, who became secretary of the Methodist Episcopal Sunday School Union in 1868. Born about 1830, Vincent became a minister in the circuit-riding system of his church, receiving his first pastorate in 1853. From that post in New Jersey, Vincent went on to a station in Joliet, Illinois, in 1857 and then rose quickly to prominence, taking successive positions in Mount Morris, Galena, and Rockford before being assigned to Trinity Church in Chicago in 1864. Despite his rapid ascent to the pastorate of a fashionable church, Vincent was bored by his pastoral duties and found an outlet for his considerable energies in the Chicago Sunday School Union. Here he began offering Sunday school addresses, lectures, model lessons, and teachers' training institutes. In 1865 he brought out a new journal, a forerunner to the *National Sunday School Teacher,* which breathed new life into the concept of a teachers' magazine. While still in Chicago, Vincent took on the duties of agent for his denomination's Sunday School Union, but by 1866 he had been called to New York to serve as general agent. Upon the departure of Daniel Wise in 1869, Vincent became corresponding secretary, not only running the Methodist Episcopal Union but also editing its teachers' magazine, the *Sunday School Journal.* He went on to found, with fellow Methodist Lewis Miller, the Chautauqua Assembly—a two-week institute for Sunday school teachers that grew into the Chautauqua Literary and Scientific Circle—develop the Oxford League for the study of Methodist doctrine and history, and eventually become a bishop of the church.[65]

Two themes that dominated Vincent's life—self-education and a distaste for revivalism—offer insight into his motivation and success. Throughout his life, Vincent expressed profound "grief, . . . regret, discouragement and mortification" because he had never attended college. To compensate, he spent much of his life studying, teaching, and devising self-education schemes for himself and others. As a twenty-year-old circuit rider, he spent much of his time reading sermons, philosophy, and the *Methodist Quarterly* in order "by force of personal resolve [to] secure many benefits of college education." As a pastor in New Jersey and Illinois, he sought the companionship of seminary professors, attending lectures and classes and using his new-found knowledge as the basis for "special classes in Biblical history, geography, and interpretation" for his flock. For a man who never tired of likening the church to "a school with many departments" where "what is generally taught in detail only in theological schools ought to be taught, in outline at least," the distinctly unenthusiastic response of his Chicago parishioners was disheartening. His intense energy soon found an outlet, however, in Sunday school work. Institutes for teachers provided a vehicle for his talents and tapped a new source of enthusiasm among teachers. The Chautauqua scheme was merely the institutional expression of a lifetime of self-education projects. Here, as in his sermons, lectures, institutes, and magazine articles, Vincent could pursue his own education while enabling similarly disposed Americans to "cover the fields of college work" like "their more favored sons and daughters."[66]

Vincent's distaste for revivalism had personal as well as intellectual roots. Not only had he had little success arousing revivals in his pastoral work, he also associated revivalism with the "gloomy," "morbid" religion of his childhood. A sensitive, solitary child, he had grown into an adult who blamed revivalistic religion for depriving him of a spontaneous "boy life" and for encouraging excessive emotionalism in others. On an intellectual level, he felt revivalism emphasized the irrational at the expense of rational understanding and led to backsliding. Thus, as a pastor he preferred the stability of the Sunday school to the upheavals of the revival and worked hard to encourage communicants of all ages to be involved in the school. "Calm, rational, intelligent, unremitting endeavor for twelve months of every year" was preferable, he believed, to occasional superficial excitements. Nonetheless, he never publicly objected to the revivalistic fervor that often surrounded the Sunday school conventions he addressed.[67]

Two other men of Vincent's generation also made their careers as Sunday school leaders after the Civil War. Both worked for the American Sunday School Union in its efforts to capitalize on the new interest in teacher training. One was Henry Clay Trumbull, member of a distinguished Connecticut family, son-in-law of the reformer Thomas H. Gallaudet, friend and student of Horace Bushnell, writer, and one of the first professional religious educators in American history. The other was Edwin W. Rice, who came from a poor New York farming family and worked his way through various schools before joining the American Union as a student missionary in 1856. Rice went on to become a regular missionary, superintendent of missions for the union in Wisconsin and Minnesota, assistant secretary of missions and assistant editor of periodicals, and finally editor of publications until his retirement. Both Trumbull and Rice were Congregationalist ministers without pastorates; both were involved in the promotion of teachers' institutes as early as the 1850s; and both had active careers in publishing. Beginning his work for the union as a missionary in 1858, Trumbull promised to work for "the increase and improvement of Sabbath Schools" in Connecticut. Improvement soon became his first priority as he traveled the state promoting a regular system of state and county conventions and institutes. In 1871 he became the union's first "normal secretary" with the job of "improving schools and training teachers for the whole country," a post he left in 1875 to edit the independent weekly *Sunday School Times*. Rice's institute work began in Wisconsin during the Civil War, when he set up a chain of institutes for "training in principles and methods of teaching as applied to moral and religious life and conduct." As the union's editor of publications after 1875, Rice supervised the production of a widely used lesson series and a variety of aids to Bible study for teachers, as well as collaborating with the well-known scholar Philip Schaff on a dictionary of the Bible. He also promoted the new Biblical scholarship in the 1870s among Sunday school teachers and worked to encourage acceptance of the new translation of the King James Bible that appeared in 1878.[68]

Rice, Trumbull, and Vincent—of nearly the same age but different social back-grounds—shared an interest in systematizing Sunday school training, encouraging the convention system, and regularizing the Sunday school curriculum. But their bonds ran deeper, for at the core of their activities was a drive to undercut the revivalistic basis of Protestant church membership and replace it with a staged process of religious growth. Vincent was the most antirevival of the three, but Trumbull—despite having been converted as a result of a revival conducted by the noted evangelist Charles G. Finney—shared his deep distrust of revivalism's em-phasis on elusive feeling. Reason alone, he believed, should be sufficient to lead individuals to see their sinfulness and confess their faith. Relying on the "Christian nurture" ideas of Horace Bushnell, who had been his spiritual advisor for a time, Trumbull stressed the gradual religious development of children. Rice was less hostile to revivals, often including revival-like "decision days" in his institute work, but the main focus of his teaching was "the development of child-mind, and the successive stages of growth of spiritual character."[69]

The lives of other convention leaders demonstrate the convention movement's broad base and the cross-denominational cooperation on which it thrived. Lacking a discrete leadership group comparable to the officers of the American Sunday School Union, the movement depended upon the expertise of diverse individuals who served on executive committees, organized meetings, determined convention pro-grams, and were responsible for the success of national conventions. They included not only ministers like Vincent and Trumbull but also businessmen like Chicagoan Benjamin F. Jacobs, Ohioan Lewis Miller and Philadelphian George Hay Stuart, as well as the revivalist Dwight Moody and the writer Edward Eggleston. The back-grounds of these men brought them together, despite their different denominational affiliations, and helped shape the convention movement. Several were Methodists, a denomination that in the past had held aloof from interdenominational efforts. To the convention movement they brought an organizational tradition which, al-though decentralized, was highly structured and enormously effective at mobilizing large numbers of people. The similarities between the Methodist system—con-gregationally based class meetings supplemented by local, regional, and national conferences—and the Sunday school conventions was no accident: the conventions had adopted the structure through the influence of their Methodist leaders. Likewise, it was Methodists like Vincent who championed the type of inter-denominational cooperation exemplified by the conventions, cooperation based on educational method and technique, not theology.[70]

But there was another dimension to the cross-denominational cooperation that proved so popular at the conventions. Many of the organizers had had experience in two other groups: the Young Men's Christian Association (YMCA) and the wartime Christian Commission. YMCAs, organized in several cities in the early 1850s, had within a few years mobilized thousands of young urbanites into prayer meetings and other cross-denominational activities designed to help them adjust to city life without losing their faith. During the revivals that occurred in many large cities in 1857–1858, members of the YMCA were especially active in hiring revivalists, leading noontime prayer meetings, and recruiting converts among the businessmen and clerks who were the associations' main constituents. One activity that YMCA members particularly encouraged was teaching Sunday school. Not only would a teaching position in a school place a young man from the country under good influences, it would also give him an immediate circle of acquaintances of the right type. And in an era when men were judged by the company they kept, having the right friends could often be an invaluable business asset. The revivals cemented this connection between the YMCA and the Sunday school because they led many association members to found mission schools in an effort to reach out to the lower classes, who remained untouched by religious enthusiasm. It is not surprising that leaders of the association became interested in the institutes and conventions that teachers were beginning to attend in the late 1850s. As a result, many YMCA workers found themselves heavily involved in the convention movement. In Chicago, men like John V. Farwell, Benjamin F. Jacobs, and Dwight L. Moody moved easily between the YMCA and the Sunday school. In 1860, for example, Farwell presided over the Chicago YMCA while also serving as superintendent of the school at Moody's mission church. Jacobs succeeded him as the Chicago association's president while continuing to serve as Sunday school superintendent at a local Baptist church. During Farwell's tenure, the Chicago YMCA assumed formal responsibility for sustaining Moody's North Market Hall Mission. In Philadelphia, George Hay Stuart, founder of that city's YMCA and a manager of the American Sunday School Union, joined with the young entrepreneur John Wanamaker to set up Bethany Sabbath School, a mission school in one of the city's poorest neighborhoods. He was also instrumental in starting the Philadelphia Sabbath School Association, a group devoted to "conference among teachers of all denominations as to the best methods of management and teaching."[71]

With the outbreak of the Civil War and the recruitment of many association members into the Union army, men like Moody, Farwell, Stuart, and Wanamaker turned their attention to organizing the Christian Commission in 1861 as the spiritual counterpart to the Sanitary Commission. While the latter would tend to soldiers' bodily wants, the former would address their spiritual needs. From an office in one of Stuart's Philadelphia warehouses, the Christian Commission sent volunteers to visit military camps and hospitals, where they supplied religious literature and held prayer meetings. The primary objects of its solicitude were ordinary soldiers, young men from the same constituency as the YMCA. Thus, the Christian Commission's work was often an extension of association work.[72]

In the postwar era, men with experience in revivalism, YMCA work, and the Christian Commission joined together to make the Sunday school convention an important focus of their evangelistic activities. The interconnections were evident at the 1864 Cook County (Illinois) Sunday school convention, organized by YMCA leaders Moody and Jacobs, who also conducted devotional exercises. John H. Vincent served as one of the meeting's two vice-presidents and sessions were adjourned to permit delegates to attend a noon prayer meeting at the YMCA rooms. Later Sunday school workers looked back on this event as a significant turning point in the convention movement for two reasons: Vincent's address urging the establishment of teachers' institutes and Moody's prayer sessions that quickly turned into revival meetings. In Vincent's call for institutes, Sunday school workers found a theme for future conventions; in Moody's prayer meetings, they discovered the appeal of YMCA-style gatherings and their potential as catalysts for revivals. Later meetings of the Illinois State Sunday School Association reflected these twin interests: after attending training sessions, delegates participated in mass meetings that were led by Moody or Jacobs and orchestrated by the hymnist Philip Phillips. The Illinois model was so influential in other states that later Sunday school historians took to referring to Moody, Jacobs, and their colleagues as "The Illinois Band" and attributing to them the success of the convention movement.[73]

There were certain paradoxes, however, in the alliance between men like Moody and Vincent. The same conventions that enabled Moody to develop his revivalistic skills offered Vincent the chance to promote his antirevival goals. Vincent saw teacher training and curriculum development as means of undercutting the role of revivals in the churches and encouraging staged religious growth throughout life. Differing purposes occasionally led to conflict between Sunday school workers who agreed with Vincent and those who sided with Moody. Edward Eggleston, for example, felt the schools were being "organized to death" by some of Vincent's methods. Still, the conventions generally accommodated the needs of both groups. At workshops, participants received the kind of training that organizers like Vincent wanted, while at mass assemblies they were subjected to Moody's revival methods. Because his revivals were conducted outside of congregational settings, in the context of large public gatherings, Moody in a sense served Vincent's purposes by eliminating the pressure on individual pastors to cultivate revivals in their churches. Pastoral energy could then be focused on improving the Sunday school and expanding its reach to all members of the congregation. Participants at Sunday school conventions went home fired by the religious zeal the mass meetings engendered and ready to put into practice the teaching techniques learned in the workshops.[74]

ecause of their success, the conventions eventually challenged the American Sunday School Union for leadership of the evangelical Sunday school cause, a challenge that churned up a good deal of turbulence beneath the conventions' surface calm. Initially, the union was actively involved in sponsoring local conventions and encouraging teachers' institutes.[75] By the early 1860s, however, opposition to the union, its officials, and its methods was evident at state convention meetings. In some states, organizers made it clear to union personnel that they had little interest in their participation. Writing from Missouri in 1867, the union missionary William P. Paxson concluded melodramatically that "out here the Amer. S S Union or the State Conventions, *one or the other must die.*" He intended, he declared, "only to go into it [the convention system] where ever I can make it useful to our interests . . . for it won't do to warm into existence an institution that may supplant us."[76] In other states, union men participated in conventions, but often only on terms set by their organizers. Thus, in Kentucky, John McCullagh played a prominent role in the state conventions of the 1870s because of his considerable fame and prestige as a long-time union missionary.[77]

Hostility to the union had two bases: organizational and doctrinal. The organizational question had confronted the union's officials since the group's early days but now posed a much larger threat to their interests. At issue was what type of organization might best achieve the dual goals of bringing teachers together for mutual self-help and fostering the growth of new schools. From the beginning, the union's officers had favored a centralized system under which local teachers' organizations were auxiliary to the union, receiving books and periodicals from it, while union missionaries worked with them to found and support new schools. The convention organizers, on the other hand, were committed from the outset to local control. They worked to keep the conventions' organizational framework simple and flexible, encouraged volunteer lay workers to start new schools, generally opposed the hiring of paid missionaries, and maintained their own sets of statistics. To provide continuity between the yearly state conventions and the triennial national conventions, they adopted an executive committee system that had the effect—intentional or not—of excluding the American Sunday School Union from direct involvement in planning or running conventions. Only occasionally were missionaries like Trumbull in Connecticut able, by dint of personality and perseverance, to circumvent the system and serve on state or national executive committees.[78]

The doctrinal issue concerned the old question of whether it was possible to establish lasting schools on the principle of common-denominator Protestantism. Reporting from the 1860 meeting of the Minnesota State Sabbath School Association, Edwin W. Rice informed the Philadelphia office of an effort to censure the union and its affiliated schools. The schools, critics charged, were "milk and water concerns" that taught "no definite truth" and should be shunned in favor of denominational schools. Although the critics lost the censure vote, they had, according to Rice, planted an "apple of discord" that would be hard to uproot. More important, the convention system resolved the problem of cross-denominational cooperation by stressing teaching techniques and avoiding doctrine entirely.[79]

Because missionary work encompassed both organizational and doctrinal issues, it became the focus of conflict. In Illinois, for example, where the convention movement was strong, critics of the union charged it with establishing weak and unsupported schools. New schools, they argued, could better be sustained by local volunteers than by traveling missionaries dispatched from Philadelphia. The debate became increasingly heated as the organizers of the Illinois State Sunday School Convention—people like Dwight Moody, B. F. Jacobs, and Edward Eggleston— attempted to exclude union spokesmen from the convention programs and, union officials charged, to take credit for schools set up by their missionaries. At stake was not merely the union's pride or statistics but its publication program, as well: should the conventions keep the American Sunday School Union from organizing new schools in Illinois—and by extension other states—the union's managers would see the effects in lost revenues to their publishing program. For their part, the convention organizers saw the union's agents as hostile to the entire convention system. Eggleston accused them of "covert and finally open attacks upon our State Association," which possessed "the best methods of missionary labor."[80]

Nowhere was the conflict over methods more evident than at the 1869 national convention. Not only did its organizers attempt to exclude American Sunday School Union officials from planning and running the meeting, but at the convention itself the union's mission program came in for explicit criticism. "Eggleston would have run the Newark Convention to the injury of the Am. S. S. Union, and for the benefit of the West and the Nat'l S. S. Teacher," reported Henry Clay Trumbull to the Philadelphia office, had he and New York secretary J. Bennet Tyler not "taken hold to head him [off]; . . . the result will be that we shall prevent him doing any harm to our Society." Still, several speakers at the convention criticized the union's methods, contending that lay volunteers established the most successful schools.[81]

Although this squabbling resulted from fundamental differences between two types of Sunday school organizations, personality clashes played a part, as well. In Illinois, some of the problems were smoothed over when the union's managers agreed to appoint as their general superintendent for the area a man recommended by Moody, Jacobs, and others. The new missionary, in turn, persuaded the Illinois Sunday School Association to conduct a statistical survey to determine whether the conventions or the union had more success in establishing permanent new schools.[82] In other instances personality conflicts revealed more deep-seated problems. When the ever-prickly William Paxson fell out with the leaders of the Missouri State Sunday School Association, the issue of union as opposed to convention schools was exacerbated by the bitterness of local political divisions. At the Missouri convention's 1867 meeting, a hullabaloo erupted over the seating of a black delegate and the presentation of speeches praising the assassinated President Lincoln. The state convention delegates, themselves hopelessly split over Reconstruction issues, associated the union missionary with one side of the split. Paxson was accused of allying himself with "the party of the Rebellion" and using his influence "on behalf of the persecuting and opposing Southern element." Under the circumstances, union officials deemed it best to pack Paxson off to Texas for a few months.[83]

Harder to paper over were long-standing differences between the managers of the American Sunday School Union, who included many Presbyterians and Episcopalians, and the Methodists, who often took leadership roles in the conventions. From the first, Methodists had declined to join interdenominational endeavors like the union, and now that many of them were emerging as convention leaders, more than one union employee professed to discern a conspiracy against their society. "Methodists and Romanists do stick to their church organizations most tenaciously," commented Trumbull dryly, lumping Methodists and Roman Catholics together as devotees of denominational exclusivity. The long-time St. Louis agent Abijah W. Corey went further, suggesting that "Eggleston and a few leading *Methodists* intend, if possible, to run off the Am. S. S. U. or at least its *missionaries*. This done, all the *itinerant* S. S. missionaries left in the field will be the *Meth. Circuit Preachers*." Sentiments like these were so common among union representatives in the 1860s and 1870s that one union official was led to caution against the "disposition to call people enemies simply because . . . their business is in competition with us. This is all wrong," he warned, "and not tolerated among Christian men in the business world."[84]

In attempting to come to terms with the convention movement, union officials had to deal not only with organizational and doctrinal questions but also with the personalities and political quirks of individual missionaries and their own limitations as an interdenominational group that was not truly interdenominational. By the 1870s state teachers' associations and conventions were handling increasing amounts of the organizational work done earlier by the union, and in the publishing arena, denominational publishing houses were reaping many of the benefits of increased interest in teacher training and curriculum development. As a result, the union was gradually but unequivocally relegated to doing missionary work in rural and remote areas or in states that did not yet have strong teachers' associations. Ironically, its publication program received a boost from one of the convention movement's major successes: uniform lessons.

dopted at the 1872 national convention, the uniform lesson plan represented a triumph for the interdenominationalism advocated by the conventions' supporters. Under the plan, a pet project of Benjamin F. Jacobs, representatives of the various denominational publishers and the American Sunday School Union met with convention leaders like Jacobs to establish a sequence of weekly lessons whereby students could study the Bible in an orderly fashion. (After 1872 a committee of the national convention oversaw the lessons.) The idea of sequential or serial lessons was not new in itself. Since the early 1860s, when Methodist publishers had begun printing lesson series covering portions of the Bible in one- or two-year plans, other publishing houses had virtually replaced their old question books with integrated lesson series. What was new was the idea of coordinating the various lesson series by prescribing the sequence of study in a seven-year cycle. Thus, under the uniform plan all Sunday school children, regardless of denominational affiliation, studied the same scriptural passage each week. Although the national convention's committee established which scriptural passage would be studied, the denominations still set the content of the lesson. This, in short, was interdenominationalism at its most successful.[85]

The uniform lessons proved a boon to the major Sunday school publishers, including the American Sunday School Union, because they enabled them to offer a variety of lesson books to fit a variety of school needs. For the small or rural school, the publisher could offer books containing a year's worth of lessons. (After 1880 they brought out four books a year, each with thirteen lessons, creating the "quarterlies" so familiar to generations of Sunday scholars.) For the larger school with several "departments"—junior, senior, adult—there were separate lessons for each. And for any school that could afford them, there were two or three students' magazines geared to different age groups and oriented around the weekly lesson, as well as teachers' magazines that included background information, explanatory material, and hints on teaching the lesson. As the major denominational publishers strove to provide solid lesson programs to their church schools, the American Sunday School Union competed to offer an attractive alternative to denominational products. The result was a revitalized publishing program for the union and an overall expansion of Sunday school publishing.[86]

But not all convention leaders were as ecstatic about uniform lessons as Jacobs and the publishers were. To some, the drive for uniformity undercut the very premises on which the convention movement had been based: local control and individuality in the schools. Perhaps the most prominent spokesman for this view was Edward Eggleston, who opposed his fellow Methodist John H. Vincent on the lessons, as well as on other issues related to the future of the convention movement. Eggleston believed that the lessons introduced too much rigidity into the schools' curriculum and discouraged further innovation, "thus quenching and squelching out the development of the individual life of our schools." After a few more years of uniform lessons, he commented sarcastically, "Dr. Vincent or Mr. Jacobs will be able to look at a watch, and tell a body just what identical printed questions they are reading simultaneously at little Baptist boys in Burmah, and little Methodist maids in Minnesota."[87] Like all caricatures, this version of Vincent's and Jacobs's vision contained elements of realism.

For similar reasons, Eggleston opposed the trend toward regularizing and system-atizing the convention process itself. Much of the basis for the convention leaders' criticism of the American Sunday School Union had focused on the union's top-down organization and its use of hired missionaries. Yet by the time the 1881 national convention met, leaders like Jacobs were pushing for a higher degree of organization in the convention system, with a permanent national secretary and state statistical secretaryships. The drive toward bureaucratizing the conventions struck Eggleston and others as wrong, not only because it robbed the conventions of the spontaneity and enthusiasm that had been their driving force, but also because it seemed calculated eventually to replace one national interdenominational organi-zation—the American Sunday School Union—with another. Although the con-ventions never quite took that road, continuing the executive committee structure into the early twentieth century, they did gradually become "international" by including delegates from Canada and Britain. Eventually, paid staffs replaced the volunteer workers of earlier days.[88]

The transition from the American Sunday School Union to the conventions as a mechanism for cross-denominational Sunday school work in the nineteenth century reverses the traditional historical wisdom about how institutions work. We tend to assume that most nineteenth-century institutions, like religious denominations or the federal government, grew from small-scale, decentralized beginnings into large-scale, national bodies. Yet the American Sunday School Union began as a cen-tralized national society; only in the late nineteenth century did Sunday school workers turn to a decentralized form of organization to achieve their goals, specifi-cally rejecting the union's structure. There is paradox in all this, of course, for the conventions' very success eventually required that they become institutionalized. The spontaneity of early days gave way to centralized organizations with all the trappings of modern bureaucracies.

Still, the differences between the union and the conventions tell us something about the changing nature of denominationalism in the nineteenth century. During the antebellum years, the men who founded and ran the American Sunday School Union convinced themselves that a truly cross-denominational organization was possible and that theirs was its model. Disregarding the Presbyterian and Low Church Episcopal character of their membership, they championed the "union principle" for all evangelicals and were genuinely surprised when they were criticized for being denominational. Envisioning their organization as the center of a web of evangelical institutions, they found the recurrence of "sectarianism" extremely frustrating and disappointing. By contrast, the conventions frankly accepted the inevitability of denominational loyalties and worked around them rather than trying to avoid them. Thus, the convention movement built an institutional structure large enough to house most evangelicals yet flexible enough to permit partitions to be drawn around divisive doctrinal issues. Uniform lessons were perhaps the conventions' most appropriate symbol, for they permitted a full range of denominational expression while uniting individual schools in the study of Scripture.

Although both the American Sunday School Union and the conventions depended upon the existence of institutional networks for their success, those networks performed different functions in different eras. During the antebellum years, the men of the American Union struggled to create the kinds of institutional supports they believed necessary for right living in a volatile society. By the time of the conventions' growth, however, a wide range of evangelical institutions—including the Sunday school, the religious press, the denominational college, the YMCA and YWCA, and the local missionary or education society—already existed. Because convention organizers operated within a much more mature institutional framework, they could concentrate on systematizing their work. The men of the American Sunday School Union had imagined evangelical institutions as vehicles for creating a Protestant America; the convention leaders saw that dream realized. Small wonder, then, that when late nineteenth-century Protestants turned their attention to evangelizing the world, the Sunday school had a key place in their plans. Just as they had once been planted in the barren valley of the Mississippi in the 1830s, Sunday schools sprang up throughout the foreign mission fields that Protestant missionaries traversed in the 1880s. And once again, they took on the job of providing an institutional framework for the faithful in a volatile world.

Chapter Four

SUNDAY SCHOOL TEACHERS

nlike the Sunday schools of the 1790s, which were founded by philanthropists and employed hired teachers, the evangelical schools of the 1810s and 1820s were started by teacher-volunteers, who formed Sunday school unions for mutual support. Teaching cemented their identification as evangelicals and provided rewards in the form of public approbation, spiritual self-improvement, expanded social experience, and broadened responsibility. These rewards facilitated the recruitment of new teachers, as Sunday school pupils emulated admired mentors by joining them in the teaching corps. Not surprisingly, women responded with greater alacrity than men to this calling, a fact which reflects both their narrower social opportunities and their acceptance of the evangelical conception of womanhood. Youth of both sexes were particularly numerous in teaching, both because new teachers were usually recruited from among students and because teaching meshed particularly well with the youthful search for identity. Thus, evangelicals conceived of teaching as more than a once-a-week obligation. They made it the keystone to a structured style of living centered on introspection and self-improvement.

he lives of Sunday school teachers, as pictured in diaries and memoirs, reveal the significance they attached to teaching and their motives for devoting themselves to it. Two examples will serve to introduce the themes that reverberate throughout teachers' lives.

Harriet Lathrop, Sunday school organizer and missionary, was born into a pious family in Connecticut in 1796. At the age of thirteen, she experienced conversion and joined her town's Presbyterian church as its youngest member. Like other evangelicals, she interpreted her conversion as a mandate to relinquish "amuse-ments" and "gay" friends and to attempt "to be useful to all around" her. "I desire," she wrote to her mother, "to spend my life in the service of my Maker." But how? She puzzled over what "a weak, ignorant female" could do, apart from prayer, to evangelize others and confessed that she was "almost ready to wish [herself] a man" so that she might become a missionary. Lathrop had begun to find an answer through activities that were not only "useful" but also in keeping with her self-definition as a converted Christian. Several hours a week were devoted to a Society for the Relief of Poor Women and Children: visiting poor women in their homes or at the almshouse, praying with them and distributing tracts, soliciting donations from well-to-do Christians, and teaching poor children in a free school. One eve-ning a week she conducted a prayer meeting that quickly metamorphosed into a missionary society, which raised funds "for the education of heathen youth." Sun-days were spent teaching the Sunday school that she organized in 1816. Founded upon her return from a trip to New York, where she had observed the work of the Female Union Society for the Promotion of Sabbath Schools, this school involved both Sunday teaching and weekly visits to her students' homes. Much of her other free time was spent writing letters to friends and relatives on religious subjects, or seeking out neighbors for "Christian conversation." At the age of twenty-three, she fulfilled her missionary dream by marrying a minister named Miron Winslow and accompanying him on a mission to Ceylon. Even after the move, Harriet Lathrop Winslow continued to correspond with her Sunday school and with individuals to whom she had delivered tracts, as well as with her family and close friends.[1]

When New Yorker Michael Floy began a diary in 1833, he was twenty-five, a graduate of Columbia College, an employee in his father's flower business, and a teacher in the Seventh Street Methodist Episcopal Church Sunday school. Like many another evangelical, Floy took special note in his diary not only of his birthday but also of the date in 1827 when he had experienced "converting grace." Resolv-ing to be a "serious" Christian, Floy filled his weeks with a variety of religious activities. Between October 8 and 16, 1833, for example, he attended two Meth-odist class meetings, a prayer meeting, the dedication of the Forsyth Street Church, gatherings of both his church's Sunday school teachers' association and the Meth-odist Episcopal Sunday School Union, and, of course, his own Sunday school, where he taught both morning and afternoon classes. As time went on, he added to this list other activities, such as distributing coal to needy neighbors through the Bowery Village Benevolent Society and teaching a class at the African Adult School on Thursday evenings. A lively young man, Floy loved to sing, was fasci-nated by the flowers his family cultivated, and fancied himself an amateur mathe-matician and astronomer. In politics he opposed "Aristocracy," endorsing both the Democratic party and the principles of the antislavery cause. Fearing that he would die young, Floy sought to be ready for that inevitable day; it came in 1837, three weeks before his twenty-ninth birthday.[2]

The life-patterns of Harriet Lathrop and Michael Floy would be familiar to readers of other nineteenth-century religious diaries and memoirs. Whether clergymen, missionaries, or lay people, their lives shared the common theme of self-mastery and the belief that evangelical Protestantism helped them achieve it. Like the American Sunday School Union manager Lewis Ashhurst (whose diary is described in chapter 3), Lathrop and Floy sought control over an alter ego, another "self" that existed before the conversion experience and that, without constant vigilance, might surface again. Thus, Lathrop recalled the "fondness for dancing" and other "amusements" that had characterized her previous life and those of her "young, gay, and attractive" friends. Anxious to detect signs of "remaining corruption" within herself, she prayed "for strength of mind to resist every emotion which is incompatible" with the life of a converted Christian. Floy was similarly worried about becoming a "backslider," as he had been at college, or behaving "immoderately" when he entertained friends.[3]

Sunday school teaching facilitated the quest for mastery and enabled Lathrop and Floy to feel they were living orderly, examined lives. Floy believed that his teaching post encouraged him to be "serious," "punctual," and "moral," while his weekly routine of prayer, teaching, visiting scholars, and attending religious events gave shape, balance, and stability to his life. A similar theme animated the diary of Hiram Peck, a young New York store clerk who taught a class at the Rutgers Street Presbyterian Church, where he was secretary of a mission school and later superintendent of the church school. Like Floy, he described a routine oriented around religious concerns and filled his diary with "needful counsel" drawn from spiritual advice books, rules for living, and religious resolutions. Sunday school work, he believed, enabled him to cultivate valuable personal qualities. "I have been Secretary to the S S for more than a year," he noted at one point, "and through the providence of God I have been enabled to be punctual every morning and afternoon. . . . [T]here is so much advantage to be derived from being punctual."[4]

It is not hard to see the appeal of such a style of life. In an era of rapid economic development and dizzying social change, evangelical Protestant institutions offered individuals a set of structures through which to achieve their personal goal of self-mastery.[5] Each in its own way, these institutions—the weekly sermon, the prayer meeting, the voluntary society, the Sunday school, and the seminary—provided guideposts by which to navigate through life. As the teacher participated in the Sunday school, he or she acquired a clearly defined social identity as an evangelical Protestant, along with a source of useful work, like-minded friends, and spiritual reinforcement. It is hardly surprising, then, that nineteenth-century Americans, who were so fond of schemes aimed at self-improvement, should find Sunday school work attractive.

As a route to spiritual self-improvement, teaching seems to have fulfilled the needs of individuals like Lathrop, Floy and Peck. There is good evidence that teachers experienced conversion at high rates. It was not unheard-of for a superintendent to report that one-half to three-quarters of his or her teachers had "professed religion" in the course of a year, although there were wide variations in patterns of conversion. In 1826, the first year that the American Sunday School Union collected statistics on teacher conversions, a total of 2.5 percent of teachers reported having "professed religion" during the preceding year. The Boston Sabbath School Union reported in 1830 that 74 percent of its teachers were "professors;" the figure rose to 93 percent by 1840. (It is impossible to know how many of these experienced conversion before beginning to teach.) Similarly, the proportion of New York teachers who reported that they had joined the church in full membership rose from 17 percent of male and 27 percent of female teachers in 1821 to 86.6 percent of all teachers in 1847.[6] Although teachers debated among themselves about whether to accept "unconverted" recruits, they generally concurred with an 1831 assessment by the secretary of the American Sunday School Union: "There are few posts of duty where the visits of the king of grace are more frequently enjoyed." Whether conversion was a side-effect of teaching or preceded it, the work enabled serious young people to express their spirituality in institutional form while also receiving positive reinforcement for the life-choice they had made as evangelical Protestants.[7]

Conversion aside, teachers felt their work offered additional spiritual benefits. In order to teach others, they themselves had to study, as New Yorker John Pintard noted when he commented that his stepgrandson was "deriving more Bible information" from his Sunday school post "than left to himself he would probably have acquired all his life." Through studying the lessons, the Princeton professor Archibald Alexander suggested, some teachers were "actually becoming accurate Bible theologians." At weekly teachers' meetings, participants engaged in "mutual instruction & prayer," learning from the lesson the portions of the Bible it covered. Most important to teachers, however, was not only the information they imbibed but also the emotions they experienced while teaching. "How often, while we have been endeavouring to instil into the children's minds a knowledge of the glorious truths of the Gospel," remarked a Baltimore woman, "have our own hearts been made to burn within us." A similar sentiment animated a letter of a Richmond teahcer in 1841:"At Sabbath-school this morning, while talking with my scholars about the Lord Jesus, my heart, which is often so cold and so stupid, seemed completely melted within me, with a view of His wonderful, wonderful love for sinners, that I almost believed I had never felt it till then. Such a blessing is worth toiling and wrestling for a whole life."

Michael Floy, who usually judged his class by the children's attentiveness, used the word "enjoyed" to describe only those sessions that moved him emotionally. "The children are very near my heart," he wrote in a typical comment; "I must pray for them every day." Attentiveness and good behavior were vital for the school to function, but Floy added, "I expect greater things, and perhaps I am not wrong for thus expecting. Addressed the children, and seldom felt such an ardent desire for their welfare." In a similar vein, Hiram Peck remarked, "I love it and I have a tender regard for all children."[8]

The emotional aspects of teaching extended beyond the individual teacher's spiritual life to embrace relationships with other teachers and with students. Teaching appealed to its practitioners not only because it confirmed their religious experiences but also because it facilitated associations and friendships with like-minded individuals. Teachers' meetings, for example, combined lesson-study with prayer sessions and sociable mixing. When the teachers of the male and female divisions at Hiram Peck's school met "to devise means for spending [their] Tuesday evening in a social manner together," they agreed to devote the time to lesson-study but no doubt found the gatherings equally conducive to mixing. Indeed, over the decades such sociability became institutionalized in teachers' parties and excursions. The members of the Bank Street Mission Sunday school in New York, for example, often ended their 1865 meetings with "season[s] of refreshment" (strawberries and cream, ice cream and cake, or watermelon); in June the teachers sponsored an excursion to Pleasant Valley Grove, where they took a boat ride and enjoyed entertainment, singing, and speeches. Friendship might motivate individuals to become teachers together, or it might blossom at the school. Michael Floy had at least three close male friends among the teachers at his school and occasionally took tea with them after classes. "Many are the sociable times that I have had with the teachers of the School," he remarked, "and I shall remember them with pleasure as long as I live." Similarly, the published memoir of Susan Bowler, a Methodist teacher in Lynn, Massachusetts, reveals a pattern of close, at times intense, friendships with other female teachers and with students, involving the exchange of letters discussing their spiritual struggles, often in intimate detail.[9]

Because teachers were generally young and single, close ties between teacher and student were common (and encouraged in advice literature). During the semicentennial celebration for the First Presbyterian Church Sunday school in Utica, New York, several former pupils recalled fondly their friendships in the 1820s with two teachers, George S. Wilson and Truman Parmele. Wilson, a teenage apprentice, had a "remarkable aptness in teaching," remarked one former pupil. "An entrance into Mr. Wilson's Sunday School Class was a desire with many boys," he remembered, and "more applied than could be received." Parmele's teaching evoked similar recollections fifty years later; friends and former pupils described his life as "exemplary" and held it up for admiration.[10] The common practice of having teachers visit students in their homes encouraged these "strong reciprocal affections" between teacher and student and laid the groundwork for long-term associations (see figure 13). Even when separated by distance, dedicated teachers frequently carried on correspondence with their former pupils, as well as with their former schools. At the Utica Presbyterian Church Sunday school's semicentennial, Susan Burchard Taintor noted that she was still in correspondence with six of the nine students in her 1816 class, several of whom had also been students in her

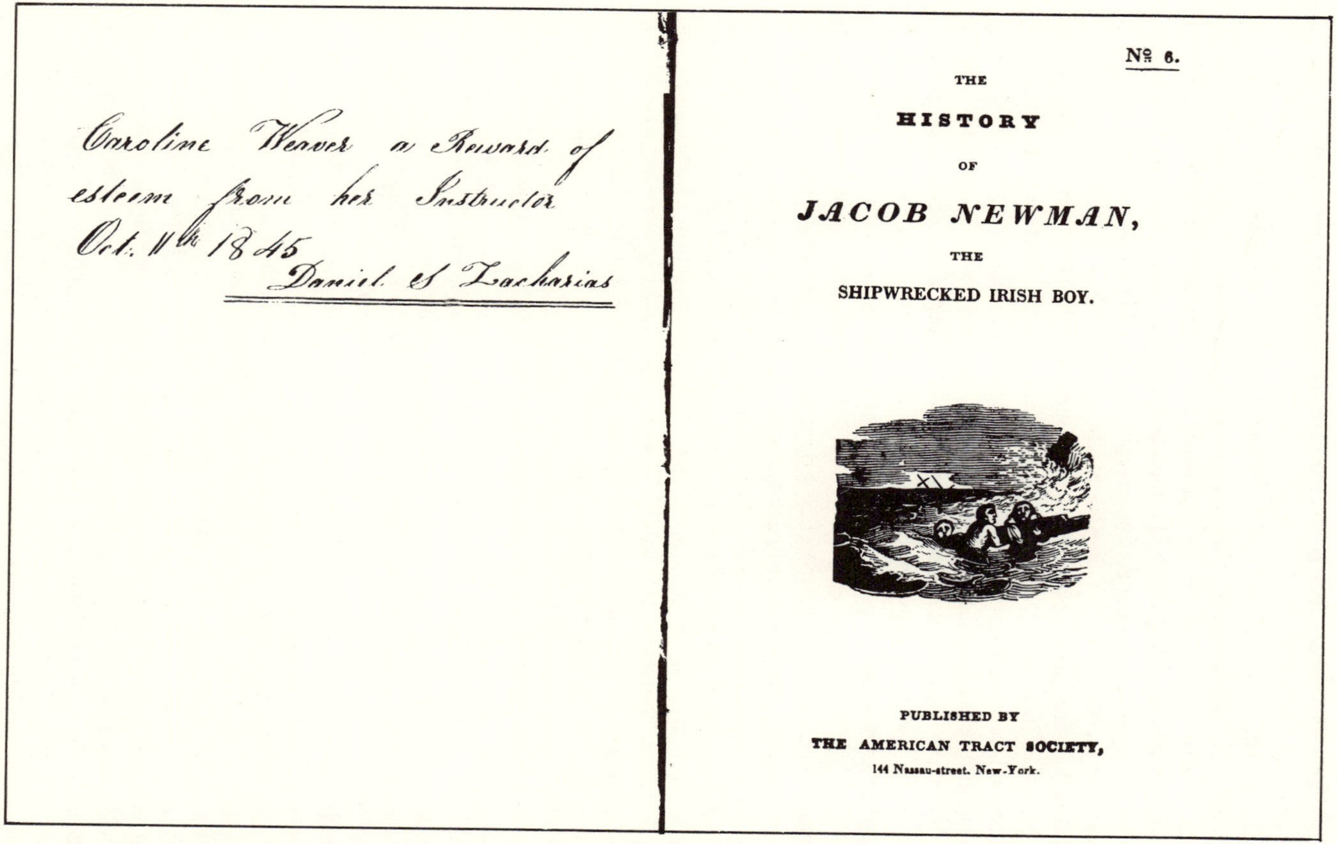

No. 6.

THE

HISTORY

OF

JACOB NEWMAN,

THE

SHIPWRECKED IRISH BOY.

PUBLISHED BY

THE AMERICAN TRACT SOCIETY,

144 Nassau-street. New-York.

Caroline Weaver, as Reward of
esteem from her Instructor,
Oct. 11th 1845.
Daniel S. Zacharias

Figure 13. This teacher inscribed a copy of The History of Jacob Newman to one of his scholars in 1845. Aside from ministers and ministerial students, men did not usually teach female pupils.

common school. From her missionary post in Ceylon, Harriet Lathrop Winslow wrote letters to her old Sunday school, as did many other men and women who undertook missionary work at home and abroad. Caroline Richards, a student and later teacher in a Canandaigua, New York, school, recorded numerous instances of female teachers and students meeting socially to make quilts or other gifts for women teachers who were leaving the school. When Richards was getting married, her class of eight girls "had their ambrotypes taken" with her, and made plans to "dress in white and sit on the first seat in church."[11]

As might be expected, and as teachers themselves recognized, teaching also provided opportunities for meeting potential mates. After school one Sunday, Michael Floy encountered a young man from another Methodist church who was apparently disappointed in his quest for a wife at his own school and had "been trying his luck up this way." Floy's own habit of evaluating the attributes of female teachers no doubt reflected common practice. "She is too overpowering for me," he confessed of one teacher, "too much for flesh and blood. She is very beautiful, lively, and possesses uncommon sense and knowledge of the world." Of two others he confided, "they are what might be called very pretty," later amending his diary entry to note, "the former excepting her feet; the latter, her shoulders. I am allowed to be a judge." When eighteen-year-old Caroline Richards developed a sudden interest in teaching, her grandmother thought she "only wanted an excuse to get out for a walk Sunday afternoon." A male teacher escorted her and a female friend home and, she confided to her diary, "Grandmother said that when she saw him opening the gate for me, she understood my zeal in missionary work." To individuals like Floy and Richards, it was important that those they courted share their world view, religious outlook, and drive for self-mastery. People whom they met at Sunday school or church were likely to fill the bill.[12]

Although it is impossible to know how often Sunday school teachers married each other, extant courtship accounts reveal that teaching did more than provide socially sanctioned occasions for meeting members of the opposite sex. It also gave them shared experiences and mutual interests that encouraged intimacy. Michael Floy's courtship of a fellow teacher offers a case in point. Attracted by "her looks, dress, earnest and plain manner of talking," Floy escorted Maria Johnston to church services, prayer meeting, the Bowery Village Benevolent Society, and the Rose Hill Church Singing Association, as well as taking long walks with her after teachers' meetings. By dating in this manner, Michael and Maria shared activities they both enjoyed in environments in which they both felt comfortable. Such mutual interests not only furthered their friendship but also promoted emotional closeness. As Floy observed Maria being "quite serious at the prayer meeting" or enjoyed "an interesting season of prayer" with her at church, his love for her blossomed. When it came time for him to propose, a religious mode seemed most appropriate. Searching for the proper words and gestures for this "one important subject," he checked his library and found a model in missionary Harriet Atwood Newell's published memoir. As a modern youth might study a screen idol's romantic technique, Floy memorized Samuel Newell's proposal and incorporated it into his own. Taking a walk with Maria after church, he popped the question: " 'If your heart be as mine, give me your hand.' She did so; I clasped it, at the same time uttering a prayer to Almighty God."[13] In a similar manner, Hiram Peck's and Caroline Richards's dates with fellow teachers revolved around church services and school events.[14]

Although the lives of people like Floy, Lathrop, Peck, and Richards provide insights into teachers' motives and concerns, they were not entirely typical of the group. Unlike most teachers, they made a mark on the historical record. Three of them kept spiritual diaries that later generations preserved, while the fourth—Lathrop—became a well-known missionary whose letters had collectible value. (In life, undoubtedly, they were not quite such paragons of virtue.) More important, their comparatively long tenures as teachers made them unusual. Throughout the nineteenth century teacher recruitment was a perennial problem. Only four years after its organization, for example, the New-York Sunday-School Union Society found that the 1819 financial panic had decimated the ranks of its teachers, many of whom had lost their jobs and left the city to seek other employment. Similarly, a Boston Sunday school worker calculated that in the first eight years of his school's existence, from 1825 to 1833, 77 different individuals had been teachers, only 2 of whom had been with the school for the entire eight years.[15] In 1839 a large New York school with 69 teachers reported that during a six-month period 12 had left and 13 entered (a turnover rate of 34 percent a year). In the following decades the same school's teaching staff fluctuated from the 1839 high of 69 to 42 in 1843, 44 in 1852, 35 in 1854, and 36 in 1860. Few other schools kept such scrupulous records of teachers' comings and goings, but complaints about "instability and decay" in teaching staffs were frequent, as were remarks about being "very much in want of good and permanent teachers."[16]

As the statistics indicate, instability was a problem integrally related to recruit-ment. For even if a school could recruit enough teachers, it could not easily keep the same people for any length of time. "There has been unhappily so great a change of teachers in the school," lamented the session of New York's Brick Presbyterian Church, "and, with few exceptions, such instability in their attachment to this particular field of labor that more than once the whole system has been not a little embarrassed." The problem of instability often cropped up unexpectedly. One Sunday school superintendent, puzzling over a sudden decline in teachers, noted that last year "every class was supplied with a teacher, and . . . the teachers and scholars were very regular in their attendance at school; but now it is quite the reverse." Not only were there few teachers, but those few displayed "much irregularity."[17]

"Irregular" teachers were as much a problem as those who quit after only a few Sundays. Lacking a system for providing substitutes, a superintendent was stuck when a teacher simply did not show up for class. Moreover, superintendents believed that teacher absence had deleterious effects on student attendance. When New York's Second Street Methodist Episcopal Church Sunday school sent a worker to check on absent scholars, he reported "that most of the scholars visited by him gave as an excuse, that their Teacher did not attend school regular, and that they (the Scholars) did not wish to come to S. S. unless their Teacher was there." The superintendent of the Allen Street Methodist Episcopal Sunday School had a similar complaint in 1873. "Yesterday afternoon," he reported, "I missed some half dozen male teachers and found they had left their classes to be gone for the remainder of that session, leaving their scholars idle."[18] Without an adequate number of teachers willing to attend faithfully every Sunday, a school's success, indeed its very existence, was in jeopardy.[19]

The causes of these recruitment problems were many. Certainly, they stemmed in part from the volunteer nature of Sunday school teaching, yet studies of paid day school teachers in the same period indicate similarly high turnover rates. The high geographical mobility of nineteenth-century Americans also provides a partial explanation: teachers simply moved away from their schools. Then, too, it remained customary throughout the antebellum period for women teachers to give up their posts upon marriage; those who remained in the teaching corps tended to be the wives of ministers or Sunday school superintendents. Whatever the causes, the recruitment issue evoked a good deal of discussion and led to the development of an institutional structure for attracting and training new generations of teachers: the Bible class.

Although Bible classes did not originate as teacher training classes, they quickly took on that character. A Boston school established one in 1822 for the "most meritorious" older students (those aged thirteen or fourteen and up) as a way to keep them in school. Soon such classes acquired the function of supplying "any vacancy that [might] occur" among the teachers, while also doing away with the "impression among the scholars, that they [could] ever be too large or too old to attend Sabbath schools." As Sunday school magazines carried articles describing such classes and annual reports enumerated them, additional classes were formed. By 1828, for example, the New Hampshire Baptist Sabbath School Union reported that eight of its thirty-three schools had Bible classes; in its 1832 survey, however, the American Sunday School Union found that questions about Bible classes elicited "vague" responses, indicating that superintendents were not very familiar with the classes. If they varied in size and composition—most were sex-segregated, but some brought "the largest Boy[s] and Girls" together—all Bible classes combined special attention to older students with efforts to retain students and prepare teachers.[20]

Bible classes multiplied and became part of the Sunday school's institutional structure during the 1820s and 1830s not merely because they were useful in training and recruiting teachers. They proliferated because they also offered a specialized structure for managing the problems of what nineteenth-century writers termed "youth." To religious educators in particular, "the elder scholars" were the group most in need of their schools' benefits, most available as teacher-trainees, yet most likely to leave school at the first opportunity. Youngsters who felt that they were "too large, or too old to remain in a school" where there were so many "younger and smaller" children, often quit the school at the age of thirteen or fourteen. Bible classes thus acquired the mission of managing adolescence, a phenomenon "discovered" and named by a nineteenth-century Sunday school teacher, the psychologist G. Stanley Hall. Well before Hall began the research that led to his massive 1904 work, *Adolescence,* Sunday school writers and promoters, wrestling with the dual issues of retaining students and recruiting teachers, drew their own portrait of volatile "youth" and devised Bible classes to counteract its excesses.[21]

Sunday school publications invariably referred to "youth" as "the most critical period of life," during which "the mind generally [took] a decided turn, and the happiness and usefulness of the character [were] ensured or destroyed." Exactly when this "eventful and critical period" began was a subject on which writers had varying opinions. but most placed it "from fourteen to eighteen or twenty" or simply in the "teens."[22] During those years, young people were "escaping from the restraints of childhood," anticipating the freedoms of adulthood, and learning "to act for themselves." At the same time, they experienced new, strong "passions" and encountered the "flattering allurements" of a world bent on "seduc[ing] them to ruin." In particular, those students who were "away from the Christian influence of home" and lacked "either religious influence or moral restraint" were left "to pursue a course that [would] end finally, in ruin."[23] If most antebellum writers left it to the reader's imagination to conjure up pictures of a youngster's "ruin," later ones provided images of youngsters who "rush[ed] to the gilded saloons or the giddy dance" in search of "sympathy, kindness and regard." Unfortunately, it was precisely at this juncture, "just when they [had] attained the age at which these instructions [became] peculiarly important," that students often left Sunday school.[24]

In this portrait of youthful behavior, nineteenth-century writers depicted adolescence as a time when crucial choices had to be made, choices that would determine the individual's entire future, both temporal and spiritual. During youth, argued Frederick Packard, "the character usually becomes fixed for life, and for the most part for eternity." Youngsters in the throes of adolescence required direction in making the necessary life-choices, yet were were quick to reject adult guidance. The challenge for the Bible class was to keep them in school as long as possible, in order to offer the right kind of influence in their lives at an especially crucial time.[25]

Like all such portraits, this one revealed as much about its creators as about its subjects. For, as historians have frequently noted, adolescence is as much socially constructed as it is physically experienced and different societies describe its essence in widely varying ways. Whereas G. Stanley Hall attributed the rebellious behavior of adolescents in his era to their struggle to recapitulate the stages of human evolution, modern psychologists often explain similar behavior by youngsters' prolonged dependence upon their families. If Hall saw idealism as the key attribute of adolescence, the twentieth-century psychologist Erik Erikson portrayed it as a search for identity. Seen in this light, nineteenth-century Sunday school writers' preoccupation with choice and their fear that unschooled youths faced potential "ruin" is explicable in terms of their view of their own society. Looking around them, they witnessed the social and economic changes of the nineteenth century, particularly the large-scale migration of young people to urban areas in search of opportunity and experience. (Many writers had no doubt made the trek themselves.) For country youngsters escaping the authority of parents and other adults, the city environment, with its emphasis on democratic social relationships and peer friendships, left them vulnerable to the wiles of "confidence men and painted women." Like authors of temperance and moral reform literature, Sunday school writers constructed a scenario in which city-bound youngsters, unprepared and unprotected, traded the values of their childhoods for the glamor and glitter of the city as easily as they took a false turn in a strange neighborhood. Such a false turn could effectively ruin the adolescent's life.[26]

Sunday school teaching (and the Bible class training that led to it) seemed to offer a panacea for these ills of youth. Above all, it was religious work, engaging the "youthful zeal and palpitating hearts" of youngsters "who formerly lounged away the Sabbath hours as having no work for them." In addition, it was demanding enough to counteract the "love of ease" that seemed to characterize adolescence and it promoted self-denial, a virtue especially "necessary to the spiritual health" and "temporal reputation" of young people. Not only did teaching mitigate the youthful tendency toward "indecision," it was work that existed in most locations, so that young people moving to new areas could, merely by visiting the local Sunday school, find the right kind of friends. Parents, ministers, and advisors concurred in listing the advantages of teaching: it promoted "a thorough acquaintance with divine truth," disciplined young people for a life of "Christian activity," cultivated a "spirit of prayer," offered a "preservative against declension," and formed "habits of Christian intimacy." Through Bible class preparation and then actual teaching, adult spiritual advisors and intimate friends could "direct the decision of the mind aright" in the individual's central life-choice: the decision to accept saving grace

and become a converted Christian. Only then would the youngster be fully pro-
tected against the dangers of adult life.[27]

Although the curriculum of the Bible class might involve anything from memorizing Bible verses to studying Hebrew or Biblical archaeology, its overall goal was
to stimulate religious conversion. Conversion, in the minds of Sunday school workers, offered not only the best preparation for becoming a teacher but also the best
protection against adolescent indecision and volatility. As a life-defining event, it
could put the adolescent's feet on the right path and perhaps guarantee his or her
future adherence to the walks of righteousness. Undergone during the "critical
period of life," conversion could be the single most important decision the youngster
made. Through the Bible class, then, Sunday school workers sought to adapt the
conversion experience—for so long the central event in an evangelical Protestant's
life—to new conditions and circumstances. In the Sunday school, conversion,
which in the seventeenth and eighteenth centuries had been closely associated with
achievement of adult independence and autonomy, would be remade to fit the
nineteenth-century adolescent's needs and experiences. More important, within
the school, the Bible class would provide a new institutional setting in which
youngsters could experience conversion while being guided through the shoals of
adolescence. Youth could then become the period of life in which childhood religious tenets and ideals were brought to fruition, not rejected. If converted and
trained as teachers before "the busy concerns of life" intruded, youngsters would be
more likely to remain faithful evangelicals, suggested a Methodist minister in 1846.
It was this widely shared view that made Bible classes an integral part of Sunday
schools in the antebellum years.[28]

Nineteenth-century religious educators thus placed a heavy burden of expectations upon Bible classes. Not only were they to make teenage students "feel special"
by setting them apart from "mere children," they were also to train youngsters to
become teachers, all the while pressing them to experience conversion. How these
varied goals were to be achieved was less clearly spelled out in the literature. Over
the years, however, teachers, ministers, and advice-givers evolved a common vision
of how Bible class experiences might shape the behavior and convictions of adolescent boys and girls. Central to this vision was a conception of the Bible class teacher
as mentor, friend, and role model, who transmitted to his or her students the values
and practices of evangelical Protestantism. Frederick Packard best summed up this
vision in his 1839 work, *The Teacher Taught*. "What can be more gratifying to a
youth," he wondered, "than to be affectionately noticed by a kind and sympathiz-
ing friend and teacher, his senior in years and superior in knowledge?" Such a
friendship would give the teacher "a moral influence over [the student], which, if
kept up and rightly employed at a time of life so peculiarly exposed to danger, may,
under the blessing of God, be attended with most beneficial and enduring results."
A Baptist minister, discussing "the perilous period" of adolescence in 1870, re-

vealed similar expectations: "The strongest grasp will be the teacher's personal hold upon the scholar. The last cord snapped will be the teacher's influence."[29]

Ideally, religious conversion would result from this mentor-pupil relationship. Even if it did not, the Bible class experience could guide youngsters through early adolescence and train them to become teachers. Unconverted youngsters were urged to "take their place among the ranks of teachers" because, as Sunday school advisors suggested and as teachers' experiences confirmed, teaching often led to conversion. Sunday school unions' practice of recording the number of teacher conversions each year reinforced the point. In the same way, Bible class members who did experience conversion were expected to take up teaching as a sign of their commitment and a means of developing it. One teacher, Lydia Bacon, expressed this view when she learned of a former pupil's conversion. "Tell her that I am happy to hear it," she wrote to a mutual acquaintance, "and that I trust she will be a firm, active Christian, taking up her cross in her youth. I presume she has a class in the Sabbath school."[30]

Thus, Bible classes, which religious educators initially developed to address the dual problems of retaining students and recruiting teachers, during the nineteenth century took on the additional tasks of managing adolescence and orchestrating conversion. How successful they were at these two jobs is unclear, but the behavior and testimony of teachers offer some positive evidence. The schedule completed by John Pintard's stepgrandson upon his arrival at a new apprenticeship certainly reflected the behavior that Sunday school workers expected of their charges. "He wrote on Sunday of his safe arrival," Pintard reported to the boy's mother, "arrangm^t of his goods & chattels & visit to the Sunday school, 48 scholars, & of his intention to commence teacher next Sunday." And Chicagoan John V. Farwell was convinced that teaching had saved him from urban temptations. "I candidly believe," he confessed in his diary in 1849, "that had I neglected this means of good since living in this city, I should have become a backslider and surrendered the practice as well as lost the power of religion." The experiences of New Yorker Charles Curtis also confirmed teachers' belief in the power of their work. "Twenty-five years ago," he wrote in 1866, "I came to this great city, entirely free from all family influence, boarding in hotels and large boarding houses, surrounded by all kinds of evil influences, and for a number of years gave myself up to all its seductive influence. But in the course of time, the beneficent influence of the Holy Spirit came to the rescue. The early lessons received were not dead, but asleep." He returned to the church, became a teacher and eventually superintendent in its Sunday school. We do not, of course, have comparable testimony from youngsters who strayed permanently from the straight and narrow path, but these three examples suggest that religious educators had some basis for believing in the efficacy of their methods.[31]

Over the years, as the number of Sunday scholars rose, so did the proportion of teachers who had at one time been students. Whereas the New-York Sunday-School Union Society, for example, reported that 10 percent of its teachers in the 1820s had once been pupils, by 1845 the figure was 50 percent and rising. Although some of these teachers had undoubtedly been scholars only briefly, a significant number had started in the Sunday school, moved on to the Bible class, and then graduated to the teacher corps. Bible classes provided a regular supply of teachers and reduced the number of complaints from superintendents about the dearth of qualified teachers. Indeed, by the 1860s and 1870s, a few schools could boast of having "reserve" or "auxiliary" teachers ready to serve as substitutes if the need arose.[32]

As might be expected, the use of Bible classes as the primary recruitment tool created a relatively youthful teacher corps. Although there were occasional reports, especially in the early decades, of extremely young teachers—the black school at St. George's Episcopal Sunday school had an 11-year-old teacher in 1820—most seem to have been in their teens and twenties. The founders of the first Sunday school in Utica, New York, for example, were five young women between the ages of 14 and 16. In Boston, a Baptist school reported in 1831 that sixteen of its twenty-two teachers were under the age of 30. Nor was it unusual for superintendents to be youthful; Michael Floy's sister Margaret was 22 when she was chosen superintendent of the female department of their school. Ironically, the same writers who urged the adoption of Bible classes for teacher training often perceived the teachers' youth as a problem. It seemed to Frederick Packard, writing in 1850, "very ill judged . . . to place a lad of 16 or 17, or a girl of 14 or 15, at the head of a class . . . without any resources except such as their own brief experience and limited attainments (intellectual and spiritual) supply." Likewise, a writer for the *Baptist Teacher* in 1877 urged older church members to get involved in the schools in order to balance teachers' youth with "more weight and dignity and gravity."[33] Despite such appeals, the average age of teachers remained low, not only because recruitment practices targeted the young but also because teaching had a special aura (as revealed in the lives of Harriet Lathrop and Michael Floy) that appealed particularly to the young. In 1907 a survey of Sunday school teachers found that a majority were between the ages of 18 and 25.[34]

Most were also female. Indeed, women dominated the ranks of Sunday school teachers and the creation of Bible classes did nothing to change that dominance. Although the ratio of men to women varied from school to school and from year to year, women constituted an overall majority virtually from the very beginning. In New York, the male Sunday-School Union Society had a slightly larger number of teachers in 1821 than the Female Union Society for the Promotion of Sabbath

Table 8
Sunday School Teachers, by Sex, 1821–1847

Year	Organization	Male teachers (N)	(%)	Female teachers (N)	(%)
1821	New-York Sunday-School Union Society (male)	429	100.0	—	—
1821	Female Union Society for the Promotion of Sabbath Schools	—	—	414	100.0
1831	New-York Sunday School Union (male and female)	840	48.4	895	51.6
1834	New-York Sunday School Union	979	48.5	1,043	51.5
1847	New-York Sunday School Union	1,375	38.4	1,403	61.6
1825	Philadelphia (all schools)	366	42.9	486	57.0
1832	American Sunday School Union	20,910	48.3	22,454	51.7

Sources: *Sunday-School Facts, Collected by a Member of the General Association of Teachers* (New York: D. H. Wickham, 1821), pp. 10–11; New-York Sunday School Union, *Fifteenth Annual Report* (New York, 1831), appendix; *Eighteenth Annual Report* (1834), appendix; *Thirty-First Annual Report* (1847), appendix; American Sunday School Union, *Eighth Annual Report* (Philadelphia, 1832), p.51.

Note: The New-York Sunday-School Union Society was all-male in 1821; later figures include men and women teachers.

Schools. By 1831, however, three years after the female union dissolved, women constituted a majority of the new Sunday School Union's teachers, and by 1847 they made up 61 percent of the teacher corps (see table 8). Within individual schools, the pattern was often varied. A New York school in which women teachers outnumbered men by three to two in 1839 had an equal ratio in 1843; in 1849 the same school had a two-to-one majority of women teachers, but in 1853 reported a slight majority of men. A Philadelphia school that began in 1817 with fifteen men and six women teachers had twenty-two men and thirty-three women by 1826; thereafter, women predominated. Allowing for individual and regional variations, women generally made up at least half of a school's teaching staff, while men constituted between 30 and 50 percent. A Connecticut superintendent's 1830 complaint that "our school has suffered, and continues to suffer, from a *deficiency of male teachers*" echoed those of numerous others. In 1920, some one hundred years after such complaints were first voiced, an Indiana survey found that 73 percent of the state's Sunday school teachers were women.[35]

Women were heavily represented in the ranks of Sunday school teachers for the same reasons that they dominated church membership rolls, benevolent society lists, and the public school teaching corps. Nineteenth-century gender ideology, combined with the rewards women gained from teaching and the use of Bible classes for recruitment, led them into the work in large numbers. Women constituted a majority of church members from the 1680s on, but it was only in the nineteenth century that this numerical preponderance was reinforced ideologically and theologically. Not only did the images and doctrines associated with evangelical Protestantism become, in Barbara Welter's words, "more domesticated, more emotional, more soft and accommodating—in a word more 'feminine,'" but women began to take up a larger share of church-related voluntary activity, such as visiting the afflicted and collecting money to buy Bibles. Denounced from the pulpit if they stepped outside their "sphere" by engaging in public reform efforts or speaking out on the issues of the day, women were nevertheless lauded for participating in benevolent projects through separate women's organizations. Church-related work became, by extension, part of women's sphere. At the same time, the nineteenth-century "cult of domesticity" increasingly glorified motherhood and established close emotional bonds between women and children, making women seem to be naturally suited not only to child rearing but also to teaching and caring for children outside the family. Just as Catharine Beecher promoted common-school teaching as a career for women by arguing that "the educating of children . . . is the true and noble profession of a woman . . . [and] worthy the noblest powers and affections of the noblest minds," so too did teaching Sunday school come to be seen as a natural extension of women's nurturing role. Women, noted the secretary of the General Protestant Episcopal Sunday School Union, made "the most willing, constant and successful teachers."[36]

Evangelical women assimilated these beliefs and acted them out in their own lives. They generally had better attendance records at teachers' meetings than did men and apparently spent more time in lesson preparation. "Our male teachers," complained a superintendent, "do not [seem to] see the importance of preparing themselves to teach their classes on the Sabbath as the females do." Another, lauding women for their attention to school visitation work, commented that their "assiduity in this duty has only been equaled by their attendance at the school." Lacking the social outlets that men in their society had, women attached more importance to close ties with students and other teachers and channeled more energy into teaching and teachers' meetings. Attending a meeting at which only two other men were present, Michael Floy observed the importance women teachers placed on socializing, though he interpreted it negatively: "Teachers' meeting . . . ; but one male present besides the Secretary; females kept up such a clack among themselves that I was disgusted."[37]

Women were also more comfortable with some of the job's trappings, particularly the emotional displays that often accompanied teaching. Just as the conversion experience itself was a highly emotional event, requiring no mere intellectual assent to doctrine but a radical "change of heart," preparing students for conversion necessitated a good deal of close communication about the state of their souls (see figure 14). Socialized to believe that they possessed more finely tuned emotional capabilities than men, women naturally found these tasks easier. Whereas women teachers' intimate conversations with students and other teachers often involved weeping, praying, and embracing, men often felt discomfited when the moment seemed to require such emotional expressions. One of Lydia Bacon's students, for example, recalled Bacon's "warm-hearted love" for God, her "tearful earnestness in the matter of our salvation," and her ability to make "an impression on the mind and heart not easily effaced." By contrast, Michael Floy's efforts to make personal appeals to students were awkward and clumsy. Meeting a pupil on the omnibus one day, Floy rode with the child in silence, "for will anyone believe it when I say that it was too great a cross for me to speak to him on religious subjects? Alas for my weakness!" Although Floy loved his pupils and wept privately upon the death of one ten-year-old, he found it difficult to convey his feelings with words.[38]

Their own statements underscore the meanings that women teachers attached to their work and reveal their interpretation of nineteenth-century gender ideology. To take one example, the speeches of successive presidents of the Baltimore McKendrean Female Sabbath School Society indicate that women saw Sunday school work as one of the few areas where they could influence, however indirectly, the course of society. Our "exertions," argued one president, multiply "the virtues that establish the comfort of society." By "fitting the present generation to act their parts upon the great stage of human action," suggested another, teachers were shaping society's future. The work of religious educators could help determine whether society "languish[ed] under a torrent of vice" or benefited from "those great moral influences upon which all prosperity and happiness" rested. It fit the "diffidence and retirement so becoming" to women, another president proposed, that their power be exerted indirectly. "What though your names may not be emblazoned on the historical page?" asked another; your influence is as great as and perhaps greater than that of those whom history does remember. You are engaged in "mighty operations" she concluded; "you are attending to the moral and intellectual culture of youthful immortals." These sentiments reflect the feeling of usefulness and importance that women derived from their teaching and their belief that they could exercise power through influence.[39]

The work's special appeal to women helps explain their dominance in the teaching corps, as does the use of Bible classes for teacher recruitment. Despite the special concern of Bible class organizers for keeping "large boys" in school, adolescent males dropped out in greater numbers than females, leading to perennial discussions of this issue. Indeed, as David Macleod points out in his study of late nineteenth-

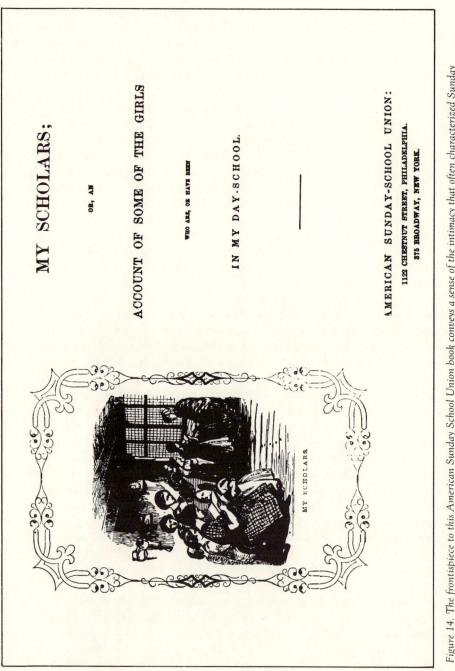

MY SCHOLARS;

OR, AN

ACCOUNT OF SOME OF THE GIRLS

WHO ARE, OR HAVE BEEN

IN MY DAY-SCHOOL.

———

AMERICAN SUNDAY-SCHOOL UNION:

1122 CHESTNUT STREET, PHILADELPHIA.

375 BROADWAY, NEW YORK.

MY SCHOLARS.

Figure 14. *The frontispiece to this American Sunday School Union book conveys a sense of the intimacy that often characterized Sunday school classes, particularly those taught by women*

century boys' organizations, it was precisely because Sunday schools could not hold adolescent boys that youth workers devised groups like the Boy Scouts. The problem of retaining boys was often attributed to the dearth of male teachers. After all, if the teacher was to serve as a mentor to the student, becoming "intimate and familiar, as . . . an elder brother or sister," then boys needed male mentors, girls female ones. Without "suitable male teachers," noted a Connecticut superintendent in 1831, it was "extremely difficult to retain the larger boys." His lament was repeated often in the ensuing years. Girls, on the other hand, having plenty of female role models, readily absorbed the expectation that they would someday be teachers. Moreover, Bible classes offered the kind of friendship and intimacy that appealed especially to girls. As a result, individual schools usually had more female than male Bible classes; even where the classes were coeducational, girls still often outnumbered boys. Aside from recruiting male teachers, schools sometimes tried to counter the feminization of Bible classes by asking the church's pastor to conduct them or by urging the establishment of classes for members of all ages. Even so, boys continued to be more likely than girls to see adolescence as a time for leaving Sunday school and other associations of childhood behind them.[40]

Even though women generally constituted a majority of Bible class scholars and Sunday school teachers, their numerical preponderance did not translate into greater power within the schools. Only when women ran their own schools and Sunday school unions did they exercise leadership. Early in the century, women founded many schools and created organizations such as New York's Female Union Society for the Promotion of Sabbath Schools (1816) and Baltimore's Female (later McKendrean Female) Sabbath School Society (1816) to bring schools together. By 1818 the New York group had auxiliaries ranging from Connecticut to North Carolina. Although most of these were single-sex schools, some female-founded schools admitted both boys and girls, at least until the women could recruit men to teach the boys separately. At a school in the working-class Southwark district of Philadelphia, women teachers accepted boys as well as girls. But, they reported to the New York society, "finding we could not manage the boys so easily as we imagined, we readily yielded to the solicitations of a committee of gentlemen, who took them off our hands." Similarly, a New York school divided in 1820, four years after its founding, "when the females thought it most beneficial." Within individual churches, it was common to have separate male and female schools, each with its own superintendent and slate of officers. In this way, women had opportunities to manage individual schools and take other leadership posts. Where women formed Sunday school unions, they acquired additional opportunities. The Female Union Society for the Promotion of Sabbath Schools, headed by Joanna Bethune, printed books and sold them at a book depository, collected statistics from schools up and down the East Coast, held large anniversary gatherings at which prominent clergymen spoke, raised annual budgets ranging from $300 to $1,800, and sponsored a committee of thirty members who regularly visited auxiliary schools in New York City. (In 1821 the Union had thirty-eight auxiliaries in the New York area, enrolling almost 2,800 pupils.)[41]

When women's schools and unions merged with men's, as became common during the course of the century, or when women and men founded a school together, women were relegated to secondary status. Whereas in 1820, for example, Philadelphia women ran almost half the city's Sunday schools, by 1859 all 219 schools had male superintendents. Although many nominally coeducational schools maintained separate male and female "departments" with male and female superintendents, the male superintendent had jurisdiction over the entire school, while the female superintendent managed only the girls' department. Thus, men always chaired teachers' meetings, even when the overwhelming majority of attendees were women, and represented the school on public occasions. Within fully coeduational schools, too, the superintendent was always male, as were the other officers, with the occasional exception of assistant superintendent and librarian. Whereas the merger of sex-segregated Sunday schools was often beneficial to boys' schools, making available a new source of teachers for the younger children (as in common schools, women were increasingly regarded as the best teachers for young boys as well as young girls), such mergers often meant the loss of leadership and visibility for female teachers.[42]

A similar process occurred when male and female Sunday school unions joined, although women's groups often resisted the blandishments of more powerful male organizations. In Baltimore, for example, the Female Sabbath School Society renamed itself the McKendrean Female Sabbath School Society in 1821, when it became affiliated with the city's Methodist Conference. Male Methodists in Baltimore organized their own association, the Asbury Sunday School Society (named, like the McKendrean, after a bishop of the church), and the two groups operated separately. In 1829, however, the Asbury Society began considering whether to admit women, largely because its own members were deficient in "regular and punctual attendance." Indeed, during the early 1830s the Asbury Society devoted considerable meeting time to the issue of disciplining delinquent teachers. In 1835 the society changed its constitution to permit women to join, thereby offering female teachers an alternative to the McKendrean group. That association, while not responding directly, did admit male teachers to one of its schools in 1843. "So far however," the group's secretary commented late that year, "the plan has been of no advantage to the female department." Finally, in 1845, with each society directing a shrinking number of schools—church-affiliated groups increasingly ran most Methodist Sunday schools, and the denomination itself was being torn by the issue of slavery—the two merged. Although the merger gave the women twelve slots on the new Asbury Society's board of managers, the women lost their autonomy, their access to leadership within the society, and even the name of their society. As they did individually when they married, the women of the McKendrean Female Sabbath School Society collectively surrendered their name and adopted that of their male partner, thus symbolizing their loss of visibility. After 1845 they were rele-gated to running their own schools under the direction of male leaders.[43]

The Female Union Society for the Promotion of Sabbath Schools, facing compara-ble pressures from the male New-York Sunday School Union, responded differ-ently. Although the groups had operated in tandem since their founding in 1816 and several of their officers and managers came from the same families, the two societies came into conflict in 1825 over the acceptance of female schools into the New-York Sunday School Union and of female pupils into previously all-male schools. In a letter protesting these policies, the members of the female union reminded the men that they had founded the city's first Sunday school union and had, by their example, spurred men to organize in order "to take . . . the boys under their direction." With the formation of the New-York Sunday-School Union Soci-ety, the women had "most cheerfully transferred" their male scholars to men's schools. After failing in 1822 to convince the women's society to merge with theirs, the men had begun accepting female schools and scholars. "And," the women's letter went on, "we have reason to believe an undue influence to have been ex-erted" in the process, as "the Male Union distributed more rewards than the Female."

Whether intentionally or not, the men had used the greater economic resources at their disposal to undermine the women's organization. After a series of negotiat-ing sessions, the two unions resolved the problem of differential rewards but could not agree on the issue of continued sex-segregation in the schools. The male union refused to stop accepting female pupils. Although soon thereafter the women's union accepted as an auxiliary a female school attended by both boys and girls, the organization encountered additional difficulties, both financial and sectarian, that led to its dissolution in 1828. Presumably, the New-York Sunday School Union would have been willing to merge with the women's group, but the ladies of the Female Union Society for the Promotion of Sabbath Schools, believing in the princi-ple of separate education of the sexes, chose not to take that route. The schools they had supervised became auxiliaries to the Sunday School Union, which remained an all-male organization. Only in 1873, when the New-York Sunday School Union reorganized in order to accommodate the newly popular Sunday school conventions and teachers' associations, did women finally acquire a place on its board of managers.[44]

The experiences of women Sunday school teachers illustrate both the pos-sibilities and limitations that women encountered in ninteenth-century Protestant-ism. From the standpoint of the teachers, Protestantism offered a positive image of womanhood, useful and engaging work in a variety of benevolent causes, and opportunities for social interactions beyond the family circle. However historical observers judge the utility of their work, we should not doubt the sincerity of the belief—widely held among evangelical women—that Christianity in general and Protestantism in particular had elevated them to a high station in life. "Gratitude becomes us for whom as a sex Christianity has done so much," proclaimed the president of the McKendrean Female Sabbath School Society in 1837. "It has asserted our claims, raised us from moral degradation, placed us in our proper sphere, secured us affection, respect, and esteem." From this perspective, many women looked upon Sunday school work as liberating and ennobling, providing an appealing vision of themselves as useful and significant individuals. For a few, it might even be a stepping-stone to full-time work, whether paid or unpaid, as benevolent society volunteers, missionaries (Harriet Lathrop became one), ministers' wives, or writers. Women applying to become missionaries of the American Board of Commissioners for Foreign Missions, for example, invariably used their Sunday school teaching as evidence of their general good character and suitability for the job; letters of recommendation from their ministers echoed this view. In addition, a large number of anonymous women teachers shaped writing careers for themselves by feeding the seemingly insatiable appetites of Sunday school publishers for books and magazine articles. All these positive associations drew women to Sunday school work in large numbers and helped assure that they would continue to volunteer as teachers.[45]

At the same time, however, their acceptance of the evangelical ideal of womanhood restricted the autonomy and independence of women teachers and limited their ability to challenge nineteenth-century gender-role prescriptions. While running their own schools and unions, women freely exercised their leadership and management abilities, acquiring public visibility and acclaim in the process. But, as with separate women's institutions in general, women's Sunday schools and unions, although enlarging the space that nineteenth-century Americans termed "women's sphere," enabled them to exercise power only over others of their sex. When women and men taught in the same school, the women, no matter how numerous, experienced few of the opportunities that accompanied single-sex schools. To take just one example, the Benton Street Mission Sunday School in St. Louis had a staff of fifty-five people in 1868, seventeen of them men (including the pastor, who taught a senior Bible class). Although they constituted almost 70 percent of the entire staff and more than 80 percent of the teachers, women had no role in running the school or representing it in public. Instead, the teaching staff husbanded its small crop of men, allocating them to the most important and visible roles in the school. Thus, eleven of the seventeen men were officers; only nine (including the pastor) actually taught classes. This pattern was not unusual. Even the language that Sunday school writers employed perpetuated the myth of male dominance. Not only did such writers routinely refer to all teachers by the male pronoun, but they usually used male models such as "father" or "minister" to describe the teacher's relationship to the student. As a rule, evangelical women seem to have accepted these arrangements, much as they accepted role prescriptions that counseled women to exercise silent influence, not public power. Even when women fought to maintain their separate institutions, as did the ladies of New

York's Female Union Society for the Promotion of Sabbath Schools, they felt the need to defend their actions on the grounds of strict separation of "spheres," not maintenance of control.[46]

It comes as no surprise to find that women who dedicated themselves to Sunday school teaching did not join the ranks of reformers or feminists. As Blanche Glassman Hersh notes in her study of early nineteenth-century feminist-abolitionists, women who became feminists in the 1840s and 1850s, although often deeply religious, uniformly rejected Calvinism and its doctrines. "This liberation from orthodox dogma and from their society's evangelical emphasis on sin and damnation," she writes, "was a crucial element in the development of the women's movement." Evangelical Protestantism unquestionably had great appeal to many women and enabled them to see themselves as significant and useful beings, but its adherents—both male and female—placed clear boundaries on the definition of womanhood. For most women, like the Sunday school teachers discussed here, those boundaries seemed broad and expansive, providing space and breathing room. But for the few who became feminists, the limits on female action were as suffocatingly narrow as the tightly laced fashions that, in their view, symbolized women's "sphere."[47]

Only in the late nineteenth century, through the convention movement, did women teachers begin to reclaim some of the authority they had exercised in the schools' early history. Women were successful as convention participants and leaders, however, only insofar as they observed established codes of feminine behavior or orchestrated their actions in familiar ways. Direct challenges to male domination simply did not work, and so Sunday school women learned how to write variations upon the standard theme of subordination.

Although the conventions' leadership was overwhelmingly male, women gradually emerged as visible participants. The proportion of women delegates to the New York State Sunday School Teachers' Convention, for example, rose from 16 percent in 1863 to 32 percent in 1878. Similarly, women made up 30 percent of the delegates to Kentucky's 1875 convention but 45 percent of the 1878 delegates. Furthermore, in contrast to the prewar years, married women remained active in teaching and many served as delegates to state conventions; at least 45 percent of the women delegates to the 1867 Illinois State Sunday School Convention were married.[48]

Women emerged most notably as leaders of institute and convention sessions, conducting workshops, running demonstration classes, and giving lectures on teaching techniques. They did so despite continuing opposition from male church workers, who invoked traditional arguments against women as superintendents of coeducational schools or as leaders at conventions or teachers' institutes. Women, claimed one minister in 1871, had special qualities that suited them to teaching but not to supervising. To another writer, it appeared "evident that God never intended that women should be public speakers; or that, in his church, and in related organizations, women should occupy the position of public teachers and rulers." He concluded that "it would be better to have a man of *very* moderate ability as superintendent, than to have a very gifted woman." At the first national teachers' summer school in Chautauqua in 1873, the organizers banned women from addressing the entire mixed assembly, requiring them instead to hold separate, women-only receptions.[49]

Nevertheless, women recaptured lost leadership roles through the conventions. They managed to do so largely by entering two new areas of activity—teacher training and temperance education—rather than threatening established male bailiwicks. In addition, these women were almost invariably normal school graduates whose expertise in new teaching techniques gave them special status at the conventions. Women were especially instrumental in adapting the principles of the Swiss educator Johann Pestalozzi to Sunday schools. Introduced into the United States during the 1820s, Pestalozzi's ideas gained wide currency only after the establishment in 1861 of the Oswego (New York) State Normal and Training School, 90 percent of whose graduates were female. Because Pestalozzi's system was predicated upon an understanding of the child's "nature" and the achievement of "empathy" between teacher and pupil, women claimed a special competence for teaching it. Thus, by the early 1870s most state Sunday school conventions had women running sessions on such Pestalozzian topics as "object teaching" and such normal-school techniques as demonstration lessons.[50]

Typical of these women leaders were Sara J. Timanus, a teacher at the Minnesota State Normal School, and Matilda H. Kriege, the principal of Boston's Kindergarten Training School. Timanus, who was one of the first women to conduct institutes and convention sessions, became well known through her articles in the *National Sunday School Teacher* and other periodicals, as well as her books on the teaching of young children. After her marriage in 1874 to fellow Sunday school worker Wilbur F. Crafts, Sara Timanus Crafts became a full time Sunday school leader, lecturing widely on child psychology, disseminating Pestalozzian principles, and campaigning for the adoption of kindergartens in Sunday schools. Kriege was even more closely associated with the kindergarten effort. Through numerous articles in teachers' magazines, addresses at institutions and conventions, and demonstrations of "model classrooms," Kriege taught techniques associated with Pestalozzi and with Friedrich Froebel, whose ideas she found particularly appealing because of their stress on the religious content of education. Like Timanus, she stressed the importance of women as teachers of Sunday school kindergartens, thus helping establish kindergarten teaching as a special area of expertise reserved for women.[51]

Women like Timanus and Kriege were neither agitators nor feminists. They did not press for their right to participate in conventions but became participants because they had the requisite expertise to teach the new pedagogy. Believing that evangelical women should defer to male (and especially clerical) authority, yet convinced that women possessed certain innate qualities that especially suited them for work with small children, they accepted contemporary ideas about women's proper "sphere" as mothers and teachers. Their achievement was to extend the boundaries of that sphere by establishing a beachhead in the conventions from which they and others could push forward as leaders.[52]

Another group of women broadened these boundaries further as they used the convention movement to promote the cause of temperance. Evangelical women had been active in temperance work since the early nineteenth century, and advocacy of temperance or abstinence was not in itself very controversial within evangelical circles (Sunday school publications had for decades included material on the virtues of temperance). Still, the issue of whether women should act publicly to promote the cause remained divisive. Thus, in the 1860s, when a group of Methodist women began teaching temperance systematically in Sunday schools, arguing that teachers could win the battle against "the rum-power" by converting children to total abstinence and forming temperance societies within the schools, they often faced criticism of their methods. For example, Jennie Fowler Willing, the Methodist temperance worker and suffragist, took the cause to the first Chautauqua meeting in 1873, where she received the moral support of fellow Methodists like John H. Vincent. Despite his own temperance beliefs, however, Vincent required that Willing follow custom and address only separate women's meetings. There, and again at the following summer's Chautauqua gathering, Willing organized women teachers and held training sessions on temperance work in Sunday schools. Out of these meetings came a call for a national women's temperance convention which met in November 1874, with Willing presiding. Here she helped organize the Woman's Christian Temperance Union (WCTU), which quickly established committees on juvenile temperance and Sunday school work. Because so many WCTU organizers, including Frances Willard and Emily Huntington Miller, had Sunday school experience, the work seemed a natural focus for their organization. During its first five years, the WCTU established two successful programs: It organized Sunday school students into the Juvenile Temperance Union, complete with banners and pledges of total abstinence, and lobbied for the adoption of temperance lessons within each denomination's schools. The lessons, written and developed by Sara Timanus Crafts and Emily Huntington Miller, were in widespread use by 1880.[53]

Although these temperance activists quickly moved into additional arenas, they left their mark on the conventions. Not only did they establish temperance and related issues as topics on which women could meet and speak, but they forced male leaders to acknowledge their competency to teach men as well as women about these subjects. As Ruth Bordin has written of Frances Willard, they "exemplified a womanliness and domesticity that did not challenge existing cultural values," yet the effect of their work was to "permit . . . women to do whatever they wished in the public sphere and compel . . . men to praise them for it." In 1876, three years after John H. Vincent had relegated women to separate Chautauqua sections, Willard became the first of many women to address the entire assembly.[54]

Feminine domination of the Sunday school teaching corps in the nineteenth century was part of the larger feminization of American Protestantism that scholars have recently chronicled. There were many ironies in both developments, not the least of which was that male evangelicals—as ministers, elders, deacons, writers, and Sunday school superintendents—increasingly presided over heavily female groups, to whom they often spoke of the virtues of feminine submissiveness. Excluded from positions of power within the church and Sunday school, women nevertheless changed those institutions permanently, often by dint of sheer numbers and dogged devotion. No doubt the softening of Calvinist dogma in the nineteenth century occurred in part because women, as Sunday school teachers and writers, were called upon to interpret theological doctrines on a regular basis. Furthermore, religious behavior seems to have served women more than men as a means of self-expression, and religious activities were increasingly associated with the feminine sphere during the course of the century. Ironically, in founding and teaching Sunday schools, evangelical women helped both to enlarge women's sphere and to entrench and prepetuate the whole notion of separate gender spheres.[55]

In the course of fulfilling their duties, Sunday school teachers received a good deal of advice. Much of it, no doubt, came informally through conversations with other teachers and discussions at teacher's meetings, where the agenda often included prayer, progress reports, and problem solving. Much of it also came through the more formal channels of teachers' magazines and advice books. Like their common school counterparts, Sunday school teachers could turn to advice literature that was especially tailored for their needs, providing encouragement, suggestions, and admonitions. Written by other teachers, ministers, magazine editors, and Sunday school superintendents, this literature not only shaped their view of the teaching job, it also expressed their concerns and reflected changes in the Sunday school curriculum over the course of the century. Thus, the study of Sunday school teachers' advice literature clarifies evangelicals' perceptions of the teacher's role and of the schools' overall goals.

Although advertised as instructing teachers "how to teach," this literature seldom offered specific pedagogical advice of the type so familiar to twentieth-century teachers. Instead, books and magazine articles provided general commentary and exhorted readers toward spiritual growth. Only after 1860 did teachers receive specific counsel on actual teaching methods; detailed guidlines were absent from the antebellum advice literature, which resembled nothing so much as self-improvement manuals. The chapter titles of W. F. Lloyd's widely circulated 1825 book, The Teacher's Manual, reveal its orientation: "The Disposition with which the Office of a Sunday-School Teacher Should be Undertaken," "On the Usefulness of a

Knowledge of Human Nature," "On Gaining the Affections of your Scholars," "Hints on Promoting their Spiritual Improvement," "On the Personal Benefits of Sunday-School Teaching," "On Preserving Unity Among Sunday-School Teachers." Lloyd's manual, originally published in England, soon had American competitors, including *The Teacher Taught* by Frederick Packard and John Todd's *Sunday School Teacher,* all of which devoted more space to counseling teachers on their spiritual lives than suggesting how or what to teach.[56]

As purveyors of the gospel of "self-culture," Sunday school teachers' magazines and guidebooks reflected the teachers' own interests. Those like Harriet Lathrop and Michael Floy, for example, envisioned their work less as an intellectual process of imparting information and more as an emotional process of sharing spiritual experiences, during which the teacher as well as the student experienced religious renewal. The goal of teaching, after all, was "the salvation of [students'] immortal souls," not the mere communication of knowledge. Thus, Sunday school workers defined success primarily in terms of the number of students (and teachers) who experienced conversion, although they simultaneously employed more conventional measures of progress, such as attendance figures and statistics on memorization. Standard lists of desirable qualities in teachers stressed the need for persons of "vital religion" who were capable of appealing directly to their students' "hearts" in order to encourage conversion. Just as teachers themselves judged the success or failure of a particular class session by the amount of feeling it generated, so advice writers emphasized qualities of heart over qualities of mind in the ideal teacher. "Those who have been called by Divine grace in early life will, in general, be found best qualified for addressing young people on the concerns of their souls," counseled the members of the New-York Sunday-School Union Society in 1817; for "the ardour of their own feelings leads them to engage in the service with delight and energy." Aside from "a competent knowledge of the Scriptures—a capability of teaching in a manner adapted to the capacities of children—and an ardent affection for young immortals," teachers needed few other qualifications. After all, the society's members concluded, God "will teach them how to impart instruction, and while they water others, they shall be watered themselves." With such views of teaching held widely by teachers, it is understandable why advice-givers seldom felt the need to describe specific teaching techniques.[57]

Although differing on some of the specifics of "self-culture," all these advisors saw it as a process of personal growth in which teachers acquired certain characteristics that enabled them better to promote student conversions. Two categories of personal qualities appeared most frequently in the literature: "earnestness" and good habits. Indeed, "earnestness" lodged near or at the top of almost every nineteenth-century list of teacher qualifications. It meant that the teacher felt a "deep interest" in his or her students' welfare, prayed for them daily, was "devoted" to them, engaged them in individual conversations about the state of their souls, and appealed directly to their "hearts and consciences" in an animated fashion. An earnest teacher would make a point of visiting his or her students during the week, praying with them, and attempting to make them feel their "sinfulness" as a first step on the road to conversion. Moreover, he or she would do all this not out of any sense of obligation but out of a deep, sincere, personal concern for the student.[58]

Under the category of good habits the advice writers subsumed a wide variety of qualities, all involving self-discipline. But they particularly stressed punctuality and orderliness. "Order *in all your plans*—and good example *in all your ways*—will crown persevering efforts with success," advised the American Sunday School Union in 1829. "The *discipline* of every *teacher* should begin with himself." Other advisors echoed this emphasis, compiling laundry lists of teacher qualifications that included, (along with "earnestness") "promptitude and strict punctuality," routine, humility, simplicity of dress, and "plain diet." In his 1825 *Teacher's Manual*, W. F. Lloyd included a chapter on the "Duty of Teachers as to Punctual Attendance." In his 1868 *Sunday-School Hand-Book*, Erwin House listed the qualities of a good teacher in the following order: punctuality, regularity, cheerfulness, patience, studiousness, correct personal habits, piety, and church membership.[59]

This emphasis on good habits and punctuality grew over the course of the century. Whereas early advisors usually discussed religious qualifications first, by the 1850s advice-givers were more likely to begin with punctuality and order, and then proceed to piety and religious knowledge. Given the growth of time-consciousness and clock discipline in the nineteenth century, this stress on punctuality is not entirely surprising. Some male teachers were, of course, young clerks making their way through the ranks in search of mercantile success; any time-management skills learned in Sunday school might further their careers. (Hiram Peck, who was a store clerk as well as a teacher, implicitly acknowledged this connection when he commented that there was "so much advantage to be derived from being punctual.") Still, it is important to keep in mind that a majority of teachers were women who, despite the growth of female employment during the century, would never have to punch a time clock or arrive at a desk promptly at nine. Moreover, the advice writers were themselves teachers, passing along the fruits of their experience. It was all very well to speak of sharing religious experiences in a Sunday school class, but if teachers and students drifted in at odd hours, how might such sharing be accomplished? The advice-givers' stress on punctuality and order is best explained not as a direct effort to inculcate in teachers—and by extension students—the work discipline of an expanding commercial and industrial economy, but as an indirect result of economic change. After all, domestic manuals, such as Catharine Beecher's *Treatise on Domestic Economy*, bristled with as much talk about efficiency and order as did other advice books. As Carl Kaestle has noted about common schools, "work discipline was not the central purpose of school discipline and is not a sufficient explanation of it." Sunday school advice literature, with its stress on self-discipline, reflected both the teachers' own interest in such qualities and their increased importance within the culture.[60]

In the advice-givers' universe, good habits went hand-in-hand with "earnestness" as necessary attributes of Sunday school teachers. When it came to explaining how to translate either quality into pedagogical technique, however, the advice writers retreated into vague generalities and pious exhortations about being good role models. "Watch over yourself," counseled New England minister John Todd, for "the eyes of the school are all upon you" and success "depends upon the opinions which children entertain of you." To be sure, these writers stressed the importance of teachers' knowledge of the Bible and their ability to explain basic theological doctrines, and they urged teachers to adapt their methods to students' general capacities or, better still, to their individual temperaments and characters. Yet specific information on what to do in the classroom itself was seldom forthcoming, except insofar as teachers were advised to "be simple" in speaking style and language and to "make sure" students understood what they learned. The most detailed advice to be found in the manuals concerned maintaining order and enforcing discipline; in fact, teachers often received much more specific advice on how to establish routine classroom procedures than on how to teach a lesson.[61]

Yet in the context of the schools' goals, the advice literature was well adapted to its readers' purposes. While pedagogically much less detailed than modern materials, it focused clearly on the goal of conversion—for both teacher and student—and advised readers on its nurturance and preservation. The process of teaching, in the minds of both advice-givers and teachers, involved more than transmitting Biblical or doctrinal information; it involved communicating a whole life-orientation and a life-style defined by specific personality characteristics (or habits). By stressing "earnestness," the advice writers were establishing religious conversion, or deep religious seriousness, as a prerequisite for teaching. (Although there was disagreement on this issue, most advisors urged unconverted individuals to become teachers, on the theory that teaching could lead to conversion.) In detailing the importance of good habits, these writers underlined the teacher's status as a role model to students.[62]

When the advice literature did become more pedagogically detailed, offering specific methodological advice, lesson plans, and classroom teaching techniques, Sunday school teachers were drawn into a debate over the relative merits of intellectual training as opposed to emotional nurturing in religious education. Precipitated by the growing popularity of teachers' institutes and Sunday school conventions during the 1850s and 1860s, the introduction of common school teaching techniques proceeded rapidly. The publication of new teachers' magazines facilitated the diffusion of these ideas. By the 1870s teachers were reading articles on new teaching techniques in Sunday school magazines, attending institutes and conventions where such new tactics were taught, and being urged to adopt new standards of professionalism in their work. No longer, it seemed, was it enough for teachers to enter their classes prepared to discuss the week's lesson. They were increasingly asked to be familiar with Pestalozzian methods, "object teaching," proper blackboard illustration, and the "art of questioning." In the words of John H. Vincent, a major proponent of professionalization, the goal was to "render . . . the work of the Sabbath-school more like that of the secular school." No doubt the effort to professionalize Sunday school teaching affected only a minority of teachers, especially those at large urban churches. Still, the new emphasis on technique led to an ongoing discussion of the schools' proper goals.[63]

Much of this discussion took place in the pages of advice books and teachers' magazines, where articles on the new pedagogy often shared space with critiques of it. In September 1869, for example, the *National Sunday School Teacher* printed two contiguous articles, one on training teachers in proper teaching methods, the other on the need for teachers to exhibit "heart-power" and love of the work, regardless of whether they were well trained. Two years later, in the same publication, one of best-known proponents of professionalization strongly criticized British Sunday school workers for inaugurating a system of competitive examinations among teachers. Such a system, Sara J. Timanus wrote, did not test "teaching ability or spirituality, the two most important qualifications of the Sabbath-school teacher. . . . It is altogether a mistake to judge the efficiency of the Sabbath-school teacher upon an intellectual basis. Intellect is cold. God's service is not one of intellect; it is of the affections through which the mind is sanctified."[64]

Perhaps the best evidence of the ongoing struggle to define "essential" as opposed to incidental qualifications of teachers was the agenda of the first Chautauqua Assembly of Sunday school teachers in 1873. The delegates, after hearing a Methodist bishop at the meeting's outset denigrate "mind-power" and extol "heart-power" as central to teaching, were encouraged at the end of the two-week assembly to take a four-and-one-half hour competitive examination, in which twenty-nine of the fifty essay questions dealt with Biblical history or geography. Whereas the bishop had warned his listeners that "if we are only intellectual, we are not soul-saving ministers or laborers," the examination asked its two hundred participants to "name the minor prophets," "give the boundaries of Palestine," and "quote the first and last verses of the Bible." (The assembly also featured a miniature "Palestine Park," devised by organizer John H. Vincent and depicting the area's geography and archeology.)[65]

In the 1870s, as in the 1830s, teachers' advice literature emphasized self-improvement. Now, however, the advice writers were unsure as to which part of the self most needed improvement. Their uncertainty stemmed both from changes in common-school pedagogy and from shifts within Sunday schools themselves. As more and more common school teachers attended normal schools and adopted new standards of professionalism for their work, Sunday school teachers (many of whom also taught school during the week) remained profoundly ambivalent about the extent to which their work should resemble that of "secular" schools. If they concentrated on improving their content and techniques by learning Biblical archaeology and history, along with the latest ideas coming out of normal schools, they ran the risk of treating the Sunday school as if it were merely a Sunday version of the common school. One observer, terming secular teachers the "rivals" of Sunday school teachers, argued that in order to "preserve their own self-respect and the respect of their pupils," Sunday school teachers would have to "equal, if not excel" their common-school counterparts "not only in breadth of mind but in capacity to instruct." John H. Vincent even established a short-lived monthly publication entitled the *Normal Class,* through which he undertook to instruct readers in Greek and Hebrew, presumably so that they could become semiprofessional Biblical scholars. For many teachers, too, it was easier to measure one's progress in terms of knowledge acquired than in the more nebulous area of character improvement. Yet teachers recognized that, because of its content, Sunday school teaching was not exactly analogous to common school teaching, and thus their qualifications were not comparable. The retired Congregationalist Sunday school leader Asa Bullard suggested that some of the best teachers had been those with few obvious credentials. "They received their qualifications," he noted, "mainly from the teachings of the Holy Spirit." Personal qualities, such as "earnest piety," were perhaps more important than acquired qualifications to the religious educator.[66]

The advice literature's ambivalence about what comprised competence in a teacher also arose from changes in the schools' goals. Whereas in the early nineteenth century teachers had known that their ultimate objective was the conversion of their pupils, by the 1860s and 1870s that aim was no longer clear. While many schools continued to stress conversion and to utilize revivalistic techniques in their curricula, others increasingly embraced the goal of "Christian nurture" for their students. As we will see in the next chapter, the shift from conversion to nurture led teachers to downplay or reject entirely the belief that one life-defining experience should be the focus of Sunday school instruction. Instead, they hoped to encourage the child's gradual growth into an adult Christian. With this shift in goals, teachers found their work both easier and harder: easier because they now had a rationale for keeping children in school indefinitely, harder because they bore a heavier burden of responsibility for the child's religious destiny. If the teacher's task was to "find . . . and fix upon . . . the *best system of teaching*," then her central work was not, as earlier generations had believed, to make children feel their innate depravity, but to discover the perfect method of nurturing religious belief.[67]

Throughout most of the nineteenth century, Sunday schools were the only American institutions for children that relied entirely on volunteer labor for their maintenance and perpetuation. Despite recurring problems with recruitment and training of teachers, the schools managed to provide enough intangible rewards to attract and retain them. If the work attracted more women than men, and if young people outnumbered older in the ranks of teachers, these patterns reflected both the particular appeal of Sunday school teaching to youth and women and the recruit- ment methods most widely used in the schools. The use of Bible classes to train new teachers virtually guaranteed that the teacher corps would be youthful, while women's attraction to the work was part of the larger process whereby Protestant- ism became "feminized" in the nineteenth century. To be sure, the use of volunteers was a source of many headaches for professional Sunday school promoters, but they considered teaching's volunteer nature one of the schools' greatest assets. Few would have entertained ideas about rewarding teachers in other than intangible ways, and virtually none envisioned the practice of hiring paid religious educators that became common in twentieth-century schools.[68] Volunteerism undergirded the schools' origins and remained a deeply held principle throughout the century.

Chapter Five

CONVERSION & CHRISTIAN NURTURE: CHILDREN AND CHILDHOOD IN SUNDAY SCHOOLS

Sunday schools were preeminently institutions for children. Like their nineteenth-century counterparts—the common school, the house of refuge, and the orphan asylum—they reflected prevailing adult beliefs about the importance of childhood and theories about its essential characteristics. Their programs and curricula manifested adult efforts to shape childhood experiences toward particular social ends, while at the same time touching the lives of the children who passed through them. Although exercising much less coercive power than either residential institutions such as asylums or public institutions such as common schools, Sunday schools nevertheless became the primary tool of Protestant religious education in the nineteenth century. Their rapid growth forced evangelicals to find a theological place for them within Protestant religious traditions and brought ministers and parents face to face with the behavioral expressions of children's religious experiences. As adult views of children's religious capabilities and needs changed, school goals and curricula underwent revision and adaptation. Through it all, children proved themselves to be decidedly resilient creatures, as some responded to and others resisted adult guidance and coercion.

The earliest goal of evangelical Sunday school workers was simply to bring religious knowledge, and the behavior associated with it, to lower-class youth. By teaching children to read the Bible, these workers believed, they would do more than impart "the truths of the Gospel" to ignorant youngsters. They would also provide a foundation upon which their charges could construct moral lives. True morality, in their view, emanated from knowledge of the individual's ultimate accountability to God for his or her actions; without that knowledge, individuals had no incentive to behave correctly. In this spirit, Sunday school workers spoke of teaching pupils "the duty required of them as social, rational and accountable beings," and of inculcating "the habit of restraining and governing corrupt nature." One commentator noted: "In exact proportion as they become acquainted with the doctrines, precepts, promises, and threatenings, of the holy Scriptures, will they find it difficult to stifle their consciences, throw off restraint, and pursue the ways of vanity and vice."[1] Although teachers did not expect their instruction to guarantee conversion—such an expectation would challenge the orthodox doctrine of inability—they did hope for subsequent conversions among pupils who participated in revivals and believed that Sunday school instruction would at the very least "rectify and enlighten their consciences," creating prudent and circumspect individuals.[2]

During the 1810s and early 1820s, the schools' curricula reflected these ideas. Students were divided into classes according to reading skill, not age, and graduated to higher classes as they mastered specific tasks. One began in the alphabet class, proceeded through the one- and two-syllable word classes, and finished in the reading classes. In the latter, pupils busied themselves memorizing prescribed portions of the Old and New Testaments and vying with each other for weekly prizes awarded to those who memorized the largest number of verses. The use of ticket rewards (described in chapter 2) reinforced the importance of memorization.[3] Moreover, most students remained in school only until they could read the Bible satisfactorily, and few had any but a passing acquaintance with their teachers. Indeed, it was common practice for schools to rotate their teaching staffs every three months or maintain different staffs for morning and afternoon school sessions.[4]

The entry of churchgoing pupils into the schools, however, along with the growth of free weekday schools, precipitated changes in both goals and curricula during the 1820s. For one thing, teaching reading assumed a secondary spot in the curriculum, as specifically religious—and occasionally denominational—education became paramount (see chapter 1). For another, some workers began attempting to keep children in the schools for lengthy indoctrination, rather than dismissing them as soon as they had learned to read. The emergence of crude age-grading in the late 1820s and early 1830s was one result of this attempt, even though most schools continued to group children by ability rather than by age. Bible classes targeted youngsters over twelve and attempted to keep them in school in order to train them as teachers, while infant classes, patterned upon the infant schools that were newly popular in cities like New York, Boston, and Philadelphia, emerged to take charge of youngsters from about eighteen months to seven years of age. Although in common schools concern about the "disease of precocity" led administrators to exclude very young children during the 1830s, Sunday schools made no such move. Indeed, both the American Sunday School Union and many local unions pressed their affiliates to form infant classes, using as a model Joanna Graham Bethune's infant school in New York (see figure 15).[5]

As the schools shifted toward more exclusively religious teaching for children of all ages and social backgrounds, Sunday school workers articulated their religious goals more explicitly and reshaped the curriculum to meet these goals. Beyond making "the deepest religious impressions" and encouraging moral behavior, teachers and writers spoke of preparing children for eventual religious conversion. Employing a horticultural metaphor in 1822, New Yorker Divie Bethune compared teachers to gardeners who remove "from nature's soil, to Zion's garden, the withering plants" which are children's souls. Finding "these scholars in their ignorant unregenerate state," in "blighted nature's barren waste," he went on, teachers move them "to a kinder soil; they plant them there; their tears bedew them; their prayers ascend for them and the Lord of the harvest returns his answer in refreshing showers of heavenly grace." In a similar vein, the Episcopal minister Gregory T. Bedell noted that through religious education "the ground becomes mellowed and softened to the reception of the seeds of truth and preparation to receive . . . copious showers of divine grace."[6] Preparation for conversion was to be a central part of the schools' agenda.

In keeping with this goal, Sunday school workers revamped the schools' organization and program. Small classes, with six to ten pupils per teacher, now became the ideal (except among "infants"). Teachers assumed a more important place in the schools' overall design; they were the gardeners in this divine field and needed to have closer personal contact with their pupils (see figure 16). The practice of rotating teaching staffs was abandoned in favor of assigning teachers to individual classes on a year-long basis. "The relation between teacher and pupil became . . . more intimate," noted one observer, as the teacher's job changed from hearing students' recitations to "imparting that religious knowledge, those religious impressions, and form[ing] . . . those religious habits, . . . which shall be crowned with the salvation of their immortal souls." Teachers and superintendents now spoke of "adapt[ing] our language to the capacities of our children" and appealing to them personally in order to stimulate religious feelings.[7]

The curriculum also changed to place more emphasis on understanding Biblical precepts and less on rote memorization. "It is a source of regret," lamented the managers of the American Sunday School Union in 1827, "that many pupils of Sunday schools are ignorant of the meaning of those passages of scripture which they commit to memory." A union author commented that "however desirable storing the memories of children may be, it is still more desirable that their minds should be enlightened, and their consciences awakened by its solemn truths." To rectify this situation, teachers and local Sunday school unions developed lesson

THE

INFANT SCHOOL

TEACHER'S ASSISTANT;

EMBRACING A COURSE OF

MORAL AND RELIGIOUS INSTRUCTION,

ADAPTED TO THE MINDS OF THE CHILDREN,

AND DESIGNED

TO DRAW ANSWERS FROM THEM.

PREPARED FOR THE AMERICAN SUNDAY-SCHOOL UNION, AND REVISED BY
THE COMMITTEE OF PUBLICATION.

AMERICAN SUNDAY-SCHOOL UNION.

PHILADELPHIA,

NO. 136 CHESTNUT STREET.

1833.

Figure 15. The American Sunday School Union published books like this one for infant schools and encouraged the formation of infant classes in Sunday schools

GROUND PLAN OF A SUNDAY SCHOOL ROOM.

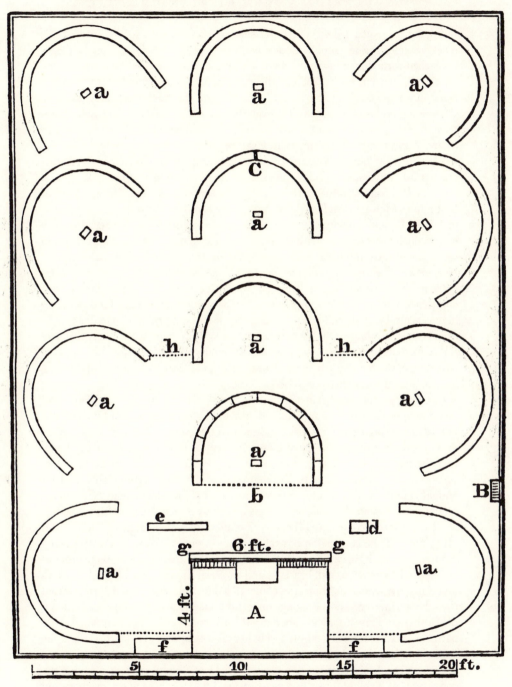

Figure 16. This plan for a Sunday school room represented an ideal: classes of six to ten students gathered in semicircles around their teachers (a), a waiting bench for new students (C), a good stove (d), a well-stocked library (f), seats for visitors (g), and a desk from which the superintendent could maintain order (A)

series, that is, sequenced sets of ten to twenty Bible verses provided to students for weekly memorization, along with question books for their teachers. Because teachers lacked formal training and "were not able to ask questions and interest the scholars," question books, such as the American Sunday School Union's *Union Questions,* enabled them to quiz their students on the week's memorized verses. Containing no answers (since all the questions could be answered by a quotation from the memorized passage), question books were supposed to "excite the mind to a careful and thorough examination of the Scriptures."[8]

In redirecting the schools' curriculum away from memorization and toward preparation for conversion, Sunday school workers began to focus their attention on emotional and spiritual rather than purely intellectual processes. The president of Baltimore's McKendrean Female Sabbath School Society stated the case succinctly in 1827. "By an assiduous attention to [students'] mental improvement, we may essentially benefit their heads and strengthen their minds," she reasoned. "But can we be content to stop here? Will we entirely neglect the culture of their hearts?" Her answer, clearly, was no. The following year, she made the point even more explicit: "The efficacy of moral and religious instruction consists more in what our children are brought to feel, than what they are taught to know." Her distinction between intellectual knowledge of religious doctrine on the one hand and emotional understanding on the other was conventional in the nineteenth century and traced its roots back to Jonathan Edwards's theology. But in stressing the centrality of feeling in the Sunday school curriculum, she and others like her made preparing for conversion a key theme in weekly lessons.[9]

Henceforth, "personal religious conversation" between teacher and pupil and "earnest appeals" from the superintendent would be as much a part of the curriculum as hymn singing and recitations. Sunday school teachers' organizations urged members to visit their students at home on a regular basis in order to get to know them better and promote their progress in religion. Increasingly, schools took censuses of teachers and students to discover who had experienced conversion and kept annual counts of conversions to report to national and denominational Sunday school organizations. Lack of conversions was cause for lamentation: "It is a melancholly [sic] fact," commented the superintendent of a New York school in 1834, "that not a single conversion has taken place in our school since our last Semi-Annual report." Religious revivals that originated in Sunday schools were promptly reported to religious publications and national organizations, which took to describing the schools as "nurseries of piety." And while most such reports stressed the schools' impact in encouraging conversions among teachers, some offered evidence that students, too, had experienced conversion. A Connecticut teacher reported in 1825 that a ten-year-old girl in her class experienced a "deep sense of the evil of her heart" and gave evidence of regeneration, while a widely circulated religious periodical criticized parents who did not "hope, or even pray for the conversion of a child four or five years of age."[10] In all these ways, teachers and their allies designated both preparation for conversion and the actual experience of conversion as the schools' central goals.

In the context of Protestant educational history, these changes in goals and curricula were singular. Ever since the Reformation, the indoctrination of youth in preparation for adult religious experience had centered on memorization of Biblical passages, catechisms, and hymns. Moreover, the purpose of such education, as Gerald Strauss has clearly shown, was to stamp childhood into a mold of docility, passivity, diffidence, and dutiful obedience to adult authority. Children were not to think for themselves but to accept the ideas and parrot the words of their teachers.[11] Although Sunday school workers valued obedience in their pupils, the whole thrust of the education they designed during the 1820s and 1830s undercut the traditional goals of Protestant schooling. By downplaying memorization and designing question books that required the teacher or student to find the answer, they necessarily permitted some measure of initiative, even spontaneity. Moreover, the practice of keeping the teacher-student ratio low and cultivating intimate ties between teachers and pupils annihilated the boundaries between intellectual knowledge and emotional understanding of Protestant doctrine, turning the Sunday school into an incubator of conversion. Sunday school education thus attempted to create an individual who was thoughtful and reflective, both self-controlled and self-directed. Sunday school teachers still expected the evangelical scholar to be obedient and dutiful, but they also hoped to give him or her possession of the inner resources and disciplined habits necessary to steer a true course in a hostile world.

Lessons and magazines aimed at scholars reflected both the goals and the tactics of evangelical pedagogy. Question books required the pupil to ponder theological points while reading specific scriptural verses. The 1829 edition of *Union Questions,* for example, offered the following questions for the consideration of older students: "What is meant by being *born again?* Eph. iv, 22–24. . . . Is the sinner, without being born again, prepared for the service and company of holy beings? . . . Why must every one be born again? Rom. viii, 7, 8. Who works this great change?" Magazines, especially those designed for children over ten, attempted to stimulate thinking about the reader's unregenerate state. Amid the advice, missionary notices, lesson questions, and obituaries of children, students read articles and poems stressing key aspects of the evangelical message. "Your heart is very wicked," wrote one author in the orthodox periodical *Youth's Companion;* "so wicked that you are unfit to go to heaven as it is; so bad that none but God can make it good."[12]

In attempting to stir children's emotions, writers most often relied upon reminders of life's fragility. Stories of youngsters experiencing conversion on their deathbeds, of children killed while playing hooky from Sunday school, of pious babes who from their sickbeds urged repentance upon their parents, of dead and dying Sunday scholars, were staple fare in these periodicals, as well as in the books that filled Sunday school libraries. Individual schools occasionally published edifying stories of the last illness and glorious death of a particular pupil, stories picked up and reprinted in the periodical literature. "Children, do you keep in constant remembrance this solemn and awful truth?" queried the editor of *Youth's Companion*. "Remember, dear children, that a large proportion of you *must* appear in eternity before your twentieth year!" Recounting a child's death, another author penned this (ungrammatical) rhyme:

> *Then let us think of death*
> *When we engage in play;*
> *For like our brother we beneath*
> *The valley's clod may lay.*[13]

We do not know, of course, what lessons nineteenth-century children derived from such reading matter. As Daniel T. Rodgers reminds us, "all children's stories are twice-told tales—the teller's words revised, elaborated, and severely edited in the intermediary of the child's imagination. The child's tale and the adult's tale are not the same story."[14] Yet because such works usually strike us as nothing less than "religious terrorism," to use E. P. Thompson's phrase, it is important to recall the context in which they were written and read. Designed to reach children through their emotions where, evangelicals believed, true religious experiences took place, stories emphasizing the nearness of death were supposed to touch their deepest emotions by engaging their deepest fears. Given the presumed difficulty of making children (or for that matter adults) feel the truth of such abstract doctrines as limited atonement, inability, and regeneration, Sunday school writers, like many a preacher and theologian before them, brought doctrine down to the concrete level of life or death. Moreover, in the nineteenth century death was a much greater everyday reality than it is today. Virtually every Sunday scholar had lost a parent, sibling, relative, friend, or acquaintance by the time he or she was ten years old. Death was both a fact of life and a very real possibility to each child who read Sunday school literature. By reminding them of death's imminence, writers were, to be sure, attempting to manipulate children's emotions, but in the context of their times such efforts were neither more nor less unusual than those of Jonathan Edwards or of modern-day advertisers who strive to "manage" consumers' "hearts."[15]

The curriculum and goals that evangelical schools laid down in broad outline during the 1820s and early 1830s remained constant over the next two decades. Preparing students for conversion, attempting to precipitate the event, and planning for revivals during which prepared students (and teachers) would undergo the experience formed the schools' underlying theme. During most of the antebellum period, teachers strove to attain an ideal whereby students entered the schools at a young age and proceeded through several age-graded (though crudely so) classes in which they studied the Bible and evangelical theology before becoming teachers. Throughout their education, students would have frequent "appeals" made to their "hearts," appeals designed to make them feel, not merely know intellectually, the doctrines of original sin, human depravity, future punishment, and regeneration. Although a few might experience conversion during their stay in the "main school" or in the boys' and girls' classes, most would graduate to Bible class at adolescence without having been "born again." In the Bible class, they would be encouraged to dwell at length on the state of their souls, all the while imbibing Biblical history and evangelical or denominational theology. Through visits with the Bible class teacher, conversations with fellow students, and private self-examination, they might become "hopefully converted," perhaps in the company of their Bible class compatriots at a general congregational revival. After finishing Bible class, they might continue as teachers or simply join the church in full membership. In some church schools, especially Methodist and Baptist ones, many would continue as scholars in adult classes.[16]

Ideals are not reality, of course. At any time during the antebellum years, a visitor could have found schools that came close to the ideal and those that were far removed from it. In most rural and frontier areas, for example, schools met only for the summer months and closed during the winter season. For many such schools, the practical difficulties of organizing and maintaining a program overshadowed any sustained effort at age-grading or other cumulative progress. "Think of a S[unday] S[chool]," wrote a rural superintendent in 1867, "in a house with cracks a cat could jump through[,] without a stove or fire place, a roof that admits half the rain and sometimes no floor but old mother earth," and you will realize why it does not meet in winter.[17] Urban mission schools sometimes had such difficulty recruiting and controlling rowdy lower-class children that teachers focused their efforts on simple, repetitive lessons. Even the best-financed and organized urban church schools had problems, frequently suspending or severely retrenching their programs during the summer months, when heat and teacher vacations took their toll. Above all, though, it was the sporadic nature of attendance and the ever-changing character of their clientele that dashed teachers' hopes for a smooth-running operation. At the Brandywine Manufacturers' Sunday School in Delaware, for example, average attendance rose from 150 in 1826 to 220 in 1831, dropped to 180 in 1832 and 150 in 1837, then rose again to 230 in 1841, dropping off to 120 in 1849. Other schools recorded similar patterns. Most Sunday scholars were probably between the ages of six and twelve and attended for a year of two.[18]

In making conversion the central focus of their work, Sunday school advocates made strong claims for themselves and their institution. Not only were many parents and ministers skeptical about the possibility of achieving true conversion in childhood or youth, but the schools themselves had no official place within the institutional frameworks of most evangelical denominations. Moreover, preparing the faithful for conversion and stimulating revivals were tasks long assigned to each sect's ordained ministers. Supporters of Sunday schools—whether they were teach-ers, administrators, writers, ministers, or paid organizers—thus faced several tasks: convincing the skeptics that children had great religious potential, weaving their lay-run institution into the fabric of their churches, and identifying the distinguish-ing characteristics of childhood religiosity.

Three common sentiments about childhood received withering glances from Sunday school workers during the antebellum years. One was the belief, summed up by the missionary Sheldon Norton in 1831, that childhood should "be the period for unrestrained indulgence and gaiety—a season which should be left to run to waste." Many parents, according to Norton and other workers, adhered to the child rearing theory that children should be permitted to do pretty much as they pleased because the difficulties of adult life would descend upon them soon enough. An Illinois man summed up this approach in 1830: "I have no opinion of keeping my children too close—For my part, if my children take a notion to go a-visiting on the Sabbath, I tell them to go." To allow children to do whatever they "took a notion to" was, in the minds of people like Norton, to allow a crucial portion of life "to run to waste."[19] Sunday school supporters thus promoted the view, common among those who advised parents on child rearing in the nineteenth century, that an individual's childhood set the course for his or her entire life. More important, as evangelicals, Sunday school supporters believed that indulgence and tolerance of children's "natural" behavior was tantamount to handing their souls, which were by nature (through original sin) corrupt, over to the devil.[20]

A related notion—that religion made children morbid—also evoked scorn. De-scribing this belief, a writer for the *Sabbath-School Magazine* recounted the story of a father who tried to remove his daughters from Sunday school because he was "fearful . . . that religion would hurt their minds" and felt that religious children were "lost to all sense of pleasure, and given over to gloom and melancholy." The daughters, however, having "looked at both sides of the question, . . . had learnt that man can only be truly happy, when he seeks to love and serve God."[21] To counteract such sentiments (which, no doubt, were reinforced by stories of pious dead and dying youngsters), Sunday school advocates argued that true happiness lay only in religion and tried to portray the institution as pleasant and appealing. "Children are disposed to see their acquaintances," noted one writer in 1824, and "would come to school, if for no other purpose than to see each other." Even William Alcott, the advice writer who was generally critical of the schools, con-ceded that, given the only feasible alternative—taking children to adult religious services—Sunday schools were "a relief to the young," who considered it "much more tolerable to spend the morning going to and returning from Sabbath school, than in constant and close confinement."[22]

A third belief—that children were incapable of true religious experiences—was so widely held that Sunday school workers focused a great deal of energy on combating it. Judging by its condemnation in religious education periodicals, this attitude seems to have been shared by parents, ministers, and Sunday school teachers alike, who needed to be convinced that children could be religiously moved and perhaps even converted. Michael Floy, for example, confessed his surprise at one student's request to join in a prayer meeting. "I had much doubt concerning children becoming religious," the teacher noted in his diary; "I thought it was sufficient to make religious impressions on their minds, and that when they grew up they would reflect on what they had been taught."

In fighting this view, one of the most popular tactics that advocates of childhood religiosity employed was to cite examples of youngsters who had experienced conversion at young ages. Stories of "a little girl" of thirteen who converted, or of a seven-year-old who experienced conversion but was required to wait until she was sixteen before being admitted to full church membership, were staple items in religious education periodicals and Sunday school speeches throughout the antebellum years. "The time was," argued a member of the Providence, Rhode Island, Association of Sabbath School Teachers in 1833, "when ministers and church members thought that children of three, five or seven years of age were too young to be converted." Now, he concluded with some exaggeration, all that had changed. In fact, it had not, judging by the volume of comments exhorting teachers, parents, and ministers to believe in children's capacity for conversion. Despite the examples Sunday school workers cited of eleven- and twelve-year-olds joining their churches in full communion, "early conversion"—by which some meant the regeneration of five-year-olds, others of twelve-year olds—remained more ideal than reality.[23]

There were other ways of making the case for genuine childhood religiosity, short of proving that children had been converted. Sunday school writers drew on a variety of contemporary theories, particularly psychological and theological, as they participated in the ongoing debate over children's essential "nature." Following the ideas of the Scottish Common Sense philosophers, evangelical Sunday school workers argued that children experienced the world primarily through their feelings. Unlike adults, whose mental faculty of reason was well developed, children were emotional and unreflective, capable of parroting reams of information because their memories were especially tenacious, but incapable of the calm, judicious contemplation that characterized adulthood. At one and the same time, then, children were foolish but malleable. Whereas their lack of reasoning ability seemed to make children unlikely candidates for serious religious thought, evangelicals seized upon their malleability and sensitivity, arguing that these qualities made children especially open to "impressions," particularly religious impressions. "Youth is the season of susceptibility," wrote W. F. Lloyd, author of a widely used Sunday school teachers' manual. "The heart is tender; the affections are lively and glowing. The wax is warmed and softened by the heat of youthful feeling, and awaits the impression which we are desirous of fixing upon it." If good impressions could be "stamped upon the hearts of our children," he argued, their characters would be correctly shaped. Lloyd's images of childhood—softness, plasticity, malleability—echoed in the literature of Sunday school teachers and organizers, as did contrasting images of adults as "heardened" and un-bending. "Adults are fixed, and with difficulty wrought on," commented the manag-ers of one school in 1819; "children are pliable."[24]

Their impressionability seemed to make children especially good candidates for religious training. Just as some Sunday school workers spoke of storing children's memories with Bible verses in order to provide them with fodder for future con-templation, others described early religious teaching as stamping children's charac-ters into permanent molds. Impressions received at a young age, suggested one writer, "can never be entirely eradicated." Sunday school children, declared the managers of the Massachusetts Sabbath School Union in 1826, are "susceptible of impressions . . . more deep, and consequently more durable, than any which can be produced at a later period of life." The teacher's task, then, was to "take advantage of this susceptibility, and imbue them with the principles of religion, that the bias of their expanding minds [might] be brought to the side of truth." Childhood plas-ticity, molded by the right hands, would harden into an adulthood of fixed princi-ples, providing fail-safe navigation through the choppy seas of life.[25]

Children's emotional sensitivity seemed to offer strong incentives to concentrate on childhood training. To the evangelicals, conversion was experienced through the "affections" or "heart." Because children were "governed in a great degree by their feelings," they would find it easier to feel the truths of evangelical doctrine than would adults "grown old in sin."[26] In arguing that children's emotional natures proved their capacity for religious conversion, Sunday school workers made no claim that children were better able than adults to become religious (unlike some of their contemporaries, who adhered to the romantic view of children as coming "from heaven, with their little souls full of innocence and peace"). They merely tried to establish children's equal capability. To adults they conceded a better capacity for intellectual knowledge of religious doctrine; for children they claimed a greater potential for emotional understanding.[27]

From the standpoint of orthodox theology, these theories were unobjectionable as long as Sunday school workers did not deny the doctrines of original sin, infant depravity, and inability. Unitarians, for example, parted company with Calvinists over these doctrines and portrayed children either as completely innocent beings whom experience corrupted or, more commonly, as blank slates (in John Locke's term) who had potential for developing either a good or an evil nature. Nineteenth-century Calvinists, especially Congregationalists, Presbyterians, and Baptists, re-tained their allegiance to the view that children were like adults in being totally alienated from God because of original sin. Despite any seeming innocence, children were as much in need of God's saving grace as adults.[28]

Orthodox doctrine was in flux, however, during the early nineteenth century, as various inheritors of the Calvinist tradition struggled to define their positions on these issues. In 1828, for example, Lyman Beecher published a series of articles reopening the question of infant damnation and asking whether good Calvinists might not hope for the salvation of all infants who die. Perhaps the most notable Calvinist revisionist of the 1820s and 1830s was Yale's Nathaniel Taylor, who reworked the doctrine of sin in general to accommodate a more benevolent view of unregenerate children's sinfulness. Taylor, who served as president of the Connecticut Sunday School Union during the 1820s, argued that individuals sinned only when they voluntarily committed sinful acts, not, as orthodox Calvinism maintained, whenever they did anything while they remained unregenerate. In other words, whereas orthodox Calvinism interpreted "sin" as both a state of being and a characteristic of individual acts, Taylor saw it only as the latter. Taylor's theology, then, assumed that as long as children remained without a sense of right or wrong, God did not hold them accountable for their acts. Once in possession of a moral sense, however, children were inclined by nature to sin (because they possessed the depraved nature common to all descendants of Adam) and needed regeneration. Taylor's position was quite close to that of the Methodists, who saw children as neither good nor bad but having the potential for either, until they became free moral agents, learned the difference between right and wrong, and were then in need of regeneration. Although Taylor did not adopt the Methodist position that God offered salvation freely to all (to do so would be to deny the doctrine of limited atonement), and although he kept the Calvinist emphasis on original sin by maintaining that children would invariably choose self over God in making their first moral choices, his theology opened the possibility that childhood training could shorten the transition from sinless child to regenerate Christian.[29]

Taylor's ideas, like Beecher's, generated controversy within the Presbyterian church and played a role in the denomination's split into Old and New School factions. In 1833, for example, the Old School Presbyterian minister Gardiner Spring attacked Taylor for his "novel speculations" and "errors" regarding the doctrine of human depravity. Defending the view that sin was an "inclination of the mind" as well as a characteristic of individual acts, Spring stated that the child was a sinner from birth, "the perfect miniature of fallen, sinning man," and "a moral and accountable being." Distinguishing between the intellectual and moral faculties of the soul, Spring argued that original sin tainted children's moral dispositions (their "hearts") just as it did adults'; one needed only look for evidence of children's "moral depravity" in their "impatience, obstinacy, pride, self-will." He went on to ask: "Where do you discover that *supreme selfishness,* which is the essence and substance of all sin, if not in a little child?" Despite their disagreements, Taylor's and Spring's arguments led in the same direction: toward early religious education. Without early training, in Spring's view, children would grow up "slave[s] of ignorance and passion," unaware of their alienation from God. If Taylor saw religious education as a means of shortening the period during which children were alienated from God, Spring saw it as a way of making them aware how deep that alienation was. Either way, children needed early and regular training.[30]

Theological debates like these reflected the growth of Sunday schools and of interest in childhood religion. In turn, the writings and speeches of Sunday school workers reflected the influence of the theological debates in offering various interpretations of childhood, depending upon the theological leanings of the writer or speaker. Thus, the minister Samuel Bacon advised children in sermons and letters that they had "a very wicked heart" and urged them to repent. The members of the Andover Theological Seminary Sunday School Association criticized teachers who allowed children to believe they could go to heaven without experiencing the "one thing needful." Reflecting the tenets of her sect, the Methodist president of the McKendrean Female Sabbath School Society of Baltimore came to a different conclusion: "Under the auspices of the Holy Spirit it must be as easy to impress the young virtuously as viciously." "Surely," she reasoned, "the lines of piety and religion, once drawn upon the heart remain as permanently as those of an opposite complexion. . . . Religious training will with rare exceptions lead to religious living." Theological differences cropped up, too, in unexpected places over less-than-crucial issues. In 1847 the members of the Providence, Rhode Island, Association of Sabbath School Teachers listened to two ministers debate the propriety of giving students rewards. In the course of the debate, the Reverend Mr. Jameson spoke against the practice on the grounds that rewards interfered with the process of conversion. Because of their hearts' natural depravity, children cared more about receiving rewards than receiving the truth and so were diverted from seeking God. The Reverend Mr. Latham, on the other hand, argued that rewards appealed to children's God-given propensities and were a useful way of getting their attention. Once teachers had students' attention, they could present them with higher motives and lead them to God.[31]

Despite such theological differences, evangelicals in the antebellum years agreed that childhood was a crucial time of preparation for adult responsibility, that children were highly impressionable, and that Sunday school instructors should use children's plasticity to prepare them for the life-defining event of conversion. Through these beliefs and their concern with teaching children self-discipline and orderly habits, Sunday school workers constructed an image of childhood very much in keeping with the ideals of their age. Growing into a good and godly adult took work, training, and self-control, because there were few external structures to help provide guidance. Children left parental homes to make their own way in the world, attending different churches as jobs and residences changed. Even ministers could no longer be relied upon to provide pastoral care for their lambs; they were becoming professionals who moved to new congregations when opportunities for advancement presented themselves. In such an environment, the individual's habits and principles had to be properly molded in childhood so they would remain "fixed" in adulthood. In a changeable and volatile world, the conversion experience could be the unchanging reference point on the individual's compass.[32]

By the 1850s, however, discussions of children's essential natures turned less and less frequently on the question of whether they were "by nature the children of wrath." Instead, new theological ideas, best exemplified by Horace Bushnell's book *Views of Christian Nurture* (first published in 1847 by the Massachusetts Sabbath School Society), along with the growth of romantic ideals of childhood, increasingly placed advocates of the old Calvinist orthodoxy on the defensive. Speaking at the American Sunday School Union's 1851 anniversary, an orthodox clergyman had to urge parents and religious educators to "abstract their own thoughts and feelings from the blooming cheeks, the laughing eye, the clear brow, the unworldly countenances" of children in order to remember that "they are condemned criminals, and they need pardoning mercy." For it was precisely that laughing eye and blooming cheek that children's writers and evangelical ministers alike had begun increasingly to emphasize.[33]

As they turned away from older notions of childhood, Sunday school workers found it necessary to remodel the institutional structure built in the antebellum years. Like a family discovering that its familiar old house no longer fits its changing circumstances, evangelicals made major alterations in the schools' curricula and goals during the 1860s and 1870s. In the remodeling process, the old goal of preparing students for conversion gave way to the new goal of Christian nurture and Sunday school workers came to see children as more capable than adults of religious sentiment. Almost as noticeable were changes in the schools' curricula which incorporated new pedagogical techniques from common schools and new types of lessons to replace the old question books. The alterations were not universally welcomed, but by 1880 they had permanently changed the institution's appearance.

The ideal of Christian nurture was in many ways a direct challenge to the ideal of conversion. Bushnell's book (intended for parents rather than Sunday school teachers) was an amalgam of psychological ideas about children's impressionability and popular notions of babies' innocence. Positing an organic union between parents and child in the early years while the child remained totally dependent upon them for physical and emotional sustenance, Bushnell described the newborn as "a bundle of possibilities" open to impressions from its immediate environment. "The spirit of the house," he wrote, "is breathed into his nature, day by day. The anger and gentleness, the fretfulness and patience, the appetites, passions and manners, all the variant moods of feeling, exhibited around him, pass into him as impressions and become seeds of character. . . . The spirit of the house is in the members by nurture, not by teaching." Given these assumptions, Bushnell went on, the "aim, effort and expectation" of parents should be to make the child "open on the world as one that is spiritually renewed, not remembering the time when he went through a technical [conversion] experience, but seeming rather to have loved what is good from his earliest years."[34]

Although Bushnell's views were controversial, elements of his theory found their way rather quickly into the thinking of some religious educators. Stephen Olin, the Methodist president of Wesleyan University, argued in 1849 that God "intends [children] to learn religion as they learn a thousand other things—from the spirit and tone of the family." With proper religious instruction, children "grow up Christians. They are sanctified from the womb." Thomas F. Curtis, a Baptist, echoed Bushnell's views in 1855 when he suggested that children could grow up holy and "insensible of any particular moment of conversion, yet being truly regenerate." Although Curtis went on to note that Baptists would still require some evidence of grace for baptism, he revealed his indebtedness to Bushnell both in his theme and in the words he used to express it. By the 1860s ministers of several denominations spoke variously of children being "religiously impressed long before they have any consciousness of it" and being reared "that they shall be converted from the cradle, and grow up in the nurture and admonition of the Lord."[35]

A corollary theme of Bushnell's, that children "are a great deal more capable" of true knowledge of God than adults, also enjoyed increasing exposure. In a lecture entitled "God's Thoughts Fit Bread for Children," delivered before a group of evangelical Sunday school teachers in 1869, Bushnell sounded very much like the exponents of the romantic view of childhood, whose ideas had been so roundly criticized in the evangelical press during the 1830s. "Tell the child how present God is, how loving he is, how close by he is in all good thoughts," Bushnell exhorted the members of the Connecticut Sunday School Teachers' Convention, "and he will take the sense a great deal better than the adult soul, that is gone a doubting so far, and speculated his mind half away in the false intellectualities miscalled reason." Because children experienced life through their feelings, he concluded, "the very highest and most spiritual things are a great deal closer to them than to us."[36] The following year, another minister entitled his article in a national Sunday school magazine "A Child's Religion, The True Religion for Men and Women."[37]

In discarding the orthodox view of children as equal inheritors of Adam's sin, and hence as much in need of conversion as adults, Bushnell had support within Sunday school circles. From Henry Ward Beecher, whose father, Lyman, had questioned the damnation of infants, came a plea for a new children's literature with heroes who were "real boys." Writing in the influential Congregationalist weekly *The Independent,* Beecher dismissed the pale protagonists of standard Sunday school literature as "impossible boys with incredible goodness. Their piety is monstrous. A man's experience [is] stuffed into a little boy." Reiterating Bushnell's argument about children's instinct for play, an 1857 article in the *Sunday-School Journal,* a publication of the American Sunday School Union that had previously hewed the orthodox line, defended children's "natural" restlessness, noisiness, and exuberance. The author of this uncharacteristic article wrote that it was "not unnatural for children to run," nor was it "a transgression of the moral law."[38] By the late 1860s and early 1870s, teachers' magazines routinely presented a view of children quite different from that which had prevailed in the antebellum years. No longer presented as obstinate, selfish, and willful, children emerged as "naturally enthusiastic" beings who "love[d] and crave[d] variety." For their part, teachers were urged to recognize children's characteristics and use them to advantage in teaching. If it was in the child's nature, for example, "to give free vent to its animal spirits and overcome them by exhaustion," then teachers needed to let children run and shout first, pray and sing later.[39]

New ideas about childhood and Christian nurture became popular among many religious educators for the same reasons that fairy tales and imaginative stories came to dominate children's literature in the late nineteenth century. As Americans witnessed the spread of industry and corporate consolidation, their fears of excessive regimentation found expression in a new emphasis on the importance of spontaneity, impulse, playfulness, and leisure within the private sphere. In this context, childhood represented the expression of emotions that were banished from the workplace and public life. In much the same way, Christian nurture appealed to those Protestants who found revivals distasteful and preferred to confine the expression of religious emotions to the private realm. Several leaders of the Sunday school convention movement, such as Methodist John H. Vincent and Congregationalist Henry Clay Trumbull, disliked the emphasis inherent in revivalistic strategies on a sudden, violent, and public upheaval in the individual's life. "Growth, not conquest" became the motto of many religious educators in the aftermath of the Civil War.[40]

It would be erroneous to assume, however, that Christian nurture quickly displaced conversion as the main goal of Sunday school instruction. The two goals existed side by side for some time and many religious educators remained profoundly skeptical of the implications of Christian nurture theory. Thus, one could read articles stressing conversion and nurture in the same publication.[41] Among Baptists in particular, theological objections to Bushnell's ideas remained strong. It was "a dangerous mistake," commented one correspondent of the *Baptist Teacher* in 1872, to teach children to sing"I am Jesus' Little Lamb" and to refer to them as "lambs of the Shepherd." Only converted and baptized children had that right, because only they were saved. Many groups combined conversion with nurture by instituting "decision days" within their Sunday schools and by ritualizing the conversion process, so that children underwent it as part of their school experience, not as a sudden jolt or radical departure.[42]

As the schools' goals changed, so too did the curriculum. The new lessons that emerged to take the place of question books emphasized the students' steady growth in religious knowledge through orderly week-by-week, year-by-year study of the Bible. Unlike the old question books, which had combined Bible study with preparation for conversion, the new lessons focused on the study of the scriptures and downplayed the conversion experience. The first big success in new-style books, Orange Judd's *Lessons for Every Sunday in the Year,* published in 1864, provided four year-long lesson sequences, each built around a specific part of the Old or New Testament. In one sequence, for example, students went through fifty-two lessons on the historical sections of the Old Testament, studying Biblical history, memorizing selected verses, and using their Bibles to answer questions posed in the lessons. Although published by the Methodist Episcopal Sunday School Union, Judd's series was nondenominational in content and printed without the designation "Methodist." Its widespread adoption by schools of all sects led other publishers to issue similar series. Eventually, through the influence of the convention movement, the major Sunday school publishers agreed to a uniform lesson plan under which all schools, regardless of denominational affiliation, would study the same sequence of Bible passages each week for seven years, although each denomination would publish its own individual lessons.[43]

The switch to new lesson series like Judd's and then to uniform lessons clearly reflected the schools' changing goals. Whereas the old question books had contained varying numbers of lessons, combined Bible study with basic evangelical theology, and assumed a relatively short student tenure in school, the new lessons were predicated on the assumption that students would remain in school for many years, that they should grow gradually in religious knowledge, and that conversion would be a minor aspect of the overall experience. (Individual schools and teachers could, of course, place greater stress on conversion if they wished.) The treatment accorded an 1878 uniform lesson, "Josiah's Early Piety," illustrates the dramatic nature of the change. Fifty years earlier, such a scriptural passage would have led naturally (perhaps exclusively) to an exposition on the subject of conversion. The writer would carefully have explained the necessity of regeneration, the importance of early conversion, and its preconditions. In 1878, without any collaboration or discussion among themselves, each of the individual lesson writers, regardless of denomination, decided that the passage on Josiah warranted only a passing reference to conversion. Even at that, the references were vague, mentioning only the importance of obeying God in one's early life. If in 1828 it would have been natural to press home the importance of experiencing conversion, in 1878 it seemed natural to pass over the subject quickly.[44]

Curricular changes like these occurred for reasons other than the schools' altered goals. They owed something to the popularity of teachers' institutes and conventions and to the growing influence of common-school pedagogy in general. Indeed, judging by the content of Sunday school teachers' publications, it was not Horace Bushnell but Johann Pestalozzi who loomed largest in teachers' minds as inspiration and model. Whereas Bushnell went unmentioned in teachers' magazines and advice books, Pestalozzi was everywhere. Teachers learned "the seven laws of teaching" and their practical application. "Never tell a child what he can discover for himself," counseled Pestalozzi's followers; proceed step by step, from the simple to the complex, the known to the unknown. Through institutes and conventions, as well as advice literature, "object teaching" and "the art of questioning" became standard parts of the Sunday school teacher's repertoire. Although the Swiss educator's ideas had enjoyed brief popularity during the 1830s among Unitarians and infant school advocates, it was only during the 1860s that his essentially romantic view of childhood became acceptable to evangelicals. In the 1860s, too, the introduction of his work into normal schools brought it wide circulation among common-school teachers and their Sunday counterparts. Moreover, Pestalozzi's ideas meshed with the new goal of nurture, while his pedagogical techniques seemed especially well suited to the new sequential lessons. For all these reasons, Pestalozzianism went hand in hand with the development of new goals and curricula.[45]

Virtually unnoticed amid the enthusiasm for Christian nurture and uniform lessons were some of the deeper implications of the new pedagogy. One was the extreme environmental determinism of Bushnell's theory, which stressed the importance of "the spirit of the house" that "is breathed into" a child's nature from birth. As another version of the "tribalism" that had characterized colonial Puritanism, Christian nurture revivified a long-standing theological distinction between children whose parents were church members and those whose parents were not. Presbyterians and Congregationalists, for example, had always described church members' offspring as "children of the covenant" and regarded them as more likely to be among the elect than other youngsters. By baptizing members' children in infancy, these churches gave children a sign of their relationship to the congregation and set them apart as its special responsibility. Even Baptists, while forbidding infant baptism, subscribed to the notion that church members' children had special promise and deserved special care. In practical terms, Bushnell's theology justified and reinforced the continuing social distinction between mission schools and church schools. For it was church members' children who were most likely to breathe in religious sentiments and grow up Christians, having "loved what [was] good from [their] earliest years." By contrast, the offspring of non-church members, born into homes where "selfishness, worldliness, and godlessness" reigned, hardly offered much material for a teacher to nurture. From a Christian nurture perspective, it was easy for teachers to turn away from the "exceedingly trying" lower-class youngsters who populated mission schools and give their attention to the more promising church scholars.[46]

"Tribalism" is indeed a fairly apt characterization of the direction in which Sunday schools were moving during the 1860s and 1870s. To be sure, the environmentalism that suffused Bushnell's theology encouraged some Sunday school workers to labor at changing the environments in which mission school children were growing up and attempt to bring to them "the joys of childhood."[47] The social programs established by large urban missions such as Boston's North End Mission were examples of such attempts. But as uniform lessons became the dominant focus of Sunday school work, as a new pedagogy took shape, and as new organizations absorbed their energies, teachers found it easy to concentrate on tilling their own church gardens and ignore the mission fields beyond. Indeed, they found another, related metaphor especially appropriate to describe their institution: "the nursery of the church."

As "nurseries," the schools affected individual children differently. Some thrived in the hothouse atmosphere of intimate conversations and appeals to the heart, while others wilted. However they reacted, students were subject to the observation of their teachers, some of whom recorded the characteristics of religious conviction in childhood. A few of the children themselves chronicled or recalled their experiences. These sources give us a picture of the institution, however sketchy, from the perspective of its clients.

Some children did, indeed, resemble the relentlessly pious youngsters of Sunday school literature. A children's magazine reported a conversation between seven-year-old Robert and his teacher. When asked if he loved God, Robert replied: "I think I do; it would be very wicked in me if I did not, after he has loved me so much as to die for me." Pressing on, the teacher inquired, "Why do you think he died for you?" "Because," Robert replied, "I am a sinner. . . . I often feel that I am one." Nine-year-old Elizabeth Payson (who grew up to write the popular religious novel *Stepping Heavenward*) used a letter to her sister in Boston to recount her Sunday school lessons and emphasize how strongly she wanted to learn her catechism. And the youngsters who wrote letters to "Uncle John's Letter-Box," an advice column for Sunday scholars published in the Baptist *Standard,* sometimes revealed concerns beyond deciphering difficult places in the Bible. One correspondent wanted to know if playing games was "sinful" for a religious child; another wondered whether she would get to see her sister's deceased baby in heaven; and a third (aged nine) informed "Uncle John": "I have given my heart to God. . . . I wish you would pray for me. I will pray for you."[48]

Although the sentiments expressed in these examples were undoubtedly genuine, children seem to have displayed the most remarkable piety during serious or fatal illnesses. Facing such traumatic events, children, like adults, coped by drawing on the experiences that were available to them. Having been told so often in Sunday school about the need to convert before it was too late, many of them experienced sickbed and deathbed conversions. More often than not, reports of a scholar's death were accompanied by a remark that there was "good evidence that the instructions she received in the S[unday] School had made an impression upon her *heart* that would bring her to the enjoyment of heaven," or that she "gave evidence of piety on her deathbed." Children in the throes of terrible illness often behaved exactly as they had been taught they should. Thus ten-year-old John Mather, a student in Michael Floy's class, "in the agonies of death" professed himself to be "happy and resigned to God's will." At the boy's wake, his father described John as being "more like *his* father than his son, always sober and serious." Floy himself was so moved by the child's death that he wrote a brief memoir which was subsequently printed.[49]

The father's comment about his son's "sober and serious" deportment points to the important role that adult expectations played in shaping the behavior of pious children. Then, as now, certain children responded more than others to adult-defined standards of "proper" behavior, mirroring the pictures held up to them as models. In the Sunday school, teachers defined for their students the characteristics of religious children, at times using examples from the deathbed conversion literature, and children who wished to become religious imitated those characteristics. In keeping with the antebellum emphasis on preparation for conversion, they almost invariably depicted converted children (and children hopeful of imminent conversion) as quiet, serious, orderly, and reflective. One typical description of a converted child portrayed her as "mild in her manners, tender and kind to her brothers and sisters and companions." Moreover, "she took great delight in good things. She loved to be with pious persons." (She was six years old.) Another writer described a child who, instead of "frolicking" with his friends, playing, or sleeping, read his Bible because it alone told him how he could "escape from sin and from its dreadful punishment."[50]

Even short of actual conversion, teachers expected certain behavioral manifestations of their work's success. As noted earlier, one favorite argument for the Sunday school was its ability to change children's behavior, to "soften down the rougher passions and asperities of their natures." Although teachers often had reason to echo Michael Floy's complaint that the students' "behavior tried my patience very much," they measured their success by the extent to which their students exhibited "amiable deportment and obedience." Likewise, parents complimented the schools when children who had been "fretful and disobedient" became "entirely changed."[51]

The reasons for this changed behavior were as varied as the pupils themselves. Certainly, some children were looking for their teachers' approval. George Wilson was such a popular teacher at the Utica, New York, Sunday school in the 1820s that there was a waiting list for his class; to please him, children would take notes on the Sunday sermon, vie for the opportunity to make a report, and join with alacrity his Juvenile Society for Doing Good. Others wanted the rewards that schools handed out for attendance and good behavior. James Aikin, attending the Brandywine Manufacturers' Sunday School in the 1820s, must have been very pleased when he finally received a storybook, after several years of forfeiting his rewards for sundry causes. (Perhaps tellingly, the book he received was *The Prodigal Son.*) His sister Mary, on the other hand, piled up her prizes: storybooks, tracts, a psalmbook, a thread case, a "collar trimmed with Nun's lace," and a "swiss collar pleated." Despite his track record, or because of his competition with Mary, James later became a teacher at the school. Still other children identified school attendance and the display of desirable character traits as part of the process of acquiring respectability. If teachers, whom the children often used as role models, defined rowdiness and lack of self-control as attributes of unrespectable, lower-class life, then children who wanted to be seen as respectable tried to behave as their teachers expected.[52]

Whether dying pious deaths, behaving as their teachers expected pious pupils to behave, or doing what was necessary to get rewards, most of these children appear in the historical record through their teachers' eyes. An occasional Sunday scholar opens a more intimate window into the schools through a diary or reminiscence. Caroline Richards was a seriously religious young girl who never quite succumbed to the pressure to convert and behave as a converted child, nor did she reject the milieu offered by her school. Growing up with her sister Anna in their grandparents' upstate New York home (they had been orphaned early in life), Caroline read the standard biographies of pious children, admired some teachers but was indifferent to others, and eventually became a teacher herself. At age eleven, she reflected on the Sunday school stories her grandmother gave her to read. "I don't see how," she confided to her diary, the characters "happened to be so awfully good. Anna says they died of 'early piety,' but she did not say it very loud." When eight-year-old Anna heard someone predict a career for her as a missionary, she "cried right out loud." Caroline "tried to comfort her and told her it might never happen, so she stopped crying." Reacting to her Sunday school teachers, Caroline saw one as a role model ("I wish I could be as good and pretty as she is") but had no compunction about disobeying another. "She said we ought not to read our S. S. books on Sunday," Caroline wrote. "I always do. Mine to-day was entitled 'Cheap Repository Tracts by Hannah More,' and it did not seem unreligious at all." When the same teacher sent for Caroline, now twelve, "to talk and pray" with her "on the subject of religion," the girl was "frightened at first," but added: "It was nice after I got used to it." As the private prayer session came to an end, the woman asked Caroline to pray. "I couldn't think of anything but 'Now I lay me down to sleep,' and I was afraid she would not like that, so I didn't say anything," Caroline recalled. Despite such pressure from the teacher and from her grandmother (who reminded her "that our mother was a Christian when she was ten years old"), Caroline molded her own version of childhood Christianity, which included neither excessively serious behavior nor overt rebellion.[53]

Even rarer than accounts like Caroline Richards's are insights by children who found the Sunday school experience wholly repelling. In one such commentary, written in 1902, Chicagoan Edwin O. Gale recalled his brief tenure at an evangelical school during the 1830s. His jaundiced adult eye visualized "those small religious books of early days, with water-paper covers of sombre hue," as he remembered their contents—"most melancholy biographies of inconceivably goody-goody boys" who invariably died young. Like Anna Richards, who whispered that such children died of "early piety," Gale could not connect "those sickly examples" with the "robust, rollicking, roguish little rascal full of animal spirits" that he had been. However he felt in later life, it was clear that the books and the lessons they represented had had their effect on him in childhood. The Sunday school, he remembered, "made a painful impression upon my sensitive nature. My frightened, rather than guilty, conscience left no doubt in my mind that I was in danger of . . . terrible doom." Sundays "became days of torture" to him as he returned home with "red, swollen eyes and [a] dejected countenance." Eventually his father, a Unitarian, forbade his further attendance, and young Edwin returned to Sunday school only when a Unitarian school was established.[54] Like Gale's father, evangelical parents also objected on occasion to the methods employed in Sunday schools. The mother of a boy in Michael Floy's school who had stayed for a special prayer meeting "disapproved of the proceeding," saying "that all those who went to be prayed for had only their feelings excited."[55] Lacking detailed accounts like Edwin Gale's, however, we cannot know how common his experiences were or how often wary parents nipped incipient religious emotions in the bud.

What Edwin Gale rejected, of course, was not religion or even Sunday schools themselves; he merely traded what his father considered the melancholy theology of evangelicalism for the more attractive approach of the Unitarians. Some children, by their ambivalent reactions to the school, taxed Sunday school workers' patience and their ability to deal with children's "animal spirits." Writing from Milwaukee in 1856, the missionary J. W. Vail described local efforts to establish a school in the city's Irish third ward. On the first Sunday fifty children appeared, and according to Vail, "a wilder, bolder uncivilized Heaven dareing company of children could not be found in any of your cities of the East." Only by telling them the story of David and leading them in singing could the teachers induce the youngsters to be quiet. Yet the tactic must have worked, for the next Sunday sixty children arrived "with their Shivey clubs an[d] Segars in their mouths. Sing[ing] S. S. Songs and telling Stories was the only exercise we could have and but little improvement in *order*." Despite Vail's frustration at the lack of order, the children continued to come, and on the third and fourth Sundays "by the assistance of a police [officer] there was signs of improvement." The teachers then began planning to offer regular lessons.

Still other children resisted all efforts to lure them into the schools and sought to sabotage the intentions of Sunday school organizers. Often, such youngsters were members of lower-class or immigrant groups who had been targeted for inclusion in a mission school. The Sunday school missionary William Bulkley described his efforts to speak at an urban school where a police officer was stationed at the locked front door to keep out a noisy group of spectators. Inside the school, things were hardly better, with "the stamping of feet and talking and whistling and hallooing rats rats rats." Bulkley sighed, "For the first time in an experience of thirty five years I failed to command the attention of children that I attempted to talk to," and so the school was dismissed "or rather broke up and when the door was unlocked they rushed pell mell out of the room." Like these youngsters, most children who resisted the appeal of the Sunday school voted with their feet and so seldom turn up in the records. Unlike these youngsters, however, most children in mission schools attended out of choice and remained because of the opportunities (whether spiritual or secular) the school offered.[56]

The rowdy children who ruined Bulkley's day stand out in the historical record, along with Edwin Gale and Caroline Richards, as flesh-and-blood individuals, giving shape and substance to the ghostly, faceless crowds of Sunday scholars whose experiences and exploits have gone unrecorded. For despite their numerical preponderance in the Sunday school and its existence for their benefit, children are often entirely missing from the institution's chronicles. Except when their names turn up in school registers or their conversions are mentioned in the minutes of a teachers' meeting, the children who spent their Sundays squirming in small chairs or reciting verses from the Bible seem to have little place in Sunday school history. Yet they exerted some influence on the institution and, in a myriad subtle ways, forced teachers and administrators to accommodate their interests.

The best example of children's influence is the persistence of rewards and premiums. Despite adult distaste for them, as reflected in the perennial discussions in teachers' meetings and Sunday school periodical literature, teachers and administrators continued to buy and award prizes. They did it for one reason: children liked them. Because children were so fond of receiving small books and religious trinkets, teachers were able to use the promise of rewards to lure children into the schools, to compel regular attendance, to discipline unruly pupils, and to reinforce desirable behavior. Thus, the Willett Street Methodist Church in New York offered a book to each student who memorized five hundred or more Scripture verses in 1866 and awarded other prizes to students who brought in new scholars. The Bank Street Mission Sunday school had a committee on rewards which in 1865 authorized the issuance of tickets that could be traded in for "*simple, yet attractive*" premiums at the end of the year. In this way the entire ticket-reward system, fed by children's love of collecting and trading, continued to thrive some forty years after it had first been denounced in teachers' literature. Most schools were more subtle, preferring to think of their premiums as incentives, not rewards. Embossed attendance certificates were popular, as were copies of children's magazines, Christmas presents, and special ribbons or badges, any of which might be, in the words of the Bank Street school's committee, "worth keeping and treasuring up for the years to come" in a scrapbook or treasure chest. Although present in all schools (as they still are), such incentives were particularly common in mission schools, where teachers felt them necessary to induce children of non-church members to attend. As part of a drive to bring in new students, for example, the Benton Street Mission Sunday school in St. Louis handed out cards in nearby neighborhoods promising free magazines "with beautiful pictures and many excellent little stories," along with "prizes in the shape of Bibles, Testaments, books, medals, or picture cards" (see figure 17).[57]

In the same vein, schools often sponsored programs designed to appeal to chil-

DAVENPORT SUNDAY SCHOOL.

BOYS AND GIRLS WILL YOU COME?

WILL YOU COME TO OUR SABBATH SCHOOL?

IT IS HELD

EVERY SUNDAY AFTERNOON AT   O'CLOCK,

IN THE

WHITING STREET PUBLIC SCHOOL HOUSE.

We have a pleasant school room ; we learn to sing beautiful hymns ; we have a library of about 200 books, written on purpose for children ; more than all, we have the HOLY BIBLE, which teaches us how we may be happy and useful while we live, and how we may be happy forever when we die.

· Will you ask your fathers and mothers, and your older brothers and sisters to come and see our Sabbath School, and all our pleasant things ?   Will you do what you can to bring in other boys and girls ?

REMEMBER EVERY SUNDAY AFTERNOON AT   O'CLOCK.

Figure 17. Advertisements like this one for the Davenport Sunday school, a mission school held in a public school house in Boston, could be handed out in nearby neighborhoods or left in streetcars

dren's love of spectacle and excitement. In the early decades, Fourth of July parades and anniversary gatherings were popular. Later, these were supplanted by Sunday school picnics, excursions, magic lantern shows, illustrated talks by missionaries from exotic lands, and annual exhibitions at which the children marched, sang, and recited for the benefit of their parents and teachers. Although teachers often complained that these events upset school routine and created a taste for short-lived pleasures, their appeal to students made them standard fixtures in nineteenth-century schools. When teachers sought ways "to increase the interest of the scholars in the school and make it more attractive," they usually turned to just such incentives (see figure 18).[58]

Although prizes, picnics, and excursions could be a means of manipulating children, they also represented a capitulation on the part of teachers to children's interests. Manipulation could be a two-way street. When Michael Floy offered some students a paper with scriptural lessons to be learned for the following Sunday, twenty of them begged to have it. When he chose one recipient, however, the others told him they would refuse to learn any lessons because he had not given them the paper. "What queer creatures children are!" Floy remarked. In another instance, a pupil's desire for a promised reward forced Floy to go out and buy the sought-after prize; the teacher who had left the promise unkept for three weeks then quit in a huff. Nor could teachers always prevent children from taking advantage of a school's free offerings and then absconding. New York's Seventh Presbyterian

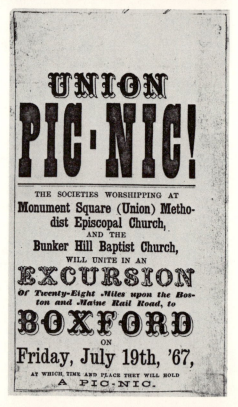

Figure 18. Exhibitions, picnics, and anniversary celebrations stimulated student interest and boosted attendance at Sunday schools

Programme.

PART FIRST.

Voluntary on the Organ.
Prayer by the Pastor
Singing.—Happy voices, — — — Sunday School
Introductory. — — — Miss Clara Duchemin
Dialogue.—On the Bible, Misses Mary Butler, Etta Williams and Etta Leonard
Declamation. — — — Miss Sarah Lundgreen
Singing.—" Nelly lost and found," — Hattie Hammond
Dialogue.—Precept vs. Practice, Ella Ricker, Clara Duchemin, W. H. Hanson.
Declamation. — — — — Fred. Orentt
Dialogue.— Love, the genius of the Sunday School, Miss Hattie Prentiss and nine Misses.
Piano Solo. — — — — Miss Dunklee
Song. — — — — Miss Poley
Dialogue.—Tattlewood, Fifteen Ladies and Gentlemen
Song.—" Beautiful birds sing on," Miss Lottie Roberts

RECESS — PART SECOND.

Singing. — — — — Infant Class
Dialogue.—Magic Lamp, Ella Stetson, Jessie Junkins
Declamation.— — — — W. H. Hanson
Song.— — Abbie Atwood, Lizzie Hamlet
Dialogue—Unhappy, Fifteen Ladies and Gentlemen
Piano Duet.— — — — Misses Dunklee
Declamation.— — — Benjamin F. Harmon
Song.— — — — Mr. Hart
Dialogue.—Peep behind the scenes, Etta Ricker, W. H. Hanson, Henry Morse
Dialogue.—The Messiah, Mrs. Bolster, Miss P. C. Holbrook and ten Misses
Song.— — — — Miss Bennett
Valedictory.— — — — Mr. Harmon
Singing.—Sunday School Volunteer Song, Sunday School
BENEDICTION.

E. F. Rollins, Printer, Scollay's Building, Boston.

A GRAND

Exhibition

Will be given in the

UNION M. E. CHURCH,

Corner High Street and Monument Square,

On Wednesday Evening, Dec. 2, 1868.

The Programme will include

SINGING, DECLAMATIONS, DIALOGUES, &C.,

And the most complete arrangements have been made by an able and efficient committee for a first-class entertainment.

A large number of sunday school scholars will participate in the exercises, and the dialogues will be found particularly interesting and instructive.

Misses Poley, Bennett, Roberts and Hammond, and Mr. Charles Hart are among those who will participate in the Singing Exercises, and Piano Solo will be given by Miss Dunklee.

The Exhibition will be given in aid of the Sunday School, and the patronage of the citizens is respectfully solicited.

The Admission Fee for Adults is only ——
Children under 11 years ——
Doors open at 7 o'clock.

UNION

PIC-NIC!

THE SOCIETIES WORSHIPPING AT

Monument Square (Union) Methodist Episcopal Church,

AND THE

Bunker Hill Baptist Church,

WILL UNITE IN AN

EXCURSION

Of Twenty-Eight Miles upon the Boston and Maine Rail Road, to

BOXFORD

ON

Friday, July 19th, '67,

AT WHICH TIME AND PLACE THEY WILL HOLD
A PIC-NIC.

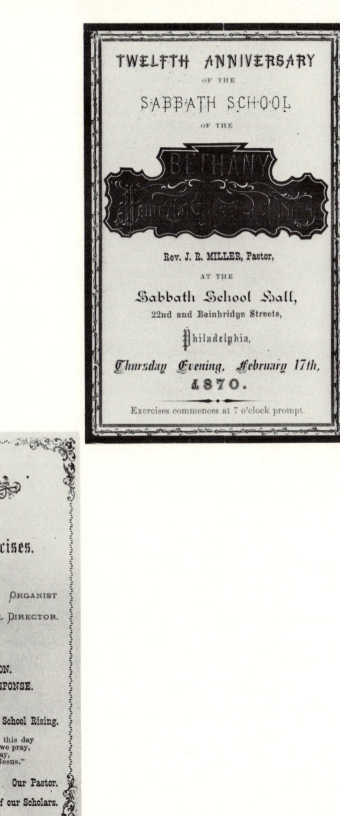

TWELFTH ANNIVERSARY

OF THE

SABBATH SCHOOL

OF THE

BETHANY

Rev. J. R. MILLER, Pastor,

AT THE

Sabbath School Hall,

22nd and Bainbridge Streets,

Philadelphia,

Thursday Evening, February 17th, 1870.

Exercises commences at 7 o'clock prompt.

Order of Exercises.

MR. H. C. EWING, - ORGANIST
MR. J. BIRKINBINE, MUSICAL DIRECTOR.

ORGAN VOLUNTARY.
SUPERINTENDENT'S INVOCATION.
SCHOLARS AND TEACHERS RESPONSE.
SILENT PRAYER.
THE CREED, - - - School Rising.

"HELP us Lord throughout this day
While we sing and while we pray,
Let thy Spirit with us stay,
While here we learn of Jesus."

PRAYER, - - - - Our Pastor.
READING SCRIPTURES, One of our Scholars.

Church Sunday school witnessed a huge enrollment increase "when it was announced that the children would be supplied with clothing." Youngsters "came flocking from all quarters" at the announcement, noted the school's secretary, but many left the school "after getting what they could." Likewise, the teachers at the December 25, 1864 session of the Willett Street Methodist Sunday school noticed an "unusually large" attendance "in consequence of tomorrow being the day on which the usual Christmas treat is to liven the school."[59]

As these examples reveal, children were not merely passive objects of Sunday school instruction; they played an active role in shaping the schools' programs. Certainly the persistence of rewards owed a great deal to children's interest in them, just as the formation of infant and Bible classes was necessitated by youngsters' collective behavior. At the same time, however, children had neither the power nor the will to reshape the schools in fundamental ways, since they were often at the mercy of their teachers and lacked the resources to resist the pressures placed upon them. If some Sunday scholars imitated the models presented to them in the conversion literature and others rejected the whole culture of conversion, most probably resembled Caroline Richards, who forged her own path, accepting most of the school's ethic while never fully capitulating to her mentors' image of the model student.

The striking thing that emerges from pupils' accounts of their Sunday school days, as well as from teachers' debates over childhood religion, is the importance this institution assumed. Whereas in 1820 Protestants had thought about children's religious experiences primarily in terms of family and church, by 1880 it was impossible to conceive of them without reference to the Sunday school. During the nineteenth century, this new institution became the primary locale—outside of the family—for religious indoctrination of Protestant youth. Moreover, its lay organizers, with no initial recourse to ministerial authority, claimed the right to prepare youngsters for conversion, the central experience of evangelical Protestant life. In the annals of church history, the saga of the Sunday school was unique, involving not only the creation of a new institution to fulfill functions previously entrusted to parents and pastors, but also the partial assumption of ministerial functions by church members. The Sunday school's success made it necessary for both congregations and denominations to make room for this unplanned offspring.

During the early decades, individual ministers and congregations responded differently to the schools' growth. For every pastor who encouraged and supported the idea, another refused his assistance in the belief that such a school was merely "the fruit of youthful inexperience and zeal." A few were openly hostile. In general, ministers in larger towns and cities in the Northeast, where a variety of lay organizations existed, were more receptive than those in rural areas and in the South, as were those clergymen who had some contact with the benevolent campaigns of their day. Charleston and Columbia, South Carolina, for example, both had vital Sunday school groups during the 1820s, largely because of their citizens' business and religious connections to Philadelphians active in the American Sunday School Union. In Virginia, the enthusiastic support of the Presbyterian minister John Holt Rice spurred the schools' growth. Although the schools prospered despite varying levels of clerical support, the active involvement of a congregation's pastor often separated the large and successful school from its smaller counterpart. The Low Church Episcopal clergyman (and later bishop) Stephen H. Tyng, for example, made the schools' growth a top priority at each of his pastoral assignments, first at St. Paul's in Philadelphia, where he became rector in 1829, and then at St. George's in New York, where he arrived in 1845. Pointing to St. George's growth—from 200 scholars in 1845 to 1,163 in 1855—and the addition of a mission school in 1856 with more than 400 pupils, the church's historian could describe Tyng's tenure as an extraordinarily successful one. Like many another clergyman, Tyng discovered that fostering the Sunday school could be as important as piling bricks upon mortar in guaranteeing oneself a place in the collective denominational memory.[60]

As these examples suggest, the minister's attitude was often crucial in determining how the congregation treated the school. When several members of St. George's Episcopal Church approached their rector in 1816 about starting a school for indigent children in New York, he refused to have anything to do with it. The group nevertheless formed two schools (male and female) without either ministerial or congregational assistance. Everything changed when James Milnor became rector in 1817. Not only did he applaud their efforts but he convinced the congregation to build a special room for the use of both the school and the church. Similarly, the women of the First Baptist Church of Nashville, Tennessee, who had started a school in 1834, were able to sustain it permanently only after the pastor stepped in as sponsor.[61]

Ministerial support aside, the level of congregational interest in the schools varied considerably. As churchgoing children began attending and church schools became differentiated from mission schools, congregations were increasingly willing to accept some responsibility for the school, although they often sought to exert some influence over it, as well. There was no one pattern. During the 1820s and 1830s, for example, a few churches, particularly in New England, began to exercise what they considered their proper authority by making the pastor president of the Sunday school teachers' association and requiring all candidates for teaching positions to be approved by the congregation. Other churches gave no formal recognition to their schools, and some pastors continued to catechize children separately from school, as if it had no role in their teaching mission. Most schools existed in a kind of limbo of ambiguity, neither fully part of the church nor entirely separate from it. A school might meet on church property, enroll most of the children of the church's members, and be permitted to hold occasional collections to raise funds, but it had no official connection to the pastor or the church's governing body. The schools' uncertain status led teachers in some cases to resist the loss of independence that accompanied the establishment of official ties to the congregation. In 1840, for example, the church session took over New York's Brick Presbyterian Church school, appointing teachers and choosing lessons as a means of undercutting the school's independence from the congregation. The session ran the school until 1846. When the governing body of the Seventh Presbyterian Church decided in 1843 to follow Brick Church's lead, several teachers objected and withdrew to form a new school.[62]

Within ten years of that incident, however, a church without a Sunday school was increasingly seen as an anomaly. By the mid-1850s most teachers and superintendents were striving to attain for the schools their "true position . . . as one of the agencies of the church." In practical terms, placing the schools in their "true position" meant getting congregations to assume financial responsibility for them and taking the schools' needs into account in the physical design of church buildings. When an Akron, Ohio, congregation included special folding dividers in its 1857 blueprints for a meeting room, Sunday school workers excitedly hailed it as a major innovation. Closer ties to the congregation meant providing more specialized doctrinal teaching in the school and greater attention to denominational concerns. Often it also meant buying more books and periodicals from a denominational publisher and fewer from the American Sunday School Union, and sending a larger portion of benevolent contributions to a denominational agency. Typical of such behavior were three decisions of Philadelphia's Fifth Baptist Church Sabbath School Teachers' Association in 1856: to pledge one hundred dollars to the American Baptist Publication Society for missionary work, to spend one Sunday every month on a denominational catechism, and to switch its subscriptions from *Youth's Penny Gazette* (a periodical of the American Sunday School Union) to the Baptist magazine *The Young Reaper*. (A few blocks away, however, the Spruce Street Baptist Sabbath School Society continued to use *Union Questions* for its students.)[63]

Congregational adoption of this "Sunday child of American Protestantism," like so many aspects of its history, proceeded on a church-by-church basis. Whereas St. Paul's Episcopal Church in Boston could claim in 1830 that its was "a parochial school," fully supervised by the rector and church vestry, a survey by the Providence, Rhode Island, Association of Sabbath School Teachers in 1847 found a variety of practices. The Beneficent Congregational Church Sunday school was managed by a church committee and used a Congregationalist catechism but subscribed to children's magazines from several publishers. At the same time, the Third Baptist Church Sunday school was under the church's direct supervision and its officers were chosen annually by the congregation. By contrast, the Fourth Baptist

Sunday school, whose teachers were virtually all members of the Fourth Baptist Church, had no official connection with the church.[64]

Variations in pastoral and congregational interest in the Sunday school can be attributed to several factors. Some pastors and church members were wary of this new institution and its lay leadership, accusing Sunday school advocates, especially in the antebellum years, of usurping clerical and parental authority. In actuality, Sunday schools did fill a void opened up by the shifting authority of both groups. As ministers lost their status as public servants and the ministry came to resemble a profession more than a "calling," individual clergymen associated mobility with success and competed for calls to the most prestigious churches. One result was that a decreasing proportion of ministers remained in one post for their entire careers. Similarly, the widespread geographical mobility of the nineteenth century meant that families attended many churches over the course of their lives, children left the parental roof at early ages, and ministers ascended their pulpits to face ever-shifting congregations. Neither parents nor ministers could exercise in such a context the kind of authority claimed by their forebears, and the Sunday school was for some an uncomfortable reminder of how things had changed.[65] Some congregations simply had other priorities, particularly if the church was new or its membership unstable. In still other cases, a dynamic minister (such as Stephen Tyng) or school superinten-dent made the difference between congregational toleration and enthusiasm for the school.

Theological factors played a role, too. How church schools fit into a denomina-tion's theology affected individual church practice, as did the educational policy statements adopted by the denominations at their periodic national gatherings. Primitive Baptists and antimission Baptists, for example, denounced the schools as "modern religious inventions" in the same category as other practices that could not be found in the Bible, such as missions, salaried preachers, and theological seminaries. In a somewhat different vein, the followers of Alexander Campbell (later the Disciples of Christ) found the schools objectionable because they were sponsored by national voluntary societies and promoted by hired missionaries. Campbell, too, had originally seen the schools as "hobbies of modern times" and "inventions of men," but changed his mind regarding church-directed schools. For all these groups, which drew their largest support from rural white southerners, the key issue was undoubtedly the northern origins of "union" schools and their texts, along with a general repugnance for the centralizing tendencies seemingly present in the Sunday school cause as a whole. Antimissionism often became a vehicle through which white southerners could express their feelings against "northern domination" in general.[66]

In the mainline Protestant denominations, theological justification for the schools was strongest among Methodists and Episcopalians, both of which had long tradi-tions of catechization. Beginning in 1824, for example, the Methodist General

Conference introduced into its rule book, the *Discipline,* a provision requiring preachers to form classes for children, and in 1828 the conference used the term "Sunday schools" to refer to such classes. After the denomination split in the 1840s, the Northern Methodist General Conference designated church school superintendents as members (along with other church officials) of its quarterly conferences, and in 1864 it empowered the quarterly conferences to supervise all schools under their jurisdictions. The Southern Methodist General Conference followed suit. Although the Episcopal church's hierarchy did not designate the church school as its official agency of religious education, the church's catechetical tradition, combined with its ready acceptance of the schools, turned practice into unofficial policy. Among Presbyterians and Congregationalists, the covenant doctrine provided room for Sunday schools. As "children of the covenant," church members' offspring were entitled to infant baptism and to special care and concern, a care increasingly expressed in church schools. Baptists, too, fit the schools into their educational traditions, stressing their utility in preparing children for baptism and helping older youths and adults live out their religious commitments.[67]

Theological status and denominational policy did not always translate into uniform practice, however. The decentralized structures of most Protestant denominations—especially of Presbyterians, Congregationalists, and Baptists—often meant that individual congregations followed very different policies toward church schools. As late as 1874, for example, the editor of the *National Sunday School Teacher* felt it necessary to urge that "the Sabbath-school should be considered as integrally and essentially a part of the church itself," with the congregation choosing its school's officers and teachers.

Despite variations in practice, the status of the church school had changed considerably in the nineteenth century. If in the 1820s some ministers and their congregations were skeptical while others were enthusiastic about this new institution, by the 1870s few Protestants could have imagined their churches without the schools, and all recognized them as a key means of recruiting new members. Who could quarrel with success? A Methodist bishop's 1854 estimate that Sunday schools accounted for "one-half the entire net increase of the membership of the church" was probably conservative, but it testified to the schools' importance. As school members swelled the ranks of church communicants, clergy and laymen alike agreed that the Sunday school had become "the nursery of the church."[68]

As an institution for children, the Sunday school reflected particular adult ideas about childhood and conveyed to children a specific set of cultural expectations by defining what it meant to be an evangelical Protestant. In the early nineteenth century, these expectations mirrored the values of self-control, obedience, good habits, and fixed principles that most Protestants believed essential to orderly living in an age of rapid market expansion and incipient industrialization. Later, as the work ethic of pre–Civil War America began to be transformed into the leisure ethic of modern America, expectations for childhood behavior increasingly stressed the importance of play and exuberance. In an era of endless smokestacks and routinized factory discipline, when more and more Americans were being turned into employees, childhood came to represent the spontaneity and emotional expression that was frowned upon in public life. No longer a period of rigorous training in which adults needed—to use the horticultural metaphors so beloved of nineteenth-century commentators—to root out the weeds of bad habits and encourage straight and sturdy growth, childhood became a time for protecting tender shoots and benevolently showering them with warmth and light.

Over the years, the Sunday school curriculum changed in accordance with new evangelical views of childhood. From a stress on preparing for conversion as the defining and direction-giving event of life, the curriculum shifted in the late nineteenth century to an emphasis on nurture and gradual growth. As evangelicals redefined conversion, they changed the Sunday school curriculum, de-emphasizing its early focus on one specific end-product (conversion) and stressing instead the process of life-long spiritual growth.

Although lacking the coercive power of public institutions and explicitly rejecting their coercive methods, Sunday schools made a difference in their pupils' lives. Small classes and personal connections between teacher and pupil created an experience that was often intimate and intense. If for some it was too intense and imposed unbearable pressures, for many it was rewarding, even pleasant. Children enjoyed the rituals of Sunday school attendance—reciting Bible verses, singing hymns, parading at anniversaries or celebrations, collecting reward tickets and religious tokens, attending picnics—and many undoubtedly found them warmly reassuring in an uncertain world. Emerging from the Sunday school after a few months or a few years, they took with them some basic knowledge of the Bible, familiarity with the tenets and morality of evangelical Protestant life, friends and advisors who felt responsible for their spiritual welfare and to whom they felt responsible, and an institutional connection that could be renewed simply by walking into another school. The evangelical Sunday school not only helped to define childhood and shape its contours, it mediated the meaning of religious experience to millions of youngsters. In short, it represented yet another example of how nineteenth-century Americans devised institutional solutions to the complex task of socializing the young.

CONCLUSION

By most reckonings, the Sunday school reached its hundredth birthday in 1880. From Robert Raikes's England, it had crossed the Atlantic and promptly floundered in American waters. Only as an evangelical, voluntaristic, and church-related phenomenon had it become a truly American institution—a fixture in church life and, by 1880, the primary recruiting ground for church members. In these and other ways, the American Sunday school differed from its British parent. Indeed, a comparison of the institution's variable appearance on two sides of the Atlantic is instructive, for it highlights the distinctiveness of the American version.

Both British and American Sunday schools rapidly lost their original form. In England, the eighteenth-century middle-class evangelicals (such as Raikes) who conceived of the schools as a philanthropic effort to elevate the condition of the poor and provide instruction in deference soon found their activities overshadowed and their schools in decline. By the 1840s working-class individuals who associated the schools with self-help and collective social advancement dominated the ranks of Sunday school founders, teachers, and promoters. Similarly, early American efforts to found Raikes-style schools, such as Philadelphia's First Day Society, quickly proved unworkable. Only with the founding of evangelical schools after 1810 did the Sunday school establish firm roots in American soil.[1]

Despite this surface similarity in their histories, however, British and American schools evolved in fundamentally different directions. In England, the nineteenth-century Sunday school was "a relatively autonomous, working-class institution," drawing its students, teachers, and financial support from local communities. Although they rejected Raikes's values and approach, British organizers did not broaden their institution's social base much beyond the groups he had targeted—the working class and the "lower orders" of society.[2] In the United States, the Sunday school was both a church and a missionary institution that enrolled children from a variety of social class backgrounds. Still, because Americans agreed that connection to a church was essential to a school's success, church schools outnumbered mission schools (except in the very early decades) and a majority of pupils came from churchgoing families. Not surprisingly, the gulf between church and mission schools often (though not always) replicated class divisions, with middle-class and "respectable working class" children attending church schools, lower-class children attending mission schools. (The major exception to this generalization were mission schools in newly settled areas, where interdenominational "union" schools often preceded the establishment of churches.)

The two institutions also differed in their local roots. The numerical strength of the English Sunday school rested more in the dissenting religious sects than in the established Church of England, more in industrial towns and country villages than in large cities such as London. American schools, on the other hand, were particularly strong in urban areas and received support virtually across the spectrum of Protestant denominations.[3]

British schools were also much more important in spreading basic literacy than their American counterparts. Because attendance at a weekday school "was not the norm for the working-class child at any age" in England, notes the historian Thomas Laqueur, Sunday schools were important supplements, adding "three, four or five years of part-time education to a very limited and discontinuous period of weekday schooling." In some manufacturing areas, he estimates, over half the children receiving any education at all received it in a Sunday school. Although British schools varied widely in their curricula over the course of the century, almost all taught reading, about 20 percent taught writing, and 5 percent still taught arithmetic as late as 1843.[4]

The American story was very different. Whereas in the 1810s and 1820s American Sunday schools did indeed reach large numbers of children who had no other schooling opportunities, teaching them reading, writing, and occasionally arithmetic, the spread of weekday schools signaled an interest in free, tax-supported public schooling that was largely absent in England. As a consequence, American Sunday schools rapidly shed any major responsibility for imparting basic literacy, leaving the bulk of that task to weekday schools. Sunday schools generally flourished wherever there were common schools; conversely, the absence of daily schools usually signaled the absence of Sunday schools. In the one area of the United States where Sunday schools might have supplied widespread literacy—the antebellum South—their potential was blocked by an official ideology committed to keeping the black population illiterate. Only during Reconstruction, when the ex-slaves' desire for literacy was unleashed, were they able to use Sunday schools to answer a pressing need. Whereas English schools provided an alternative system of schooling, American Sunday schools simply plugged temporary gaps in existing school networks.

Literacy aside, Sunday schools on both sides of the Atlantic were significant agents of cultural transmission. Both spread books, magazines, and libraries among the population at large. All of these taught a complex of Protestant virtues, foremost among them being good reading habits. Whether or not they actually taught students to read, the schools imparted a culture of literacy and prepared children for life in a print-oriented world. In both countries, too, Sunday scholars learned the importance of good habits, orderliness, cleanliness, punctuality, and neatness.[5] The differences between English and American schools in this regard were primarily ones of emphasis. Concern about personal habits was more prominent in English than in American schools, perhaps reflecting the particularly British association of cleanliness with godliness. In American schools, the culture of evangelical Protestantism, with its message of both spiritual and behavioral reformation, took center stage.

In the United States, Sunday schools were much more important as a source of new church members than they were in England. Thus, although both English and American schools were organized and run by lay people, and although both English and American ministers complained about lay usurpation of clerical authority, American schools established stronger claims to denominational recognition and support. Church schools trained children of the congregations for eventual church membership, while mission schools often served as foundations on which churches were later built. Long after many American schools had found homes in church buildings and garnered regular financial support from the congregations to which they were attached, British schools continued to meet in school buildings and to seek funds from the public at large.[6]

Indeed, efforts to use the Sunday school for national evangelization, so important a part of the American story, were wholly absent in nineteenth-century Britain. The largest nationwide organization in England, the Sunday School Union, while performing the same teacher services and publishing functions as its American counterpart, did virtually no missionary work. The group did hire a missionary in 1828 to travel around and contact teachers' organizations, but its main activity was publishing. (It also—unlike the American Sunday School Union—served as a political pressure group for dissenting sects.)[7] There was simply no counterpart on the English scene for the massive missionary efforts of American organizers in rural and frontier areas during the nineteenth century or the national fund-raising campaigns that accompanied them.

The reasons for this contrast are rooted in the structures of the two societies and the different functions the schools assumed in them. In England, where long-established institutions such as the Anglican church and the monarchy served to promote national unity, the Sunday school was basically a local enterprise. Its working-class base reflected the strength of social stratification in English society and contrasted strongly with the egalitarian aspirations of American schools. Particularly popular among the Methodists and other dissenting sects, it represented a form of collective self-help by one social group. By providing literacy and access to basic values, English Sunday schools may have promoted a common sense of Englishness, but that result was more incidental than intentional. No one thought or spoke of the schools as agents of national cohesion; no one associated the success of the schools with the fate of the nation. More important, the training that English schools provided to their clients could fuel working-class radicalism as easily as it promoted acquiescence in middle-class values. Not only were many labor activists the products of English Sunday schools, but their publications, which routinely employed scriptural imagery, depended for their success upon the Sunday-school-bred literacy of their readers.[8]

In the United States, the Sunday school was both a community fixture and part of a national network. Individual schools fulfilled important local functions, providing religious instruction to children and an evangelical Protestant identity to adolescent and adult teachers. In addition, urban mission schools delivered important social services to pupils and their families through employment agencies, free classes, and winter relief. On the frontier, mission schools brought the familiar rituals and symbols of Protestant life to newly settled areas. But beyond their local importance, evangelical schools were connected through their associations with the American Sunday School Union and other national societies. When students in a local school read a national society's periodical, donated money to support a missionary in the West, or heard a teacher read the missionary's letters of thanks, they became part of a national community defined not by location but by common evangelical concerns.

The national significance that Sunday schools acquired during the course of the nineteenth century was not accidental. As we have seen, the schools were part of a larger process of evangelical institution building begun in the antebellum years and consolidated after the Civil War. Like their counterparts in other endeavors, Sunday school leaders explicitly promoted the notion that the fate of the republic depended upon the triumph of evangelical ideals and institutions. By capturing the republican values of the Revolutionary era and dressing them in evangelical garb, they cemented the connection between church and nation and denied legitimacy to other republican traditions (such as that of Thomas Paine). In this process, evangelical institutions such as Sunday schools became both symbols and agents of nationalism. It is hardly surprising, then, that when American missionaries in the late nineteenth century headed for foreign lands, they took the Sunday school with them. If the central symbols of British efforts to bring their brand of enlightenment and civilization to the world were the army officer and the bureaucrat, American "civilizers" were more likely to be missionaries bearing Bibles and Sunday school books.[9]

Their belief in the efficacy of evangelical institutions to fulfill crucial social goals arose out of personal experience more than abstract theorizing. To their organizers, Sunday schools and other evangelical institutions represented effective ways of ordering individual lives in an increasingly disorderly society. Convinced by their own experience that a life organized around evangelical concerns offered protection against individual and national chaos, Sunday school promoters hoped to construct a network of evangelical institutions to achieve this social goal. In such a network, Sunday schools were to play a crucial role by introducing children to evangelical Protestantism, training them in proper habits and values, and guiding them through the treacherous waters of adolescence. They believed that being a Sunday scholar or teacher would offer sources of like-minded friends and associates and an evangelical identity that was transferable across space and time.

While the schools provided individuals like Lewis Ashhurst, Michael Floy, and Harriet Lathrop with roadmaps on their trek through life, they also created opportunities for individuals to rewrite the maps. Women founders of Sunday schools and Sunday school unions, for example, exerted an authority to preach and teach on the most sensitive religious topics that was remarkable by comparison to their role in the eighteenth century. Although they lost some of that authority when schools became coeducational, their importance as teachers nevertheless distinguished them markedly from their silent (and often silenced) predecessors. In the latter part of the century, as speakers for the causes of temperance and pedagogical improvement, women reassumed the mantle of authority. Young people, too, were able to find their niche in the schools, usually as teachers but sometimes as officers, acquiring the right to cultivate young souls in the nursery of the church. And through unions and publishing houses, ordinary merchants and professional men found a forum by which to disseminate their values and touch the lives of unseen millions in the name of evangelical influence.

The Sunday school was, to be sure, only one part of the institutional world that nineteenth-century evangelicals created. In their desire to provide new forms of social order, they wove organizational threads into dense pieces of fabric, then stitched them all together to form an overall design. Missionary, educational, and social welfare groups belonged to the pattern, as did youth groups, YMCAs and YWCAs, temperance societies, choral groups, and women's organizations. Each had its place in the drive to make America a Christian nation. In recent times, the stitches binding this institutional world have unraveled, destroying the once-clear pattern and changing the significance of the individual elements. Particularly notable is the passing of the mission school, which was once such an important part of evangelical outreach efforts. Although the church school remains an important part of Protestant life, it draws its social significance primarily from its role in training the children of the congregation. The Sunday school is still an American institution, but it no longer draws its institutional rationale from efforts to evangelize the nation and the world.

NOTES

The locations of manuscript collections frequently cited in the notes have been identified by the following abbreviations:

HSP	Historical Society of Pennsylvania, Philadelphia
LLMM	Lovely Lane Methodist Museum, Baltimore
NYPL	New York Public Library
PHS	Presbyterian Historical Society, Philadelphia
RIHS	Rhode Island Historical Society, Providence

INTRODUCTION

1. Arthur M. Schlesinger, *Paths to the Present* (New York: Alfred A. Knopf, 1949), pp. 23–50; Stanley M. Elkins, *Slavery: A Problem in American Institutional and Intellectual Life,* 3d ed. (Chicago: University of Chicago Press, 1976), pp. 28–29; David Donald, "An Excess of Democracy: The American Civil War and the Social Process," in *Lincoln Reconsidered: Essays on the Civil War Era* (New York: Random House, 1961), p. 234. A recent restatement of this view can be found in Paul E. Johnson, *A Shopkeeper's Millennium: Society and Revivals in Rochester, New York, 1815–1837* (New York: Hill and Wang, 1978), p. 10.

2. John R. McKivigan, *The War against Proslavery Religion: Abolitionism and the Northern Churches, 1830–1865* (Ithaca, N.Y.: Cornell University Press, 1984), pp. 74–92. See also Charles I. Foster, *An Errand of Mercy: The Evangelical United Front, 1790–1837* (Chapel Hill: University of North Carolina Press, 1960); Clifford S. Griffin, *Their Brothers' Keepers: Moral Stewardship in the United States, 1800–1865* (New Brunswick, N.J.: Rutgers University Press, 1960); David J. Rothman, *The Discovery of the Asylum: Social Order and Disorder in the New Republic* (Boston: Little, Brown, 1971); Carroll Smith Rosenberg, *Religion and the Rise of the American City: The New York City Mission Movement, 1812–1870* (Ithaca, N.Y.: Cornell University Press, 1971); Lois W. Banner, "The Protestant Crusade: Religious Missions, Benevolence, and Reform in the United States, 1790–1840" (Ph.D. diss., Columbia University, 1970); Mary

P. Ryan, *Cradle of the Middle Class: The Family in Oneida County, New York, 1790–1865* (New York: Cambridge University Press, 1981); and Nancy A. Hewitt, *Women's Activism and Social Change: Rochester, 1822–1872* (Ithaca, N.Y.: Cornell University Press, 1984).

3. Michael B. Katz, "Origins of the Institutional State," *Marxist Perspectives* 1 (Winter 1978), p. 6. See also Katz, "The Origins of Public Education: A Reassessment," *History of Education Quarterly* 3 (Winter 1976), pp. 381–407; and Carl F. Kaestle, *The Evolution of an Urban School System: New York City, 1750–1850* (Cambridge: Harvard University Press, 1973).

4. For the view expressed in the preceding paragraph, see Griffin, *Their Brothers' Keepers*, pp. 3–22; Raymond Mohl, "The Urban Missionary Movement in New York City, 1800–1825," *Journal of Religious History* 7 (Dec. 1972), pp. 110–28; and Paul Boyer, *Urban Masses and Moral Order in America, 1820–1920* (Cambridge: Harvard University Press, 1978), pp. 34–55. For the second view, see Rosenberg, *Religion*, pp. 7–8; Lois W. Banner, "Religious Benevolence as Social Control: A Critique of an Interpretation," *Journal of American History* 60 (1973), pp. 23–41; Donald M. Scott, *From Office to Profession: The New England Ministry, 1750–1850* (Philadelphia: University of Pennsylvania Press, 1978), esp. chap. 3; and Daniel Walker Howe, *The Political Culture of the American Whigs* (Chicago: University of Chicago Press, 1979), esp. chap. 7. In his analysis of the 19th-century "organizational revolution," John S. Gilkeson, Jr., tends to portray voluntary societies as middle-class efforts to control the poor; see *Middle-Class Providence, 1820–1940* (Princeton: Princeton University Press, 1986), pp. 8–13.

5. Howe, *Political Culture*, p. 159; Rosenberg, *Religion*, p. 8; Rhys Isaac, "Evangelical Revolt: The Nature of the Baptists' Challenge to the Traditional Order in Virginia, 1765 to 1775," *William and Mary Quarterly*, 3d ser., 31 (1974), pp. 345–68; Robert T. Handy, *A Christian America: Protestant Hopes and Historical Realities* (New York: Oxford University Press, 1971), p. 39. See also Gilkeson, *Middle-Class Providence*, pp. 28–32, 52–53.

1. THE ORIGINS OF EVANGELICAL SUNDAY SCHOOLS

1. On British Sunday schools, see Thomas W. Laqueur, *Religion and Respectability: Sunday Schools and Working Class Culture, 1780–1850* (New Haven: Yale University Press, 1976), esp. pp. 4–33; on American Sunday schools, the basic reference is still Edwin W. Rice, *The Sunday-School Movement, 1780–1917, and the American Sunday-School Union, 1817–1917* (Philadelphia: American Sunday-School Union, 1917). On Slater's school, see Barbara Tucker, *Samuel Slater and the Origins of the American Textile Industry* (Ithaca, N.Y.: Cornell University Press, 1984), pp. 44, 75–76, 163–74. The quotation is from Albert Mathews, "Early Sunday Schools in Boston," *Publications of the Colonial Society of Massachusetts* 21 (1919), p. 280.

2. Throughout this book, I use the term *evangelical* to denote those Protestant denominations that emphasized the need for a personal conversion experience for church membership. I also use the term *Sunday school* rather than the variant *Sabbath school* that some 19th-century writers preferred. Strictly speaking, of course, the Sabbath is the seventh day of the week.

3. First Day Society, Constitution and Rules, in Board of Visitors, Minutes, Feb. 1, 1791, PHS; Benjamin Rush to Jeremy Belknap, Jan. 5, 1791, in *Letters of Benjamin Rush,* ed. L. H. Butterfield (Princeton: Princeton University Press, 1951), vol. 1, p. 573; First Day Society, Board of Visitors, Minutes, Feb. 1, 1791, PHS. See also John K. Alexander, *Render Them Submissive: Responses to Poverty in Philadelphia, 1760–1800* (Amherst: University of Massachusetts Press, 1980), pp. 145–46; and Jacqueline Reusser Reinier, "Attitudes toward and Practices of Childrearing: Philadelphia, 1790–1830" (Ph.D. diss. University of California, Berkeley, 1977), pp. 288–94.

4. Biographical information on the First Day Society's managers is derived from a variety of sources. Among the most important are Abraham Ritter, *Philadelphia and Her Merchants* (Philadelphia: n.p., 1860); *Hazard's Register of Pennsylvania* 6 (Sept. 1830), pp. 204–05; Joseph J. McCadden, *Education in Pennsylvania, 1801–1835, and its Debt to Roberts Vaux* (Philadelphia: University of Pennsylvania Press, 1937), p. 123; Alfred Poor, *A Memoir and Genealogy of John Poore* (Salem, Mass.: n. p., 1881), pp. 121–22; "Charles Marshall," *The National Cyclopedia of American Biography,* 62 vols. to date (New York; J. T. White, 1892–1984), vol. 5, p. 343; "Matthew Carey," ibid., vol. 6, p. 278; "Thomas Pym Cope," *The Dictionary of American Biography,* 20 vols. (New York: Scribner's, 1928–1936), vol. 4, pp. 421–22; "Benjamin Rush," ibid., vol. 16, pp. 227–31; "William White," ibid., vol. 20, pp. 121–22; "John Poor," ibid., vol. 15, pp. 71.

5. On the concept of republican education, see Carl F. Kaestle, *Pillars of the Republic: Common Schools and American Society, 1780–1860* (New York: Hill and Wang, 1983), pp. 3–12. The quotations are from: Memorial to the Pennsylvania Legislature, in First Day Society, Board of Managers, Minutes, Dec. 29, 1791; and "Address to the Public," in First Day Society, Board of Visitors, Minutes, Dec. 6, 1799, PHS. See also Alexander, *Render Them Submissive,* pp. 154–55, which presents a different view of the managers' motives; and Jacqueline S. Reinier, "Rearing the Republican Child: Attitudes and Practices in Post-Revolutionary Philadelphia," *William and Mary Quarterly* 39 (Jan. 1982), pp. 156–62.

6. First Day Society, Board of Managers, Minutes, Dec. 17, 1790–Apr. 11, 1804; Board of Visitors, Minutes, Jan. 18, 1791–July 19, 1810, PHS.

7. On declining enrollments, see First Day Society, Board of Visitors, Minutes, Aug. 1800–Feb. 5, 1818, PHS. The quotation is from the minutes of May 2, 1817. On the society's operations after 1819, see First Day Society, Board of Managers, Minutes, July 28, 1819–July 9, 1823. See also Reinier, "Practices of Childrearing," pp. 322–24.

8. Kaestle, *Pillars of the Republic,* pp. 30–61; Isaac Ferris, *Semi-Centennial Memorial Discourse of the New-York Sunday School Union, 25 February 1866* (New York: n.p., 1866), pp. 11–14; Mathews, "Early Sunday Schools in Boston," p. 280; Addie Grace Wardle, *History of the Sunday School Movement in the Methodist Episcopal Church* (New York: Methodist Book Concern, 1918), p. 53 (Asbury quotation); Joanna Bethune to Frederick A. Packard, Aug. 4, 1829, Packard Letters, Gratz Collection, HSP; *Semi-Centennial Celebration of the First Sabbath-School Society in Massachusetts, and the First Parish Sabbath School, Charlestown, October 14, 1866* (Boston: n.p., 1867), p. 77; Clifton Hartwell Brewer, *A History of Religious Education in the Episcopal Church to 1835* (New Haven: Yale University Press, 1924), pp. 150–61. For more information on catechizing practices, see Jessie Dell Crawford, "The Status of the Child in American Baptist Churches" (Ph.D. diss., Yale University, 1940), p. 285; "Archibald Alexander,"

in *Annals of the American Pulpit; or, Commemorative Notices of Distinguished American Clergymen of Various Denominations*, ed. William B. Sprague, 9 vols. (New York: Robert Carter, 1857–1869), vol. 3, p. 617; and *Life of Ashbel Green* (New York: Robert Carter and Bros., 1849), pp. 257–58.

9. James H. Blodgett, "Sunday Schools," in *Annual Report of the Department of the Interior, 1897*, vol. 1: *Report of the Commissioner of Education* (Washington, D.C.: Government Printing Office, 1898), p. 351; William Arthur Maddox, *The Free School Idea in Virginia Before the Civil War* (New York: Teachers' College, Columbia University, 1918; New York: Arno Press, 1969), pp. 38–40; Sadie Bell, *The Church, The State, and Education in Virginia* (Philadelphia: Science Press Printing Company, 1930), p. 249; Raymond F. Betts, "Eleuthère Irénée du Pont and the Brandywine Sunday School," *Delaware History* 29 (1959), p. 349 n. 30; Blodgett, "Sunday Schools," p. 351; William M. Brabham, "A History of Sunday-School Work in the North Carolina Conference, Methodist Episcopal Church, South" [Address before the North Carolina Conference Historical Society, 1916] (Greensboro, N.C.: Published by the North Carolina *Christian Advocate*, 1925), pp. 7–10. See also "Sabbath Schools in New York," *Religious Intelligencer* 9 (Aug. 28, 1824), pp. 204–05 (advocating public funds for Sunday schools); and Ernest Trice Thompson, *Presbyterians in the South, I: 1607–1861* (Richmond, Va.: John Knox Press, 1963), pp. 237–38.

10. See, for example, Boston Society for the Moral and Religious Instruction of the Poor, *Third Annual Report* (Boston, 1819), pp. 14–15; Philadelphia Sunday and Adult School Union, *Third Annual Report* (Philadelphia, 1820), p. 8; Female Union Society for the Promotion of Sabbath Schools, *Third Annual Report* (New York, 1819), pp. 7–8. The quotation is from McKendrean Female Sabbath School Society, Minutes, Nov. 3, 1821, LLMM.

11. Baltimore Female Sabbath School Society, Constitution, 1816, LLMM; Boston, Second Baptist Church Female Sabbath School Society, *Constitution* (Boston, 1817); Philadelphia, First Presbyterian Church [Kensington] Sabbath School Association, Constitution, in 1817 Minutes, PHS; "Third Annual Report of Western Sunday School Union," *American Sunday-School Magazine* 5 (Nov. 1828), p. 339.

12. See, for example, Female Union Society for the Promotion of Sabbath Schools, Minutes, 1825–1828, Brooklyn Historical Society, Brooklyn, N.Y..

13. *Historical Statistics of the United States, Colonial Times to 1970* (Washington, D.C.: Government Printing Office, 1972), series A119–34, A143–57; Philadelphia Sunday and Adult School Union, *Seventh Annual Report* (Philadelphia, 1824), pp. 68–72; American Sunday School Union, *First Annual Report* (Philadelphia, 1825), pp. 22–27, and *Eighth Annual Report* (1832), pp. 43–51.

14. Clifford S. Griffin, *Their Brothers' Keepers: Moral Stewardship in the United States, 1800–1865* (New Brunswick N.J.: Rutgers University Press, 1960); Charles I. Foster, *An Errand of Mercy: The Evangelical United Front, 1790–1837* (Chapel Hill: University of North Carolina Press, 1960); Carroll Smith Rosenberg, *Religion and the Rise of the American City: The New York City Mission Movement, 1812–1870* (Ithaca, N.Y.: Cornell University Press, 1971), esp. pp. 29–75; Lois W. Banner, "The Protestant Crusade: Religious Missions, Benevolence, and Reform in the United States, 1790–1840" (Ph.D. diss., Columbia University, 1970); Martha Tomhave Blauvelt, "Society,

Religion and Revivalism: The Second Great Awakening in New Jersey, 1780–1830" (Ph.D. diss., Princeton University, 1975); Anne M. Boylan, "Women in Groups: An Analysis of Women's Benevolent Organizations in New York and Boston, 1797–1840," *Journal of American History* 71 (Dec. 1984), pp. 497–523; Kenneth D. Miller and Ethel Prince Miller, *The People Are the City: 150 Years of Social and Religious Concern in New York City* (New York: Harper and Row, 1962); J. Leslie Dunstan, *A Light to the City: 150 Years of the City Missionary Society of Boston, 1816–1966* (Boston: Beacon, 1966), esp. pp. 3–69.

15. Rice, *Sunday-School Movement,* p. 51; "The Presbyterian Evangelical Society of Philadelphia," *Presbyterian Historical Society Journal* 5 (1909–1910), pp. 150–54; Ashbel Green, *Memoir of the Life of Rev. Joseph Eastburn, Stated Preacher in the Mariners' Church, Philadelphia* (Philadelphia: G. W. Mentz, 1828), pp. 34–42. See also Anne M. Boylan, "Presbyterians and Sunday Schools in Philadelphia, 1800–1824," *Journal of Presbyterian History* 58 (Winter 1980), pp. 299–310.

16. "Presbyterian Evangelical Society," p. 152.

17. Ibid.; Robert May Sunday School, Minute book, Oct. 20, 1811–Jan. 26, 1812, PHS; Philadelphia Sunday and Adult School Union, *First Annual Report* (Philadelphia, 1818), p. 10 (footnote on May's school). See also Reinier, "Practices of Childrearing," pp. 324–30.

18. Rice, *Sunday-School Movement,* pp. 61–69; John Bankson to Divie Bethune, July 18, 1817, in Philadelphia Sunday and Adult School Union, Letterbook, PHS. On adult schools in New York, see Female Union Society for the Promotion of Sabbath Schools, *Second Annual Report* (New York, 1818), pp. 43–44.

19. Rosenberg, *Religion,* pp. 136–40; Joseph W. Phillips, *Jedidiah Morse and New England Congregationalism* (New Brunswick, N.J.: Rutgers University Press, 1983), pp. 174–75; "Sunday Schools," *Religious Intelligencer* 1 (May 10, 1817), p. 789; John Henry Hobart, *The Beneficial Effects of Sunday Schools Considered* (New York: New York Protestant Episcopal Sunday School Society, 1818), p. 28; "Sabbath School in Nantucket, Mass.," *Religious Intelligencer* 5 (Jan. 6, 1821), pp. 521–22; *Sunday School Repository* 2 (June 1818), pp. 71–72; Philadelphia Sunday and Adult School Union, *Fifth Annual Report* (Philadelphia, 1822), p. 11. For a discussion of Hobart's views on interdenominational cooperation, see Robert Bruce Mullin, *Episcopal Vision / American Reality: High Church Theology and Social Thought in Evangelical America* (New Haven: Yale University Press, 1986).

20. Male Adult Association, Minutes, Constitution, 1815, PHS; Male Adult Association, Minutes, Aug. 10 and Dec. 12, 1816; June 12 and 13, Oct. 9, and Nov. 13, 1817; Philadelphia Sunday and Adult School Union, *First Annual Report* (Philadelphia, 1818), pp. 22–24.

21. Auxiliary Evangelical Society, Minutes, Jan. 29, 1818, PHS; Boston Society for the Moral and Religious Instruction of the Poor, *Third Annual Report* (Boston, 1819), p. 11; New-York Sunday-School Union Society, *Fourth Annual Report* (New York, 1820), p. 29; "Sabbath Schools at Whitehall, New York," *Religious Intelligencer* 4 (June 26, 1819), p. 63; "Sunday School Gleanings," *American Sunday-School Magazine* 1 (June 1824), pp. 20–21; George Kelly, *A Sermon Preached in the First Baptist Meetinghouse in Haverhill, May 31, 1829* (Haverhill, Mass.: n.p., 1829), pp. 13–14; Archibald Alex-

ander, *Suggestions in Vindication of Sunday Schools* (Philadelphia: American Sunday-School Union, 1829), p. 8; "Sketch of a Sabbath School," *American Sunday-School Magazine* 5 (Nov. 1828), p. 325.

22. Shepherd Knapp, *A History of the Brick Presbyterian Church in the City of New York* (New York: Trustees of Brick Presbyterian Church, 1909), p. 215; Mathews, "Early Sunday Schools in Boston," pp. 266–67; Brewer, *Religious Education in the Episcopal Church to 1835,* p. 210; General Protestant Episcopal Sunday School Union, *Fourth Annual Report* (New York, 1830), pp. 20–21; *Fifth Annual Report* (1831), pp. 79–80. See also Boston Society for the Moral and Religious Instruction of the Poor, *Second Annual Report* (Boston, 1818), p. 9.

23. "Pastoral Letter," *Religious Intelligencer* 3 (July 4, 1818), p. 73; ibid., 1 (May 24, 1817), p. 823; Philadelphia City Sunday School Union, Annual Meeting, 1827, clipping attached to minutes, PHS. On the connections between maternal associations and Sunday schools, see *Diary of Sarah Connell Ayer, 1805–1835* (Portland, Maine: Lefavor-Tower, 1910), pp. 209–99. See also Mary P. Ryan, "A Women's Awakening: Evangelical Religion and the Families of Utica, New York, 1800–1849," *American Quarterly* 30 (Winter 1978), pp. 602–23; and Ralph R. Smith, " 'In Every Destitute Place': The Mission Program of the American Sunday School Union, 1817–1834" (Ph.D. diss., University of Southern California, 1973), pp. 27–30.

24. "Philadelphia Association of Male Sunday School Teachers," *American Sunday-School Magazine* 1 (November 1824), pp. 142–45; Massachusetts Sabbath School Union, *First Annual Report* (Boston, 1826), p. 6; "Sunday Schools not for the Poor Only," *American Sunday-School Magazine* 2 (Jan. 1825), p. 13; "Sabbath School Beneficial to the Rich as well as the Poor," *Religious Intelligencer* 13 (Sept. 27, 1828), p. 279; "Ought Heads of Families to Enlist as Teachers in Sabbath Schools," ibid., 9 (Feb. 19, 1825), p. 598.

25. "The Local System," *American Sunday-School Magazine* 2 (Jan. 1825), p. 4; Joseph Thomas, *A Discourse Dedicated to the World, on the Benevolent Institutions of Sunday Schools, October 18, 1818* (Winchester, Va.: n.p., 1818), p. 27; "Sunday Schools for the Rich as well as the Poor," *Religious Intelligencer* 10 (Nov. 26, 1825), p. 411; "Philadelphia Association of Male Sunday School Teachers," *American Sunday-School Magazine* 1 (Nov. 1824), p. 144; "Sabbath Schools Beneficial to the Rich as well as the Poor," *Religious Intelligencer* 13 (Sept. 27, 1828), p. 279.

26. William Bacon Stevens, *The Past and Present of St. Andrew's* (Philadelphia: C. Sherman, 1858), p. 50. The Beecher story is repeated in many places, among them Marianna C. Brown, *Sunday School Movements in America* (New York: Fleming H. Revell Co., 1901), p. 23. On British schools, see Laqueur, *Religion and Respectability,* pp. 87–89.

27. *American Sunday-School Magazine* 7 (October 1830), p. 312; Providence Association of Sabbath School Teachers, Records, Aug. 20, 1832, RIHS; Boston Society for the Religious and Moral Instruction of the Poor, *Eighth Annual Report* (Boston, 1824), p. 10.

28. Carl F. Kaestle, *The Evolution of an Urban School System: New York City, 1750–1850* (Cambridge: Harvard University Press, 1973), pp. 75–111; James P. Wickersham, *A History of Education in Pennsylvania* (Lancaster, Pa.: Inquirer Publishing Co., 1886), pp. 269–301 (quotation, 275); *Nineteenth Annual Report of the Public Schools of the*

First District of the State of Pennsylvania (Philadelphia: The District, 1837), p. 10. On the proportion of students in private as opposed to public schools, see Kaestle, *Evolution,* pp. 89–90.

29. New-York Sunday-School Union Society, *Hints on the Establishment and Regulation of Sunday Schools* (New York, 1817), p. 5; William Oland Bourne, *History of the Public School Society of the City of New York* (New York: William Wood, 1870), pp. 108–11. For a discussion of whether arithmetic should be taught in Sunday schools, see Philadelphia Association of Male Sunday School Teachers, Minutes, Jan. 17, 1825, PHS.

30. Kaestle, *Pillars of the Republic,* pp. 93–103; Timothy L. Smith, "Protestant Schooling and American Nationality, 1800–1850," *Journal of American History* 53 (1967), pp. 679–95.

31. Boston Society for the Religious and Moral Instruction of the Poor, *Fourth Annual Report* (Boston, 1820), pp. 1–3; Rice, *Sunday-School Movement,* pp. 81–87.

2. SUNDAY SCHOOLS AND AMERICAN EDUCATION

1. Three studies that have been influential in redefining the history of education to include all methods of cultural transmission, formal and informal, are: Bernard Bailyn, *Education in the Forming of American Society* (Chapel Hill: University of North Carolina Press, 1960); Lawrence Cremin, *American Education: The Colonial Experience, 1607–1783* (New York: Harper and Row, 1970); and Cremin, *American Education: The National Experience, 1783–1876* (New York: Harper and Row, 1980). The following works assign a significant schooling role to Sunday schools: Robert W. Lynn and Elliott Wright, *The Big Little School: Sunday Child of American Protestantism* (New York: Harper and Row, 1971); Carl F. Kaestle, *Pillars of the Republic: Common Schools and American Society, 1780–1860* (New York: Hill and Wang, 1983), esp. chap. 3; Raymond F. Betts, "Eleuthère Irénée du Pont and the Brandywine Sunday School," *Delaware History* 29 (1959), pp. 343–53; and James Anderson, "Ex-Slaves and the Rise of Universal Education in the New South, 1860–1880," in *Education and the Rise of the New South,* ed. Ronald Goodenow and Arthur O. White (Boston: G. K. Hall, 1981), pp. 8–10. On British Sunday schools, see Thomas W. Laqueur, *Religion and Respectability: Sunday Schools and Working Class Culture, 1780–1850* (New Haven: Yale University Press, 1976), pp. 95–102.

2. Stanley K. Schultz, *The Culture Factory: Boston Public Schools, 1789–1860* (New York: Oxford University Press, 1973), p. 35; New-York Sunday-School Union Society, *Hints on the Establishment and Regulation of Sunday Schools* (New York, 1817), p. 3. Vera Butler provides statistics on Boston city schools during 1819–1820 in *Education as Revealed by New England Newspapers Prior to 1850* (Ph.D. diss., Temple University, 1935; New York: Arno Press, 1969), pp. 283–88. For statistics on First Day schools, see First Day Society, Board of Managers, Minutes, Apr. 9, 1800, PHS. On adult Sunday schools, see Philadelphia Sunday and Adult School Union, *Second Annual Report* (Philadelphia, 1819), p. 29; and Thomas Pole, *A History of the Origin and Progress of Adult Schools,* 2d ed. (Bristol, England: n.p., 1816), esp. pp. 30–34.

3. New-York Sunday-School Union Society, *First Annual Report* (New York, 1817), p. 4; *Semi-Centennial of the Sunday School of the First Presbyterian Church of Utica* (Utica, N.Y.: The Church, 1866), pp. 173–75; Philadelphia Sunday and Adult

School Union, *Fifth Annual Report* (Philadelphia, 1822), pp. 50–54; New-York Sunday-School Union Society, Methodist Branch, Minutes, May 1816, NYPL; Philadelphia Sunday and Adult School Union, *Second Annual Report* (Philadelphia, 1819), pp. 4, 29–31; *Sunday-School Facts, Collected by a Member of the General Association of Teachers* (New York: D. H. Wickham, 1821), pp. 10–11; Philadelphia Sunday and Adult School Union, *First Annual Report* (Philadelphia, 1818), p. 9. See also Allen Hartvik, "Catherine Ferguson: Black Founder of a Sunday School," *Negro History Bulletin* 35 (Oct. 1972), pp. 176–77.

4. On the Brandywine Manufacturers' Sunday School, see Betts, "Eleuthère Irénée du Pont," pp. 351–53; and Ruth C. Linton, "To the Promotion and Improvement of Youth: The Brandywine Manufacturers' Sunday School, 1816–1840" (Master's thesis, University of Delaware, 1981), pp. 88–91. The Brandywine school taught arithmetic, too, but seems to have abandoned the practice early in its history. The school building still stands and has been restored as part of the Hagley Museum outside Wilmington, Delaware. For a discussion of a closely related factory school, see Anthony F. C. Wallace, *Rockdale: The Growth of An American Village in the Early Industrial Revolution* (New York: Alfred A. Knopf, 1978), pp. 308–12. Responses to the American Sunday School Union's 1832 questionnaire are on file in the union's papers at the PHS. For a summary of the questionnaire's findings, see *Sunday-School Journal and Advocate of Christian Education* 2 (Oct. 10, 1832), pp. 162–63. The quotation is from American Sunday School Union, *Eighteenth Annual Report* (Philadelphia, 1842), p. 43. On the relationship between common schools and Sunday schools, see *Sunday-School Journal* 10 (Dec. 19, 1849), p. 198.

5. "Union Adult Society," *American Sunday-School Magazine* 1 (July 1824), p. 30; Abraham Martin, *Sketch of the Mission and Other Sabbath Schools Established Under the Auspices of the Philadelphia Sabbath School Association* (Philadelphia: William S. Young, 1860), pp. 18–19; New-York Sunday School Union, *Fifteenth Annual Report* (New York, 1831), appendix.

6. Baltimore, Asbury Sunday School Society, Minutes, Feb. 7, 1820, LLMM; M. B. Goodwin, "History of Schools for the Colored Population in the District of Columbia," *1868 Report of the U. S. Commissioner of Education* (Washington, D.C.: Government Printing Office, 1871), pp. 100–101; *Sunday-School Facts*, pp. 10–11; New-York Sunday School Union, *Thirty-First Annual Report* (New York, 1847), appendix.

7. Goodwin, "Schools for the Colored Population," p. 220; Asbury Sunday School Society, Minutes, Mar. 12, 1824, LLMM; Elizabeth, N.J., First Presbyterian Church Sunday School Teachers' Association, Minutes, Apr. 23, 1838, PHS. See also Albert J. Raboteau, *Slave Religion: The "Invisible Institution" in the Antebellum South* (New York: Oxford University Press, 1978), pp. 178–210; and Ernest Trice Thompson, *Presbyterians in the South, I: 1607–1861* (Richmond, Va.: John Knox Press, 1963), p. 206. On segregation in northern common schools, see Kaestle, *Pillars of the Republic*, pp. 172–79. Black newspapers offer evidence of sustained interest in Sunday schools; see, for example, *Freedom's Journal*, Apr. 13, 1827, p. 18, and Jan. 18, 1828, p. 170; and *The Colored American*, Apr. 15, 1837, p. 2.

8. Paul M. Harrison, ed., *Forty Years of Pioneer Life: Memoir of John Mason Peck, D.D.; Edited from his Journals and Correspondence by Rufus Babcock* (Carbondale: Southern Illinois University Press, 1965), pp. 93–94 (quotation, 210); Charles C. Jones,

The Religious Instruction of Negroes in the United States (Savannah, Ga.: Thomas Purse, 1842), pp. 229–66; E. T. Winkler, *Notes and Questions for the Oral Instruction of Colored People* (Charleston, S.C.: Southern Baptist Publication Society, 1857), p. v; A. W. Chambliss, *The Catechetical Instructor. Designed for the Use of Families, Sabbath Schools, and Bible Classes, and Especially for the Oral Instruction of the Colored Population* (Montgomery: Press of the Daily Alabama Journal, 1847), pp. ii, xiv–xv; Mrs. Mary Winans Wall, essay in *The Gospel Among the Slaves: A Short Account of Missionary Operations Among the African Slaves of the Southern States,* comp. W. P. Harrison (Nashville: Publishing House of the M. E. Church, South, 1893), p. 370; "Sabbath Schools Among the Slaves," New York *Observer* 34 (Apr. 10, 1856), p. 114. For a discussion of white religious teaching for slaves, see Thomas L. Webber, *Deep Like the Rivers: Education in the Slave Quarter Community, 1831–1865* (New York: W. W. Norton, 1978), pp. 43–58. See also Raboteau, *Slave Religion,* pp. 152–78 and 212–88.

9. Frederick Douglass, *Life and Times of Frederick Douglass* (1892; reprint, New York: Collier-Macmillan, 1962), pp. 111, 151–53.

10. American Sunday School Union, *Forty-Third Annual Report* (Philadelphia, 1867), pp. 43–44; J. M. Marsh to Maurice A. Wurts, Dec. 4, 1865, American Sunday School Union Papers, PHS; W. J. Farrow to Maurice A. Wurts, Dec. 18, 1865, American Sunday School Union Papers, PHS; "Sunday Schools Among the Freedmen," *Sunday-School World* 13 (Feb. 1873), 17–18; Benjamin W. Arnett, ed., *The Budget. Containing Annual Reports of the General Officers of the African Methodist Episcopal Church* (N.p., 1886), pp. 231–39; Anderson, "Ex-Slaves and the Rise of Universal Education," p. 9. See also Peter Kolchin, *First Freedom: The Responses of Alabama's Blacks to Emancipation and Reconstruction* (Westport, Conn.: Greenwood Press, 1972), pp. 87–88.

11. American Sunday School Union, *Eighth Annual Report* (Philadelphia, 1832), pp. 43–55; *Historical Statistics of the United States From Colonial Times to 1970* (Washington, D.C.: Government Printing Office, 1972); *First International (Sixth National) Sunday-School Convention, Baltimore, May 11–13, 1875* (Newark, N.J.: W. F. Sherwin, 1875), pp. 134–35. For a general discussion of 19th-century literacy rates, see Lee Soltow and Edward Stevens, *The Rise of Literacy and the Common School in the United States: A Socioeconomic Analysis to 1870* (Chicago: University of Chicago Press, 1981), esp. chap. 4. For a comparison of northern and southern attitudes toward schooling, see William H. Pease and Jane H. Pease, *The Web of Progress: Private Values and Public Styles in Boston and Charleston, 1828–1843* (New York: Oxford University Press, 1985), pp. 108–14.

12. Harrison, *Forty Years of Pioneer Life,* pp. 184–221; Edward H. McCullagh, *"The Sunday-School Man of the South." A Sketch of the Life and Labors of the Rev. John McCullagh* (Philadelphia: American Sunday-School Union, 1889), pp. 58–166; Edmund L. Starling, *History of Henderson County, Kentucky* (Henderson, Ky.: n.p., 1887), pp. 412–61; "An Appeal from the West," *American Sunday-School Magazine* 7 (Oct. 1830), pp. 310–11; Asa Bullard, *Incidents in a Busy Life. An Autobiography* (Boston: Congregational Sunday-School and Publishing Society, 1888), p. 21. See also Kaestle, *Pillars of the Republic,* pp. 182–217; David Tyack and Elisabeth Hansot, *Managers of Virtue: School Leadership in America, 1820–1980* (New York: Basic Books, 1982), pp. 39–63; Ellen Harriet Thomsen, "The Interest of the Eastern Churches in Western Emigration, 1830–1839" (Master's thesis, Columbia University, 1947), pp. 21–22; and

David Marion McCord, "Sunday School and Public School: An Exploration of their Relationship with Special Reference to Indiana, 1790–1860" (Ph.D. diss., Purdue University, 1976), pp. 58–79.

13. *The Sunday Schools of the First Presbyterian Church in Newark, New Jersey* (Newark: n.p., 1914), pp. 3–12; *Semi-Centennial of the Sunday School of the First Presbyterian Church in Utica,* pp. 5–40, 173–76 (quotations, 26 and 175); East Boston, Meridian Street Methodist Episcopal Sunday School, Minutes, 1878, New England Methodist Historical Society, Boston University School of Theology Library. See also Philadelphia Sabbath-School Association, *Annual Report* (Philadelphia, 1859), pp. 3–5; and George Stewart, Jr., *A History of Religious Education in Connecticut to the Middle of the Nineteenth Century* (New Haven: Yale University Press, 1924), p. 339.

14. American Sunday School Union, *Thirty-Fifth Annual Report* (Philadelphia, 1859), p. 21; American Sunday School Union Missions Committee, "Report on Educational Work in Wisconsin," 1843–1857, compiled by J. W. Vail, American Sunday School Union Papers; "Corey manuscript" (autobiography), American Sunday School Union Papers, PHS.

15. John Adams, *Testimony of the Value of the Labors of Sunday School Missionaries* (Philadelphia: American Sunday-School Union, [1855]), p. 6; J. M. Peck to Frederick A. Packard, Sept. 3, 1845, Packard correspondence, American Sunday School Union Papers, PHS.

16. "Sabbath-School in Nantucket, Massachusetts," *Religious Intelligencer* 5 (Jan. 6, 1821), pp. 521–22; Stephen Paxson to Mr. Willet's Church, June 30, 1859, American Sunday School Union Papers, PHS; "Sabbath Schools in Marietta," *Religious Intelligencer* 3 (Jan. 23, 1819), pp. 540–41.

17. John Henry Hobart, *The Beneficial Effects of Sunday Schools Considered* (New York: New York Protestant Episcopal Sunday School Union, 1818), p. 28; "Bible, Charity and Sunday School Society of the County of York, Pa.," *Religious Intelligencer* 3 (Feb. 27, 1819), p. 630; Boston Society for the Moral and Religious Instruction of the Poor, *First Annual Report* (Boston, 1817), p. 5; New-York Sunday-School Union Society, *Fourth Annual Report* (New York, 1820), p. 28; "Virginia," *American Sunday-School Magazine* 5 (November 1828), p. 341; American Sunday School Union, *Twenty-Ninth Annual Report* (Philadelphia, 1853), p. 47. See also Methodist Episcopal Sunday School Union, *Annual Report* (New York, 1870), p. 33. Urban missionary groups sponsored Sunday schools at houses of refuge and prisons. By 1833, reported prison reformer E. C. Wines, "a Sabbath school had come to be looked upon as an essential element in a good system of prison discipline" ("Sabbath Schools in Prisons," Prison Association of New York, *Twenty-Fourth Annual Report, 1868* [Albany: Argus, 1869], p. 391).

18. *Sabbath School Treasury* 1 (July 1828), p. 5; Philadelphia Sunday School Union, Minutes, Oct. 24, 1840, PHS; Daniel Walker Howe, ed., *Victorian America* (Philadelphia: University of Pennsylvania Press, 1978), p. 24. For 19th-century views on the relationship between common schools and social order, see Carl F. Kaestle, *The Evolution of an Urban School System: New York City, 1750–1850* (Cambridge: Harvard University Press, 1973), chap. 4; Schultz, *The Culture Factory,* chap. 5; and Soltow and Stevens, *The Rise of Literacy,* pp. 16, 71–73.

19. E. P. Thompson, *The Making of the English Working Class* (New York: Pantheon, 1964), pp. 375–79; Laqueur, *Religion and Respectability,* pp. 147–58, 241–45. Two

works that adopt Thompson's position, erroneously in my view, are Anthony F. C. Wallace, *Rockdale: The Growth of an American Village in the Early Industrial Revolution* (New York: Alfred A. Knopf, 1978), pp. 308–12, 318–22; and Barbara M. Tucker, *Samuel Slater and the Origins of the American Textile Industry* (Ithaca, N.Y.: Cornell University Press, 1984), p. 44. Throughout her book, Tucker argues that worker culture helped shape industrial practices. Yet in discussing Sunday schools, she reverses the argument, claiming that they were "the principal agency" through which workers' children learned specific values. A more consistent interpretation might view the schools' teachings as expressions of family values.

20. Tucker, *Samuel Slater,* pp. 75–76, 163–74.

21. Bruce Laurie clarifies divisions within the antebellum working class and demonstrates the appeal of evangelical religion to one segment in *Working People of Philadelphia, 1800–1850* (Philadelphia: Temple University Press, 1980).

22. *The Texas Banner,* Oct. 21, 1847, clipping in Scrapbook no. 1, American Sunday School Union Papers, PHS; W. H. Simpson to the American Sunday School Union, July 4, 1858, American Sunday School Union Papers, PHS. On Paxson, see B. Paxson Drury, *A Fruitful Life: A Narrative of the Experiences and Missionary Labors of Stephen Paxson* (Philadelphia: American Sunday-School Union, 1882), pp. 18–50. The quotations are from Paxson's letters to Richard B. Westbrook, Feb. 22, 1861, and A. W. Corey, Aug. 13, 1861, American Sunday School Union Papers, PHS.

23. Philadelphia Sabbath School Association, Minutes, [Jan. 1856], PHS; Philadelphia, Pine Street Third Presbyterian Church Sunday School, Minutes and Reports, Jan. 17, 1859, PHS; *A Visit of One Thousand Sabbath School Teachers of Massachusetts to New York and Brooklyn* (Boston: Published by the Committee of Arrangements, 1855), p. 64; E. D. Jones, "The Mission Sunday-School," *Sunday School Workman* 1 (Jan. 1, 1870), p. 2; E. D. Jones, *The Benton Street Mission Sunday School* (St. Louis: Published for the School, 1861), pp. 52–53, 13–14; Philo Adams Otis, *The First Presbyterian Church, 1833–1913: A History of the Oldest Organization in Chicago* (Chicago: Fleming H. Revell, 1913), pp. 294–304; North End Mission, *The North Street Beacon Light* (Boston: E. Tourjee, 1874), p. 3; *The North End Mission* (Boston: n.p., 1870), pp. 3–8; Philadelphia, Bethany Sabbath School Association, Executive Board, Minutes, Feb. 23, Mar. 8, 1875; Bethany Sabbath School Teachers' Association, Minutes, Dec. 28, 1874, PHS.

24. Baltimore, McKendrean Sabbath School Society, Minutes, Nov. 3, 1821, LLMM; Philadelphia Sunday and Adult School Union, *Second Annual Report* (Philadelphia, 1819), p. 36; "Pittsburgh Sabbath School Association First Annual Report," *Religious Intelligencer* 3 (Mar. 13, 1819), p. 660; Boston Society for the Moral and Religious Instruction of the Poor, *Third Annual Report* (Boston, 1819), pp. 14–15; Baltimore, McKendrean Sabbath School Society, Minutes, Nov. 1, 1823, LLMM. See also Providence Association of Sabbath School Teachers, Records, Nov. 15, 1847 RIHS; and Kaestle, *Pillars of the Republic,* pp. 45–46.

25. Letters of Andrew Adgate to the Rev. A. Hemphill, in Asbury Sunday School Society, Minutes, July 14, 1821, LLMM; *Semi-Centennial of the Sunday School of the First Presbyterian Church of Utica,* pp. 57–58. See also Frank Glenn Lankard, *A History of the American Sunday School Curriculum* (New York: Abingdon Press, 1927), p. 134; and Edwin Wilbur Rice, *The Sunday-School Movement, 1780–1917, and the American Sunday-School Union, 1817–1917* (Philadelphia: American Sunday-School Union, 1917), pp. 52 and 76.

26. "The Reward System," *American Sunday-School Magazine* 5 (Nov. 1828), p. 322; [Robert Baird], "American Sunday-School Union," *Biblical Repertory and Princeton Review* 2 (1830), p. 220; letter of S. Wells Williams in *Semi-Centennial of the Sunday School of the First Presbyterian Church of Utica*, pp. 35–36; Lankard, *Sunday School Curriculum*, pp. 142–49.

27. "Plan for the Management of a Class," *American Sunday-School Magazine* 2 (Jan. 1825), p. 9; Boston Society for the Religious and Moral Instruction of the Poor, *Eleventh Annual Report* (Boston, 1827), pp. 9–10.

28. Baltimore Female [McKendrean] Sabbath School Society, Constitution, 1816, LLMM; Elizabeth, N.J., Sunday School Teachers' Association, Minutes, Apr. 2, 1827, PHS; *Constitution of the Female Sabbath School Society of the Second Baptist Church* (Boston, 1817), p. 6; *Semi-Centennial of the Sunday School of the First Presbyterian Church of Utica*, p. 97.

29. J. H. Temple, *History of the First Sabbath School in Framingham, Mass., from 1816 to 1868* (Boston: Printed for the Author, 1868), p. 67; Sabbath School Missionary Association of the Fourteenth Street Presbyterian Church of New York, *First Report* (New York, 1857), pp. 3–4; Henry Anstice, *History of St. George's Church in the City of New York, 1752–1811–1911* (New York: Harper and Bros., 1911), pp. 204–5; *Sunday-School World* 7 (April 1867), p. 54. See also Providence Association of Sabbath School Teachers, Records, Oct. 18, 1852, RIHS.

30. New-York Sunday-School Union Society, *Second Annual Report* (New York, 1818), p. 5; American Sunday School Union, *Seventh Annual Report* (Philadelphia, 1831), pp. 28–29.

31. Philadelphia Sunday and Adult School Union, *Sixth Annual Report* (Philadelphia, 1823), pp. 11–12; Methodist Episcopal Sunday School Union, Board of Managers Minutes, Feb. 10, 1829 and May 26, 1829, NYPL; American Sunday School Union, *Directions for the Formation of Sunday Schools* (Philadelphia, 1829), p. 11; American Sunday School Union, *Second Annual Report* (Philadelphia, 1826), pp. xxv–xxxii; New-York Sunday School Union, *Fifteenth Annual Report* (New York, 1831), appendix; "Tabular Statement," Cook County Sabbath School Convention, *Proceedings* (Chicago: Church, Goodman and Donnelley, 1864), unpaginated; Rice, *Sunday-School Movement*, pp. 146–47, 186–87. On the relationships among libraries, literacy, and character training, see Soltow and Stevens, *Rise of Literacy*, pp. 62–65, 81–82.

32. *Sunday School in the Mountains* (Philadelphia: American Sunday-School Union, 1862), p. 25; Robert Baird, *Religion in America* (New York: Harper and Bros., 1844), p. 154; Baltimore, McKendrean Sabbath School Society, Minutes, Nov. 1, 1828, LLMM.

33. New York, Seventh Presbyterian Church Sunday School Teachers' Association, Minutes, Dec. 3, 1857, PHS; Providence Association of Sabbath School Teachers, Records, July 26, 1847, RIHS. The book titles are taken from American Baptist Publication Society, *Thirty-Eighth Annual Report* (Philadelphia, 1862), pp. 19–23. See also Anne Scott Macleod, *A Moral Tale: Children's Fiction and American Culture, 1820–1860* (Hamden, Conn.: Archon, 1975), p. 158.

34. Kaestle, *Pillars of the Republic*, pp. 76–99; Massachusetts Sabbath School Union report, in American Sunday School Union, *Second Annual Report*, p. 10; *Sunday-School Journal and Advocate of Christian Education* 2 (Mar. 14, 1832), p. 42.

35. American Sunday School Union, *Ninth Annual Report* (Philadelphia, 1833), p.

18; Benjamin W. Chidlaw, *The Story of My Life* (Cleves, Ohio: Published for the Author, 1890), p. 190. See also Stewart, *Religious Education in Connecticut*, p. 333. For examples of Fourth of July speeches, see Gabriel P. Disosway, "Oration at the Sunday Schools of Petersburg, Virginia, on the Fourth of July, 1826," *Christian Advocate* 1 (Sept. 23, 1826); and "Sunday-School Celebration," in *The Works of William H. Seward*, ed. G. E. Baker (Boston, 1884), vol. 3, pp. 208–10. On secular republican celebrations of the Fourth, see Laurie, *Working People of Philadelphia*, p. 82.

36. William Oland Bourne, *History of the Public School Society of the City of New York* (New York: William Wood, 1870), p. 27; *American Sunday-School Magazine* 1 (July 1824), p. 2; James Milnor, *Address Delivered Before the Superintendents, Teachers and Pupils of the Sunday Schools Attached to St. George's Church, Sunday, November 9, 1817* (New York: Published at the Request of the Board of Officers of the New-York Sunday-School Union Society, 1817), p. 10; Boston Society for the Moral and Religious Instruction of the Poor, *Third Annual Report*, (Boston, 1819) p. 14; *Ninth Annual Report* (Boston, 1825), p. 4.

37. The text of the 1827 law is printed in William Kailer Dunn, *What Happened to Religious Education? The Decline of Religious Teaching in the Public Elementary School* (Baltimore: Johns Hopkins Press, 1968), pp. 96–97. American Sunday School Union, *Sixth Annual Report* (Philadelphia, 1830), p. 29; *Sunday-School Journal and Advocate of Religious Education* 5 (May 20, 1835), p. 89; *Address of Thomas S. Grimké, at a Meeting in Charleston, South Carolina, March 29, 1831* (Philadelphia: American Sunday-School Union, 1831), pp. 4 and 9.

38. Charles Hodge, "Introductory Lecture Delivered in the Theological Seminary, Princeton, Nov. 7, 1828," *Biblical Repertory and Princeton Review* 1 (1829), pp. 86–87.

39. On "moral education," see Kaestle, *Pillars of the Republic*, pp. 31–61, 66–71; and Michael B. Katz, *The Irony of Early School Reform: Educational Innovation in Mid-Nineteenth-Century Massachusetts* (Cambridge: Harvard University Press, 1968), pp. 109–11, 128–29.

40. American Sunday School Union, *Fourteenth Annual Report* (Philadelphia, 1838), p. 23. The Mann-Packard correspondence is printed in Raymond Culver, *Horace Mann and Religion in the Massachusetts Public Schools* (New Haven: Yale University Press, 1929), pp. 241–84; the quotation is from p. 242.

41. Culver, *Horace Mann*, pp. 247, 246, and 249.

42. Ibid., pp. 273, 267, 242, 267, and 266. Packard expanded on these views in *The Question, Will the Christian Religion Be Recognized as the Basis of the System of Public Instruction in Massachusetts? Discussed in Four Letters to the Rev. Dr. Humphrey, President of Amherst College* (Boston: Whipple and Damrell, 1839), esp. pp. 10–11. For other expressions of this viewpoint, see Lyman Beecher's address in *Proceedings of the Public Meeting Held in Boston, to aid the American Sunday School Union in their Efforts to Establish Sunday Schools Throughout the Valley of the Mississippi* (Philadelphia: American Sunday-School Union, [1831]), pp. 16–19; and Baltimore, McKendrean Sabbath School Society, Minutes, Oct. 16, 1837, LLMM.

43. Culver, *Horace Mann*, pp. 278 and 281 (italicized in the original); letter of Richard S. Storrs to Mann, Feb. 20, 1839, printed in ibid., pp. 98–101 (quotation, 99).

44. On the 1840 controversy, see ibid., pp. 134–36; and Carl F. Kaestle and Maris A. Vinovskis, *Education and Social Change in Nineteenth-Century Massachusetts* (Cam-

bridge: Cambridge University Press, 1980), pp. 208–32. The quotation is from [Packard], *Four Letters to Dr. Humphrey*, p. 6.

45. Charles Hodge to Frederick A. Packard, April 25, 1841, Packard letters, American Sunday School Union Papers, PHS. On the New York legislature's decision, see Cremin, *American Education: The National Experience*, p. 168. On denominational schools, see Lewis Joseph Sherrill, *Presbyterian Parochial Schools, 1846–1870* (New Haven: Yale University Press, 1932), pp. 20–29. See also James W. Alexander to John Hall, August 1840, in *Forty Years' Familiar Letters of James W. Alexander, D.D., Constituting, with the Notes, A Memoir of His Life*, ed. John Hall (New York: Charles Scribner, 1860), vol. 1, p. 312.

46. James W. Alexander to John Hall, Aug. 21, 1834, in Hall, *Familiar Letters*, vol. 1, p. 217; Theodore Dwight, Jr., to Frederick A. Packard, Aug. 23, 1841, Packard letters, American Sunday School Union Papers, PHS.

47. Sermon of George W. Bethune in American Sunday School Union, *Twenty-Third Annual Report* (Philadelphia, 1847), p. 20; Sermon of H. V. D. Johns in *Twenty-Fourth Annual Report* (Philadelphia, 1848), pp. 6–24; [Frederick A. Packard], "Religious Instruction in the Common Schools," *Biblical Repertory and Princeton Review* 13 (July 1841), p. 322; Packard, *The Daily Public School in the United States* (Philadelphia: J. B. Lippincott, 1865).

3. SUNDAY SCHOOL ORGANIZATIONS

1. For example, New York teachers had formed the Female Union Society for the Promotion of Sabbath Schools and the New-York Sunday-School Union Society in 1816. Bostonians had formed the Society for the Moral and Religious Instruction of the Poor in 1817, the same year Philadelphians organized the Sunday and Adult School Union. See Joanna Bethune to Frederick A. Packard, Aug. 4, 1829, Packard Letters, Gratz Collection, HSP; Boston Society for the Moral and Religious Instruction of the Poor, *First Annual Report* (Boston, 1817), p. 1; Philadelphia Sunday and Adult School Union, Constitution and Minutes, May 13–July 1, 1817, American Sunday School Union Papers, PHS.

2. Philadelphia Sunday and Adult School Union, *Seventh Annual Report* (Philadelphia, 1824), pp. 68–72. On the formation of the American Sunday School Union, see Edwin W. Rice, *The Sunday-School Movement, 1780–1817, and the American Sunday-School Union, 1817–1917* (Philadelphia: American Sunday-School Union, 1917), pp. 78–79; Ralph R. Smith, Jr., "'In Every Destitute Place': The Mission Program of the American Sunday School Union, 1817–1834" (Ph.D. diss., University of Southern California, 1973), pp. 124–51; Philadelphia Sunday and Adult School Union, Constitution and Minutes, Oct. 14, 1817–Mar. 4, 1824; and Philadelphia Sunday and Adult School Union, Letterbook, May 6–Dec. 11, 1823, both in American Sunday School Union Papers, PHS. The Philadelphia Union had been formed by a group of young teachers (including two women—Sarah Brown and Emma Whitehead) who quickly recruited an older and more prominent all-male group to be its officers. See Philadelphia Sunday and Adult School Union, Constitution and Minutes, May 13, 1817–Jan. 4, 1818, PHS; and Anne M. Boylan, "Presbyterians and Sunday Schools in Philadelphia, 1800–1824," *Journal of Presbyterian History* 58 (Winter 1980), pp. 299–310.

3. Lists of managers appeared in the yearly *Annual Reports* of the American Sunday School Union. The most important sources for information on their backgrounds are: *The Dictionary of American Biography*, 20 vols. (New York: Scribner's, 1928–1936); *The National Cyclopedia of American Biography*, 62 vols. to date (New York: J. T. White, 1892–1984); *The Biographical Encyclopedia of Pennsylvania* (Philadelphia: Galaxy Publishing Co., 1874); *The Pennsylvania Magazine of History and Biography* 3 (1879), p. 165; 4 (1880), pp. 414–500; 32 (1908), p. 399; 35 (1911), pp. 276–89; and 55 (1931), pp. 174–86; *The Philadelphia Directory for 1817* (Philadelphia: n.p., 1817); *The Philadelphia Index, or Directory for 1824* (Philadelphia: Robert Desilver, 1824); *The Philadelphia Directory and Stranger's Guide for 1825* (Philadelphia: Bioren, 1825); Henry Simpson, *Lives of Eminent Philadelphians* (Philadelphia: William Brotherhood, 1859); Abraham Ritter, *Philadelphia and her Merchants* (Philadelphia: n.p., 1860); Stephen N. Winslow, *Biographies of Successful Philadelphia Merchants* (Philadelphia: n.p., 1864); Rice, *Sunday-School Movement*, pp. 51, 95–99, 136–38; "Presbyterian Evangelical Society of Philadelphia," *Presbyterian Historical Society Journal* 5 (1909–1910), pp. 150–54; Anna M. Holstein, *Swedish Holsteins in America* (Norristown, Pa.: n.p., 1892); Samuel Small, *Genealogical Records of . . . William Geddes Latimer . . .* (Philadelphia: J. B. Lippincott, 1905); Emily Claxton, ed., *John Claxton and his Family, 1791–1900* (1968); *In Memory of Levi Knowles, 1813–1898* (Privately printed, 1898); and Robert Ellis Thompson, ed., *The Life of George H. Stuart, Written by Himself* (Philadelphia: J. M. Stoddart, 1890).

4. On Porter, see Philadelphia Sunday and Adult School Union, Minutes, Apr. 1 and May 6, 1824, PHS; American Sunday School Union, Board of Managers, Minutes, June 3 and 14, 1824, American Sunday School Union Papers, PHS; Joseph W. Porter, *A Genealogy of the Descendants of Richard Porter* (Bangor, Maine: Buna and Robinson, 1878), p. 275; and Smith, " 'In Every Destitute Place,' " pp. 59–60. On Packard, see *The Dictionary of American Biography* 7, pp. 127–28; "Frederick A. Packard," *Princeton Review*, index volume, 1868, pp. 265–71; and George H. Griffin, *Frederick A. Packard. A Memorial Discourse Given in the First Church, Springfield, October 19, 1890* (Philadelphia: American Sunday-School Union, 1890). See also Rice, *Sunday-School Movement*, pp. 91–99, 136–38, 174–75; and Anne M. Boylan, " 'The Nursery of the Church': Evangelical Protestant Sunday Schools, 1820–1880" (Ph.D. diss., University of Wisconsin, 1973), pp. 157–64. A few other men held full-time positions with the union for briefer periods: John Hall was assistant publications editor from 1832 to 1841; Robert Baird was general agent from 1829 to 1834; and Richard B. Westbrook was secretary of missions during the 1850s. On Baird, see Michael R. H. Swanson, "Robert Baird and the Evangelical Crusade in America, 1820–1860" (Ph.D. diss., Case Western Reserve University, 1971).

5. In addition to the sources cited in n. 3, see Edward Pessen, *Riches, Class, and Power before the Civil War* (Lexington, Ky.: D. C. Heath, 1973), esp. pp. 327–31.

6. See sources cited in n. 3 and Boylan, "Presbyterians and Sunday Schools," pp. 306–07.

7. Norris Stanley Barratt, *An Outline History of Old St. Paul's Church* (Philadelphia: n.p., 1917), pp. 226–80; E. P. Beadle, *The Old and the New, 1743–1876: The Second Presbyterian Church of Philadelphia* (Philadelphia: n.p., 1876), pp. 129 and 136ff.; Hughes Oliphant Gibbons, *A History of Old Pine Street* (Philadelphia: John C. Winston,

1905), pp. 147–79; Stephen Tyng, *Forty Years' Experience in Sunday Schools* (New York: Sheldon, 1866), pp. 40–41; Alexander Henry to Thomas Latimer, Nov. 25, 1810, Gratz Collection, HSP. On the split between High and Low Church Episcopalians, see Robert Bruce Mullin, *Episcopal Vision/American Reality: High Church Theology and Social Thought in Evangelical America* (New Haven: Yale University Press, 1986), pp. 26–59.

8. First Day Society, Board of Managers, Minutes, Jan. 9 and July 9, 1823; Jan. 12, 1825; and Jan. 1826, PHS; Philadelphia Association of Male Sunday School Teachers, Minutes, June 30, 1824–Mar. 21, 1831, PHS; Philadelphia City Sunday School Union, Minutes, 1826–1829, PHS; Philadelphia Sunday School Union, Minutes, May 8 and July 10, 1841, and Mar. 26 and esp. Sept. 24, 1842, PHS.

9. In addition to the sources cited in n. 5, see James P. Wickersham, *A History of Education in Pennsylvania* (Lancaster, Pa.: Inquirer Publishing Co., 1886), pp. 286–89; Joseph J. McCadden, *Education in Pennsylvania, 1801–1835* (Philadelphia: University of Pennsylvania Press, 1937), pp. 156, 182, and 202; *Hazard's Register of Pennsylvania* 2 (1828), pp. 28–29, and 3 (1829), pp. 187–89; Philadelphia House of Refuge, *First Annual Report* (Philadelphia, 1829), p. 14, and *Eighth Annual Report* (1836), pp. 22–23; *An Account of the Origins, Progress, and Present Condition of the Philadelphia Society for the Establishment and Support of Charity Schools* (Philadelphia, 1831), pp. 47–60; *The Ludwick Institute, 1799–1947, with a Biographical Sketch of Christopher Ludwick* (Philadelphia: n.p., 1947), pp. 10–12; O. A. Pendleton, "Poor Relief in Philadelphia, 1790–1840," *Pennsylvania Magazine of History and Biography* 70 (Apr. 1946), pp. 168–69; and Young Men's Colonization Society of Pennsylvania, undated broadside, American Sunday School Union Papers, PHS.

10. The historical literature interpreting the social ideology of these men and others like them is voluminous. Works presenting them as conservative defenders of a hierarchical order include Clifford S. Griffin, *Their Brothers' Keepers: Moral Stewardship in the United States, 1800–1865* (New Brunswick, N.J.: Rutgers University Press, 1960), pp. 3–22; Paul Boyer, *Urban Masses and Moral Order in America, 1820–1920* (Cambridge: Harvard University Press, 1978), pp. viii and 34; Anthony F. C. Wallace, *Rockdale: The Growth of an American Village in the Early Industrial Revolution* (New York: Alfred A. Knopf, 1978), pp. 318–22; and Raymond Mohl, "The Urban Missionary Movement in New York City, 1800–1825," *Journal of Religious History* 7 (Dec. 1972), pp. 110–28. Other historians have viewed them in a more positive light; see Lois W. Banner, "Religious Benevolence as Social Control: A Critique of an Interpretation," *Journal of American History* 60 (1973), pp. 23–41; Carroll Smith Rosenberg, *Religion and the Rise of the American City: The New York City Mission Movement, 1812–1870* (Ithaca, N.Y.: Cornell University Press, 1971), pp. 6–8; and M. J. Heale, "Humanitarianism in the Early Republic: The Moral Reformers of New York, 1776–1825," *Journal of American Studies* 2 (1968), pp. 161–75.

The quotations are from Archibald Alexander, *Suggestions in Vindication of Sunday Schools* (Philadelphia: American Sunday-School Union, 1829), pp. 8–9; *American Sunday-School Magazine* 5 (Nov. 1828), p. 341; James W. Alexander to Frederick A. Packard, Dec. 18, 1840, Gratz Collection, HSP; and Philadelphia Sunday and Adult School Union, *Fifth Annual Report* (Philadelphia, 1822), p. 81.

11. Packard was active in the Whig party in an effort to nominate Theodore Frelinghuysen for vice-president because he believed Frelinghuysen to be a representative of

"public virtue, morality and religion." Porter was briefly involved in a nativist Protestant association. See Lucius Q. C. Elmer to Packard, Jan. 24 and Jan. 30, 1843; and Henry W. Green to Packard, Mar. 1844, both in Packard letters, American Sunday School Union Papers, PHS. On Whig politics, see Daniel Walker Howe, *The Political Culture of the American Whigs* (Chicago: University of Chicago Press, 1979), esp. pp. 23–42.

12. Frederick A. Packard to Samuel Lathrop, Feb. 11, 1826, Hartmann Manuscripts, New-York Historical Society; James W. Alexander to Packard, Dec. 18, 1840, Gratz Collection, HSP; Henry W. Green to Packard, Mar. 1844, Packard Letters, American Sunday School Union Papers, PHS; Ezra Stiles Ely, *"The Duty of Christian Freemen to Elect Christian Rulers." A Discourse Delivered on the Fourth of July in the Seventh Presbyterian Church in Philadelphia, With an Appendix, Designed to Vindicate the Liberty of Christians and of the American Sunday School Union* (Philadelphia: n.p., 1828). The charter fight is covered in Smith, " 'In Every Destitute Place,' " pp. 189–96; Rice, *Sunday-School Movement*, pp. 130–32; and Charles I. Foster, *An Errand of Mercy: The Evangelical United Front, 1790–1837* (Chapel Hill: University of North Carolina Press, 1960), p. 185. On the evangelicals' critics, see Wallace, *Rockdale*.

13. James W. Alexander, *The American Sunday School and its Adjuncts* (Philadelphia: American Sunday-School Union, 1856), p. 282; Joseph H. Dulles to Frederick A. Packard, Aug. 20, 1835, Packard Letters, American Sunday School Union Papers, PHS; John Henry Hobart, *The Beneficial Effects of Sunday Schools Considered* (New York: New York Protestant Episcopal Sunday School Union, 1818), p. 28; American Sunday School Union, *Seventeenth Annual Report* (Philadelphia, 1841), pp. 25–28. See also Robert T. Handy, *A Christian America: Protestant Hopes and Historical Realities* (New York: Oxford University Press, 1971), pp. 27–64.

14. Lewis Ashhurst Journal, 4 vols., 1834–1874, Richard Ashhurst Papers, HSP.

15. Ibid., Jan. 10 and 21–22, and Nov. 12, 1834; Nov. 26, 1840; June 7, 1841; and Sept. 16–Oct. 6, 1857. For a fuller discussion of the Porter scandal and its aftermath, see Boylan, " 'The Nursery of the Church,' " pp. 118–27. The managers' handling of the scandal is detailed in American Sunday School Union, Board of Managers, Minutes, Sept. 21–Nov. 24, 1857, and in the minutes of a series of special meetings between Oct. 6 and Nov. 17, 1857, box 130 of American Sunday School Union Papers, PHS. The quotations are from John McCullagh to R. B. Westbrook, Oct. 7, 1857, and S. B. S. Bissell to Westbrook, Oct. 1, 1857, American Sunday School Union Papers, PHS. For analyses of other antebellum moralists like Ashhurst, see Howe, *American Whigs*, pp. 30–34, and Daniel T. Rodgers, *The Work Ethic in Industrial America, 1850–1920* (Chicago: University of Chicago Press, 1978), pp. 11–12.

16. Mohl, "Urban Missionary Movement," p. 110; Donald M. Scott, *From Office to Profession: The New England Ministry, 1750–1850* (Philadelphia: University of Pennsylvania Press, 1978), pp. 33–48. For examples of the thinking of these men, see James W. Alexander to John Hall, July 5, 1838, in *Forty Years' Familiar Letters of James W. Alexander, D.D., Constituting, With the Notes, a Memoir of his Life*, ed. John Hall, (New York: Charles Scribner, 1860), vol. 1, p. 266; and L. Q. C. Elmer to Frederick A. Packard, Jan. 30, 1843, Packard Letters, American Sunday School Union Papers, PHS.

17. On the importance of self-control to antebellum moralists, see Rodgers, *Work Ethic*, pp. 14–17; and Daniel Horowitz, *The Morality of Spending: Attitudes toward the*

Consumer Society in America, 1875–1940 (Baltimore: Johns Hopkins University Press, 1985), pp. 6–13.

18. James W. Alexander to John Hall, Sept. 14, 1832, in Hall, Familiar Letters, vol. 1, p. 196. On the Protestant press in the 19th century, see Joan Jacobs Brumberg, *Mission for Life: The Story of the Family of Adoniram Judson* (New York: Free Press, 1980), pp. 44–78. For statements on the importance of influencing children, see Alexander, *The American Sunday School,* pp. 42–44, 276–86; New-York Sunday-School Union Society, *Fourth Annual Report* (New York, 1820), pp. 28–29; "Extract from a Report from Carlisle, Pennsylvania," *Religious Intelligencer* 3 (Oct. 1818), pp. 316–17; *Sunday-School Journal and Advocate of Christian Education* 2 (Mar. 14, 1832), p. 42; American Sunday School Union, *Tenth Annual Report* (Philadelphia, 1834), pp. 23–25, and *Seventeenth Annual Report* (1841), pp. 27–28. See also, Howe, *American Whigs,* pp. 157–59.

19. See Rice, *Sunday-School Movement,* pp. 92–94; Smith, " 'In Every Destitute Place,' " pp. 124–51.

20. See American Sunday School Union, *First Annual Report* (Philadelphia, 1825), appendix, pp. 58–94. For evidence on how the web of connections worked, see the folder of responses to a questionnaire sent out by the union in 1832, American Sunday School Union Papers, PHS. The results of the questionnaire are summarized in *Sunday-School Journal and Advocate of Christian Education* 2 (Oct. 10, 1832), pp. 162–63.

21. Paul M. Harrison, ed., *Forty Years of Pioneer Life. A Memoir of John Mason Peck, D.D. Edited from his Journals and Correspondence by Rufus Babcock* (Carbondale: Southern Illinois University Press, 1965), pp. 55–71, 184–210; Smith " 'In Every Destitute Place,' " pp. 129, 134–36.

22. On the Mississippi Valley Enterprise, see Smith, " 'In Every Destitute Place', " pp. 110–15; Bertram Wyatt-Brown, *Lewis Tappan and the Evangelical War Against Slavery* (Cleveland: Case Western Reserve University Press, 1969), pp. 49–52; American Sunday School Union, *Sixth Annual Report* (Philadelphia, 1830), pp. 3–4, and *Eighth Annual Report* (1832), p. 35. On the Southern Enterprise, see John Wells Kuykendall, *Southern Enterprize: The Work of National Evangelical Societies in the Antebellum South* (Westport, Conn.: Greenwood Press, 1982); American Sunday School Union, *Ninth Annual Report* (Philadelphia, 1833), p. vi.

23. "Instructions to Missionaries," Feb. 23, 1825, Minutes of the Committee on Missions, American Sunday School Union Papers, PHS; *Instructions of the Committee on Missions of the American Sunday School Union to its Missionaries* (Philadelphia, 1862); Swanson, "Robert Baird," pp. 148–55.

24. Boylan, " 'The Nursery of the Church,' " pp. 193–98. See also, Joseph H. McCullagh, *"The Sunday-School Man of the South." A Sketch of the Life and Labors of the Rev. John McCullagh* (Philadelphia: American Sunday-School Union, 1889), pp. 72–109.

25. B. Paxson Drury, *A Fruitful Life: A Narrative of the Experiences and Missionary Labors of Stephen Paxson* (Philadelphia: American Sunday-School Union, 1882), pp. 105–12; B. W. Chidlaw, *The Story of My Life* (Cleves, Ohio: published for the author, 1890), p. 155; Shepherd Knapp, *A History of the Brick Presbyterian Church in the City of New York* (New York: Trustees of Brick Presbyterian Church, 1909), pp. 229–30; letter to the editor, *Daily State Journal* (Indianapolis), Jan. 15, 1849, in scrapbook no. 1, American Sunday School Union Papers, PHS; Swanson, "Robert Baird," p. 163.

26. For examples of an author's work, see Hall, *Familiar Letters,* vol. 1, pp. 184, 192–93, 195, 203–5, 215, and 219; the quotation is from Frederick A. Packard, *The Teacher Taught; An Humble Attempt to Make the Path of the Sunday-School Teacher Straight and Plain,* 2d ed. (Philadelphia: American Sunday-School Union, 1861), p. 14. Materials in the Gratz Collection, HSP, offer insights into how the union's publications editor solicited and received contributions. See, for example, the letters to Frederick A. Packard from Mary M. Cornelius of the 1840s; from Frederick A. Adams, 1836–1842; from Mary Anne Hooker, Mar. 11, 1842; from Charles Hodge, 1842–1845; and from T. H. Gallaudet, Oct. 7, 1829.

27. American Sunday School Union, *Catalog,* 3d ed. (Philadelphia, 1825), 25th ed. (1840), and 60th ed. (1863); Rice, *Sunday-School Movement,* pp. 160–64. See also Ellen Shaffer, "The Children's Books of the American Sunday School Union," *American Book Collector* 17 (Oct. 1966), pp. 20–28.

28. Smith, " 'In Every Destitute Place,' " pp. 173–74; Judith Wellman, "The Burned-Over District Revisited: Religion and Social Reform in Upstate New York, 1820–1850" (Ph.D. diss., State University of New York, Buffalo, 1976), pp. 167–70; American Sunday School Union, *Fourteenth Annual Report* (Philadelphia, 1838), pp. 23–25; B. W. Chidlaw to George Scofield, Apr. 7, 1852, American Sunday School Union Papers, PHS.

29. For an analysis of the long-distance flow of information through newspapers and the mail, see Allan R. Pred, *Urban Growth and the Circulation of Information: The United States System of Cities, 1790–1840* (Cambridge: Harvard University Press, 1973), pp. 20–103.

30. In their book, *Managers of Virtue: School Leadership in America, 1820–1980* (New York: Basic Books, 1982), p. 36, David Tyack and Elisabeth Hansot suggest that the union possessed a "complex bureaucracy" with "an elaborate organization" and "national marketing system." "Because of its centralized corporate structure," they write, "the American Sunday School Union was far more bureaucratized in operation than any state public-school system, at least until the Progressive era. Indeed, it anticipated the bureaucratization of city schools in the latter part of the nineteenth century." For the view that the union was part of a "benevolent empire" in which "leadership . . . was exercised through a series of interlocking directorates, composed of a relatively small number of prominent clergymen and philanthropists," see Gilbert Hobbs Barnes, *The Antislavery Impulse, 1830–1844,* 2d ed. (New York: Harcourt, Brace and World, 1964), pp. 18–19.

31. Smith, " 'In Every Destitute Place,' " pp. 143–44, 177–90; American Sunday School Union, *Sixth Annual Report* (Philadelphia, 1830), p. 22. As late as 1876, the union had more missionaries in New York, Pennsylvania, and Ohio than in, for instance, Missouri, Arkansas, or Indian Territory (see Minutes of the Committee on Missions and List of Missionaries, 1876), PHS. Relations with the New York auxiliary can be traced in the New York Sunday School Union, Board of Managers, Minutes, 1865–1875, PHS.

32. Wellman, "Burned-Over District," pp. 158–62; Rhode Island Sunday School Union Records, Apr. 7, 1830; May 12 and 19, 1834; Oct. 20, 1836; May 4 and July 21, 1847; Jan. 19, 1849; and April 30, 1860, RIHS; American Sunday School Union, Board of Managers, Minutes, Nov. 18, 1851; June 8, 1855; and Jan. 4, 1856, PHS; Smith, " 'In Every Destitute Place,' " pp. 256–57.

33. I. B. Parlin to F. W. Porter, Jan. 4, 1858; Frederick A. Packard to Porter, July 3 and

Aug. 7, 1848, American Sunday School Union Papers, PHS. See also Smith, " 'In Every Destitute Place,' " pp. 130–31.

34. American Sunday School Union, Board of Managers, Minutes, Dec. 21, 1827, PHS; American Sunday School Union, *Eighteenth Annual Report* (Philadelphia, 1842), p. 46; American Sunday School Union, Board of Managers, Minutes, Nov. 14, 1847, PHS; Richard Westbrook to F. W. Porter, Oct. 16, 1854, American Sunday School Union Papers, PHS. See also Swanson, "Robert Baird," pp. 159–66.

35. Smith, " 'In Every Destitute Place,' " p. 129; J. H. Dulles to Frederick A. Packard, Aug. 20, 1835, Gratz Collection, HSP; Edwin W. Rice, "A Short History of the Union's Finances," pp. 3–9 (typescript in American Sunday School Union Papers, PHS); Swanson, "Robert Baird," pp. 167–71. On the Porter scandal, see Boylan, " 'The Nursery of the Church,' " pp. 118–22; American Sunday School Union, Board of Managers, Minutes, Sept. 21, 1857–June 15, 1858, PHS. See also American Sunday School Union, Board of Managers, Minutes, Oct. 15, 1855 (on finances); and Minutes of the Committee on Depositories, 1853–1860, PHS.

36. "Address of the Committee of Publication," *American Sunday-School Magazine* 1 (Oct. 1824), p. 97; "The Publication Department of the American Sunday School Union—Its Scope and Design," *Sunday-School Journal* 26 (June 6, 1855), p. 84; American Sunday School Union, Minutes of the Committee of Publication, 1850–1857, Oct. 14, 1874, PHS; Packard, *The Teacher Taught*, pp. 33–34.

37. Robert Baird to F. W. Porter, Sept. 20, 1832; H. Dyer, H. Boardman, and John W. Dulles to the American Sunday School Union, Nov. 1854; R. B. Westbrook to Porter, Dec. 16, 1854, American Sunday School Union Papers, PHS. "The West," *Sunday-School Journal* 6 (Jan. 20, 1836), p. 149; Swanson, "Robert Baird," pp. 156–62.

38. General Protestant Episcopal Sunday School Union, *First Annual Report* (New York, 1827), pp. 17–21; Clifton Hartwell Brewer, *A History of Religious Education in the Episcopal Church to 1835* (New Haven: Yale University Press, 1924), pp. 152–53; Addie Grace Wardle, *History of the Sunday School Movement in the Methodist Episcopal Church* (New York: Methodist Book Concern, 1918), p. 72; Methodist Episcopal Sunday School Union, Board of Managers, Minutes, Mar. 6–May 30, 1827, NYPL; Massachusetts Sabbath School Union, *First Annual Report* (Boston, 1826); Marianna C. Brown, *Sunday School Movements in America* (Chicago: Fleming H. Revell, 1901), pp. 140–42; Daniel Gurden Stevens, *The First Hundred Years of the American Baptist Publication Society* (Philadelphia: American Baptist Publication Society, [1924]), pp. 21–23; Willard M. Rice, *History of the Presbyterian Board of Publication and Sabbath School Work* (Philadelphia: Presbyterian Board of Publication, [1887]), pp. 8–19.

39. Methodist Episcopal Sunday School Union, Board of Managers, Minutes, May 30, 1827, NYPL; Brewer, *Religious Education*, pp. 183–85 (quotation, 184); "Second Circular to Members of the Protestant Episcopal Church in the United States," in General Protestant Episcopal Sunday School Union, *First Annual Report* (New York, 1827), pp. 17–18.

40. *Review of the Annual Report of the St. Louis Sunday Schools Auxiliary to the Sunday School Union of the Methodist Episcopal Church* (Philadelphia: American Sunday-School Union, 1831), p. 7; American Sunday School Union, *Fourteenth Annual Report* (Philadelphia, 1838), pp. 26 and 29; Smith, " 'In Every Destitute Place,' " p. 218. See also American Sunday School Union, Board of Managers, Minutes, Apr. 8, 1828, PHS, and *Ninth Annual Report* (Philadelphia, 1833), pp. 16–17.

41. For a good discussion of how doctrinal controversies within a denomination affected its Sunday schools, see Clifton Hartwell Brewer, *Early Episcopal Sunday Schools (1814–1865)* (Milwaukee: Morehouse, 1933), pp. 121–26.

42. American Sunday School Union, *Eighth Annual Report* (Philadelphia, 1832), pp. 36–37, footnote; J. E. Welch to F. W. Porter, Aug. 23, 1830, American Sunday School Union Papers, PHS; Swanson, "Robert Baird," pp. 165–66. The quotations are from L. B. Tousley to Porter, Oct. 15, 1851, and Rufus Babcock to Porter, Nov. 1850, American Sunday School Union Papers, PHS.

43. American Sunday School Union, *Eighth Annual Report* (Philadelphia, 1832), p. 14 (list of missionaries' religious affiliations); Rufus Babcock to F. W. Porter, Aug. 18, 1851, American Sunday School Union Papers, PHS.

44. Rhode Island Sunday School Union, Records, Jan. 31, 1843, RIHS; Massachusetts Sabbath School Society, *First Annual Report* (Boston, 1833), p. 5; William Ewing, *The Sunday-School Century. Containing a History of the Congregational Sunday School and Publishing Society* (Boston: Pilgrim Press, 1918), pp. 16–22; New England Sabbath School Union, *First Annual Report* (Boston, 1837); C. R. Blackall, *A Story of Six Decades* (Philadelphia: American Baptist Publication Society, 1885), p. 48. When the Massachusetts Sabbath School Union split, one-third of its capital went to the Baptists, who later organized the Massachusetts Baptist Sabbath School Union, which became the New England Baptist Sabbath School Union in 1836 and was absorbed by the American Baptist Publication Society in 1856. Two-thirds went to the Congregationalists, who founded the Massachusetts Sabbath School Society. In New York, Methodists maintained their own "Methodist branch" within the male and female unions, but separated to form the Methodist Episcopal Sunday School Union in 1827.

45. Massachusetts Sabbath School Society, *Sixth Annual Report* (Boston, 1838), p. 7; *Eighteenth Annual Report* (1850), pp. 6–7; Board of Managers, Minutes, June 10 and 24, 1844, Congregational Library, Boston.

46. Massachusetts Sabbath School Society, *Sixth Annual Report* (Boston, 1838), pp. 6–7; Methodist Episcopal Sunday School Union, Board of Managers, Minutes, May 30, 1827, NYPL. For examples of doctrine found in magazines for children, see *The Well-Spring* (published by the Massachusetts Sabbath School Society) 1 (Jan. 4, 1844), and 7 (July 26, 1850).

47. Wilson Smith, *Professors and Public Ethics: Studies of Northern Moral Philosophers before the Civil War* (Ithaca, N.Y.: Cornell University Press, 1956), pp. 204–8; Timothy L. Smith, *Revivalism and Social Reform: American Protestantism on the Eve of the Civil War* (2d ed., New York: Harper and Row, 1965), pp. 80–94; Handy, *A Christian America*, pp. 30–42.

48. American Sunday School Union, *First Annual Report* (Philadelphia, 1825), p. 88; M. B. Goodwin, "History of Schools for the Colored Population in the District of Columbia," *Report of the U.S. Commissioner of Education, 1868* (Washington, D.C.: Government Printing Office, 1871), pp. 193–300; Smith, " 'In Every Destitute Place,' " pp. 205–7 (quotation, p. 205).

49. Smith, " 'In Every Destitute Place,' " pp. 221 and 223. See also Kuykendall, *Southern Enterprize*, pp. 76–77.

50. "Instructions to Missionaries," American Sunday School Union, Minutes of the Committee on Missions, Feb. 23, 1825, American Sunday School Union Papers, PHS; ibid., June 25, 1833, quoted in Smith, " 'In Every Destitute Place,' " p. 224. See also

American Sunday School Union, *Eighth Annual Report* (Philadelphia, 1832), p. 32; and Kuykendall, *Southern Enterprize,* pp. 78–79.

51. American Sunday School Union, *Sixteenth Annual Report* (Philadelphia, 1840), p. 8; Kuykendall, *Southern Enterprize,* pp. 98–115 (quotation, 108).

52. Wyatt-Brown, *Lewis Tappan,* pp. 49–52; F. A. Packard to Tappan, Feb. 11, 1848, in Tappan, ed., *Letters Respecting a Book "Dropped from the Catalogue" of the American Sunday School Union in Compliance with the Dictation of the Slave Power* (New York: American and Foreign Anti-Slavery Society, 1848), pp. 23–25.

53. Tappan, *Letters,* pp. 101–2, (footnotes 23–26). See also Boylan, " 'The Nursery of the Church,' " pp. 103–6. Other national societies, such as the American Tract Society, had similiar experiences with abolitionists like Tappan; see Louis Filler, *The Crusade Against Slavery, 1830–1860* (New York: Harper and Row, 1960), pp. 259–63; Kuykendall, *Southern Enterprize,* pp. 133–45; and John R. McKivigan, *The War against Proslavery Religion: Abolitionism and the Northern Churches, 1830–1865* (Ithaca, N.Y.: Cornell University Press, 1984), pp. 120–25.

54. On abolitionist tactics, see Aileen S. Kraditor, *Means and Ends in American Abolitionism: Garrison and his Critics on Strategy and Tactics, 1834–1856* (New York: Pantheon, 1969), pp. 239–40; and Ronald G. Walters, *The Antislavery Appeal: American Abolitionism after 1830* (Baltimore: Johns Hopkins University Press, 1976), pp. 37–53. On the Wisconsin episode, see J. W. Vail to F. W. Porter, Oct. 5, 1852, American Sunday School Union Papers, PHS.

55. E. B. Cleghorn to R. B. Westbrook, Feb. 1, 1858; E. S. Robinson to F. W. Porter, Aug. 14, 1856; W. B. Truax to J. Henry Burtis, Aug. 1, 1860, American Sunday School Union Papers, PHS.

56. American Sunday School Union, Board of Managers, Minutes, Oct. 20, 1857–Jan. 10, 1861; Missions Committee, Minutes, Feb. 18 and 28, 1861, PHS; Lewis Ashhurst Journal, Jan. 17, 1860–Jan. 10, 1861, HSP; James Alexander quoted in F. A. Packard to W. J. Cheyney, [Sept. 1859?], American Sunday School Union Papers, PHS. The 1857–1861 crisis is discussed in more detail in Boylan, " 'The Nursery of the Church,' " pp. 122–27.

57. E. E., "The National Sunday School Convention of 1869," *National Sunday School Teacher* 4 (June 1869), pp. 161–64. On the convention movement in general, see Robert W. Lynn and Elliott Wright, *The Big Little School: Sunday Child of American Protestantism* (New York: Harper and Row, 1971), pp. 56–60.

58. On early conventions, promoted by the Methodist Sunday school editor Daniel P. Kidder and the American Sunday School Union editor Frederick A. Packard, see "Normal Classes for Teachers," *Sunday School Advocate* 7 (Oct. 3, 1848), p. 1; "Training Schools for S. S. Teachers," *Sunday-School Journal* 26 (Mar. 7, 1855), p. 36; "Training Classes for Teachers," ibid. 29 (Oct. 6, 1858), pp. 148–49; Methodist Episcopal Sunday School Union, *Annual Report* (New York, 1847), pp. 46–48, 111–15; *Annual Report* (1849), pp. 83–91; American Sunday School Union, *Thirty-Fifth Annual Report* (Philadelphia, 1859), pp. 9–10; and *A Visit of One Thousand Sabbath School Teachers of Massachusetts to New York and Brooklyn, 1855* (Boston: Published by the Committee of Arrangements, 1855). On the 1859 convention, see "National Sunday-School Convention," *Sunday-School Times* 1 (Jan. 22, 1859), p. 1; "The Great National Convention of Sunday School Teachers," ibid. (Mar. 5, 1859), entire issue.

59. "Great National Convention," *Sunday-School Times* 1 (Mar. 5, 1869); *The Third National Sunday-School Convention of the United States, Newark, April 28–30, 1869* (Philadelphia: J. C. Garrigues, 1869), pp. 10–11, 153–54. [This was referred to as the third convention because organizers counted one held in 1832 as the first national convention and the one held in 1859 as the second.]

60. *Third National Sunday-School Convention*, pp. 153–60. See also E. Morris Fergusson, *Historic Chapters in Christian Education in America* (New York: Fleming H. Revell, 1935), pp. 30–36; and George S. Cottman, "Indiana's First Sunday-School Convention," *Indiana Magazine of History* 6 (June 1910), pp. 89–90.

61. Rev. John Vincent speech, in Cook County Sabbath School Convention, *Proceedings* (Chicago: Church, Goodman and Donnelley, 1864), pp. 10–12; New York State Sunday School Teachers' Association, *Proceedings of the Annual Convention* (various places: Published for the Association, 1862–1869); Pennsylvania State Sabbath School Association, Manuscript Records, 1862–1880, 2 vols., HSP, vol. 1, unpaginated; Lynn and Wright, *Big Little School*, pp. 56–58.

62. *Proceedings of the New York Sunday School Institute* (New York, 1867); New York State Sunday School Teachers' Association, *Proceedings of the Thirteenth Convention* (Elmira: Published for the Association, 1868), pp. 1–105. See also Ned Harland Dearborn, *The Oswego Movement in American Education* (New York: Teachers' College, Columbia University, 1925; New York: Arno Press, 1969), pp. 48–51.

63. Rice, *Sunday-School Movement*, pp. 165–69; Wardle, *History of the Sunday School Movement*, pp. 99–100; Rice, *History of the Presbyterian Board of Publication and Sabbath-School Work*, pp. 74–113; Lemuel Clark Barnes and Mary Clark Barnes, *Pioneers of Light: The First Century of the American Baptist Publication Society, 1824–1924* (Philadelphia: American Baptist Publication Society, [1924]), pp. 320–21.

64. H. Clay Trumbull to Maurice A. Wurts, Mar. 2, 1865, American Sunday School Union Papers, PHS.

65. Leon H. Vincent, *John Heyl Vincent: A Biographical Sketch* (New York: Macmillan, 1925), pp. 81–133, 234–39; J. H. Vincent, "The Autobiography of Bishop Vincent," *Northwestern Christian Advocate* 58 (Apr. 13, June 1, June 22, June 29, July 13, July 20, Aug. 3, and Aug. 24, 1910); J. H. Vincent, *The Chautauqua Movement* (Boston: Chautauqua Press, 1886), pp. 2–32.

66. J. H. Vincent, "How I Was Educated," *The Forum* 1 (June 1866), pp. 338, 346, and 341; L. H. Vincent, *John Heyl Vincent*, pp. 82 and 90; J. H. Vincent, "Autobiography," *Northwestern Christian Advocate* 58 (1910), pp. 974 and 847.

67. J. H. Vincent, "Autobiography," *Northwestern Christian Advocate* 58 (1910), pp. 562, 715, 846–47.

68. H. Clay Trumbull, "Circular Letter," Sept. 1858, American Sunday School Union Papers, PHS; Philip E. Howard, *The Life Story of Henry Clay Trumbull: Missionary, Army Chaplain, Editor and Author* (New York: International Committee of YMCAs, 1906), pp. 10–18, 42–44, 136–72, 292–340; Trumbull to M. A. Wurts, Aug. 31, 1871, American Sunday School Union Papers, PHS; Edwin Wilbur Rice, *After Ninety Years* (Philadelphia: American Sunday-School Union, 1924), pp. 39–93; *Sunday-School World* 17 (Oct. 1878), entire issue devoted to the new Bible translation.

69. Howard, *Henry Clay Trumbull*, pp. 81–90, 255–59; Rice, *After Ninety Years*, pp. 58–60.

70. On Jacobs, See John Richard Sampey, *The International Lesson System: The History of its Origin and Development* (New York: Fleming H. Revell, 1911), pp. 56–57; on Lewis Miller, see Ellwood Hendrick, *Lewis Miller: A Biographical Essay* (New York: G. P. Putnam's Sons, 1925), pp. 50–53, 90–94; on Stuart, see Robert Ellis Thompson, ed., *The Life of George H. Stuart, Written by Himself* (Philadelphia: J. M. Stoddart, 1890).

71. On the YMCAs and the 1857 revival, see Marion L. Bell, *Crusade in the City: Revivalism in Nineteenth-Century Philadelphia* (Lewisburg, Pa.: Bucknell University Press, 1977), pp. 178–88. On the Chicago and Philadelphia YMCAs, see Emmett Dedmon, *Great Enterprises: 100 Years of the YMCA of Metropolitan Chicago* (New York: Rand-McNally, 1957), pp. 20–55; James F. Findlay, Jr., *Dwight L. Moody: American Evangelist, 1837–1899* (Chicago: University of Chicago Press, 1969), pp. 72–73, 106, 118–19; and Thompson, *George H. Stuart*, pp. 94–102. See also David I. Macleod, *Building Character in the American Boy: The Boy Scouts, the YMCA and their Forerunners, 1870–1920* (Madison: University of Wisconsin Press, 1983).

72. Thompson, *George H. Stuart*, pp. 110–70; Griffin, *Their Brothers' Keepers*, pp. 260–63.

73. Cook County Sabbath School Convention, *Proceedings* (1864), pp. 2–4, 9–12; Illinois State Sunday School Convention, *Proceedings of the Ninth Annual Convention* (Decatur, 1867), pp. 41–42; Henry C. McCook, "From our Muster-Roll of Heroes," *The Development of the Sunday-School, 1780–1905* (Boston: Executive Committee of the International Sunday-School Association, 1905), pp. 24–36.

74. Edward Eggleston, "Organized to Death," *Sunday School Teacher* 1 (Oct. 1866), pp. 297–98; Fergusson, *Historic Chapters*, pp. 30–34.

75. On union missionaries' involvement in local conventions during the 1850s, see Mrs. W. E. Boardman, *Life and Labors of the Rev. W. E. Boardman* (New York: D. Appleton and Co., 1887), pp. 101–5; Circular Letter of the Connecticut State Sunday School Teachers' Association, Sept. 1858, American Sunday School Union Papers, PHS; and H. Clay Trumbull to Richard B. Westbrook, June 24 and 30, 1859, American Sunday School Union Papers, PHS.

76. W. P. Paxson to Maurice A. Wurts, Dec. 12 and Sept. 30, 1867, American Sunday School Union Papers, PHS.

77. Kentucky State Sabbath School Association, *Proceedings of the Ninth Convention* (Lexington, 1874), pp. 3–30.

78. Fergusson, *Historic Chapters*, pp. 36, 44–46.

79. E. W. Rice to Richard B. Westbrook, June 14, 1860, American Sunday School Union Papers, PHS.

80. W. R. Port to A. W. Corey, Jan. 18, 1869; Port to M. A. Wurts, Feb. 19, 1869; H. Foote to Adams, Blackmer and Lyon (publishers of *The National Sunday School Teacher*), Mar. 1, 1869, copy; Edward Eggleston to Rev. H. L. Hammond, Mar. 6, 1869, copy, all in American Sunday School Union Papers, PHS.

81. H. Clay Trumbull to M. A. Wurts, Apr. 12, 1869; G. Lentz to Wurts, Apr. 29, 1869, American Sunday School Union Papers, PHS.

82. B. F. Jacobs, D. L. Moody, William Reynolds, A. G. Tyng, and P. G. Gillett to J. Bennett Tyler, Nov. 5, 1869, American Sunday School Union Papers, PHS. In this letter, they recommended Frederick G. Ensign for the job of superintendent of missions in the

Midwest. He accepted and became one of the union's stalwart workers for 35 years. See Rice, *Sunday-School Movement,* pp. 279–80. For Ensign's idea of a statistical survey, see F. G. Ensign to M. A. Wurts, June 10, 1870, American Sunday School Union Papers, PHS.

83. E. D. Jones, Clinton B. Fisk, Henry C. McCook, J. M. Brawner, and H. M. Blossom, Memorial to the American Sunday School Union, [St. Louis?] (1869); A. W. Corey to M. A. Wurts, Dec. 14, 1868; William P. Paxson to Wurts, June 16, 1870; J. Bennett Tyler to Wurts, June 18, 1869, all in American Sunday School Union Papers, PHS.

84. H. Clay Trumbull to M. A. Wurts, Apr. 12, 1869; A. W. Corey to Wurts, Mar. 5, 1869; J. Bennett Tyler to Wurts, June 29, 1869, all in American Sunday School Union Papers, PHS.

85. For a fuller discussion of precursors to the uniform lessons, see Boylan, " 'The Nursery of the Church,' " pp. 309–12; Frank Glenn Lankard, *A History of the American Sunday School Curriculum* (New York and Cincinnati: Abingdon Press, 1927), pp. 179–234; and Rice, *Sunday-School Movement,* pp. 304–7.

86. Rice, *Sunday-School Movement,* pp. 298–301.

87. *The Fifth National Sunday-School Convention, Held at Indianapolis, April 16, 17, 18, 19, 1872* (New York: A. O. Van Lennep, 1872), pp. 91–93; Edward Eggleston, "Unpopular Words," *Sunday School Times* 18 (May 20, 1876), p. 321; Lankard, *Sunday School Curriculum,* pp. 233–34.

88. Fergusson, *Historic Chapters,* pp. 36, 44–46; Gerald E. Knoff, *The World Sunday School Movement: The Story of a Broadening Mission* (New York: Seabury Press, 1979), pp. 1–97.

4. SUNDAY SCHOOL TEACHERS

1. Miron Winslow, *Memoir of Mrs. Harriet L. Winslow, Thirteen Years a Member of the American Mission in Ceylon* (New York: American Tract Society, 1840), pp. 29–30, 34, 37–40, 64–66.

2. Richard Albert Edward Brooks, ed., *The Diary of Michael Floy, Jr. Bowery Village, 1833–1837* (New Haven: Yale University Press, 1941), November 8–9, 1833, pp. 14–17; October 8–16, 1833, pp. 3–5; Dec. 5, 1834, p. 123; January 7–14, 1836, pp. 212–13.

3. Winslow, *Memoir,* pp. 18 and 25; Brooks, *Diary of Michael Floy, Jr.,* Nov. 8, 1833, p. 14. For a concise analysis of conversion narratives, see Martha Tomhave Blauvelt, "Society, Religion, and Revivalism: The Second Great Awakening in New Jersey, 1780–1830" (Ph.D. diss., Princeton University, 1975), pp. 212–28.

4. Brooks, *Diary of Michael Floy, Jr.,* Feb. 28–Mar. 2, 1834, p. 65; Hiram Peck Diary, 1830–1847, New-York Historical Society, New York, first leaves contain his lists of "needful counsel," rules for living, and resolutions; the quotation is from the entry of Dec. 31, 1830. See also B. K. Peirce, *One Talent Improved: or, The Life and Labors of Miss Susan B. Bowler, Successful Sunday School Teacher* (New York: Carlton and Porter, 1845).

5. See Paul Boyer, *Urban Masses and Moral Order in America, 1820–1920* (Cambridge: Harvard University Press, 1978), pp. 62–65.

6. American Sunday School Union, *Second Annual Report* (Philadelphia, 1826), pp. xxv–xxxii; Boston Sabbath School Union, *First Annual Report* (Boston, 1830), p. 5, and *Eleventh Annual Report* (1840), p. 29; *Sunday-School Facts: Collected by a Member of the General Association of Teachers* (New York: D. H. Wickham, 1821), pp. 10–11; New-York Sunday School Union, *Thirty-First Annual Report* (New York, 1847), appendix.

7. American Sunday School Union, *Eighth Annual Report* (Philadelphia, 1832), p. 18. Writing in 1889, the Baptist pastor Nathan Wood suggested that teacher conversions were so common that "it might almost seem as if the chief good of the Sabbath-school was not to the pupils but to the teachers" (*The History of the First Baptist Church of Boston (1665–1889)* [Philadelphia: American Baptist Publication Society, 1889], p. 358).

8. Dorothy C. Barck, ed., *Letters from John Pintard to his Daughter, Eliza Noel Pintard Servoss, 1816–1833* (New York: New-York Historical Society, 1940), vol. 3, p. 87; Archibald Alexander, *Suggestions in Vindication of Sunday Schools* (Philadelphia: American Sunday-School Union, 1829), p. 7; McKendrean Female Sabbath School Society of Baltimore, Records, 1816–1843, Nov. 6, 1819, LLMM; George L. Prentiss, *Life and Letters of Elizabeth Prentiss* (New York: Anson D. F. Randolph, 1882), p. 35; Brooks, *Diary of Michael Floy, Jr.,* Nov. 6, 1833, p. 13; Dec. 3, 1833, p. 26; and Oct. 4, 1835, p. 187; Hiram Peck Diary, Nov. 28, 1830, New-York Historical Society. See also Andrew Lester Diary, 14 vols., 1836–1888, vol. 2, April 16, 1843, New-York Historical Society.

9. Hiram Peck Diary, Aug. 23, 1831; Bank Street [Methodist Episcopal] Mission Sunday School, Minutes, 1865–1868, June 12, July 10, Aug. 1, and Oct. 9, 1865, NYPL; Brooks, *Diary of Michael Floy, Jr.,* Oct. 25, 1833, p. 9; Nov. 24, 1833, p. 22 (quotation); Peirce, *One Talent Improved,* chap. 3, 5, 10–12. For an example of how teachers' meetings were conducted, see Philadelphia, Spruce Street Baptist Sabbath School Society Minutes, 1855–1857, American Baptist Historical Society, Rochester, N.Y. Of course, teachers also quarreled: see Brooks, *Diary of Michael Floy, Jr.,* Jan. 26, 1834, pp. 54–55, and Jan. 2, 1835, p. 131.

10. *Semi-Centennial of the Sunday School of the First Presbyterian Church of Utica* (Utica: The Church, 1866), pp. 65–67, 99–100 (on George Wilson; quotation, 65); pp. 14, 25, 29–30, 176–81 (on Truman Parmele).

11. Letter of Susan Burchard Taintor, ibid., pp. 41–43; Winslow, *Memoir,* pp. 203–30; Caroline Cowles Richards, *Village Life in America, 1852–1872* (New York: Henry Holt, 1912), pp. 198–99. Women teachers seem to have received gifts more often than men, but for an example of a male recipient, see Asbury Sunday School Society Records, 1817–1877, Jan. 11, 1846, LLMM.

12. Brooks, *Diary of Michael Floy, Jr.,* Dec. 1, 1833, p. 25; Nov. 24, 1834, pp. 120–121; July 5, 1835, p. 162 and footnote; Richards, *Village Life in America,* p. 133. Floy (pp. 248–50) also recorded the elopement of two teachers.

13. Brooks, *Diary of Michael Floy, Jr.,* Feb.–Mar. 1836, pp. 220–24; the proposal is recorded on Apr. 10, p. 230.

14. Diary of Hiram Peck, Nov. 28 and Dec. 5, 1830, New-York Historical Society; Richards, *Village Life in America,* pp. 132–33, 180.

15. New-York Sunday-School Union Society, *Fourth Annual Report* (New York,

1820), p. 8; *An Address Delivered Before the Sunday School of the Twelfth Congregational Society at their Sixth Anniversary, March 29, 1833. By one of the Superintendents* (Boston: n.p., 1833), p. 8.

16. New York, Seventh Presbyterian Sunday School Teachers' Association, Minutes, Nov. 29, 1839; May 26, 1843; May 28, 1852; Nov. 24, 1854; and May 31, 1860, PHS; *Address Delivered Before the Sunday School of the Twelfth Congregational Society*, p. 11; Asbury Sunday School Society Minutes, Apr. 10, 1855, LLMM.

17. Quoted in Shepherd Knapp, *A History of the Brick Presbyterian Church in the City of New York* (New York: Trustees of Brick Presbyterian Church, 1909), p. 223; New York, Seventh Presbyterian Church Sunday School Teachers' Association, Minutes, May 26, 1854, PHS. See also Asbury Sunday School Society, Minutes, Feb. 18, 1825, and Apr. 10, 1855, LLMM.

18. New York, Second Street Methodist Episcopal Church Sunday school, Minutes, 1867–1872, Oct. 14, 1867, NYPL; New York, Allen Street Methodist Episcopal Sunday School Society, Minutes, 1870–1880, Dec. 15, 1873, NYPL. See also Second Street Methodist Episcopal Church Sunday school, Minutes, June 14, 1869; New York, Dry Dock Mission Methodist Episcopal Sunday School Association, Minutes, 1847–1850, Sept. 8, 1847, NYPL; Boston, Harvard Street Baptist Sunday school, Records, 1860–1864, Jan. 15, 1860, Andover Newton Theological Seminary, Newton, Mass.; and Charlestown, Mass., Union Methodist Episcopal Sunday school, Records, 1847–1870, Aug. 13, 1865, Boston University School of Theology Library.

19. American Sunday School Union, *Sixth Annual Report* (Philadelphia, 1830), pp. 26–27.

20. Boston Society for the Religious and Moral Instruction of the Poor, *Sixth Annual Report* (Boston, 1822), pp. 10–12; Massachusetts Sabbath School Union, *First Annual Report* (Boston, 1826), p. 8; "New Hampshire Baptist Sabbath School Union," *American Sunday-School Magazine* 7 (Oct. 1828), p. 317; "Sunday-School Teachers' Convention—Report of the Committee on Interrogatories," *Sunday-School Journal and Advocate of Christian Education* 2 (Oct. 10, 1832), p. 162; New York, Seventh Presbyterian Sunday School Teachers' Association, Minutes, Mar. 16, 1831, PHS. For examples of schools that had a preponderance of female Bible classes, see Providence Association of Sabbath School Teachers, Records, 1827–1854, Feb. 15, 1830, and Nov. 15, 1847, RIHS. For an example of a coeducational Bible class, see Blandford, Mass., Methodist Episcopal Sunday school, Annual Reports, 1846–1866 and 1868–1881, esp. 1865, Boston University School of Theology Library.

21. "The Elder Scholars," *American Sunday-School Magazine* 2 (Feb. 1825), pp. 37–44 (quotation, 38). See also Philadelphia Association of Male Sunday School Teachers, Minutes, 1824–1831, Apr. 16, 1827, PHS, recommending Bible classes for "youth above the age of thirteen years," especially "those who begin to feel themselves men."

22. W. F. Lloyd, *The Teacher's Manual; or, Hints to a Teacher upon Being Appointed to the Charge of a Sunday School Class* (Philadelphia: American Sunday-School Union, 1825), p. 82; Frederick A. Packard, *The Teacher Taught: An Humble Attempt to Make the Path of the Sunday School Teacher Straight and Plain* (Philadelphia: American Sunday-School Union, 1839), p. 87; John Todd, *The Sabbath School Teacher: Designed to Aid in Elevating and Perfecting the Sabbath School System* (Northampton, Mass.: n.p., 1837), p. 68. For an article defining the "critical period" as ages eighteen to twenty,

see "Advice to Youth," *Youth's Instructor and Guardian* 4 (Apr. 1826), p. 114. Another Methodist publication defined sixteen and seventeen as problem ages; see "Our Elder Scholars," *Sunday School Advocate* 8 (June 19, 1849), p. 142. Most discussions, however, referred to "elder" pupils as thirteen- and fourteen-year-olds.

23. Lloyd, *Teacher's Manual*, p. 82; "The Elder Scholars," *American Sunday-School Magazine* 2 (Feb. 1825), p. 38; Packard, *Teacher Taught*, p. 89; Philadelphia Sunday School Union Minutes, 1840–1852, Feb. 13, 1845, PHS.

24. R. G. Pardee, *The Sabbath-School Index* (Philadelphia: J. C. Garrigues, 1868), p. 146; "The Elder Scholars," *American Sunday-School Magazine* (Feb. 1825), p. 38; "Western [New York] Sunday School Union," *Religious Intelligencer* 13 (Nov. 15, 1828), p. 390. See also Asa Bullard, *Fifty Years with the Sabbath Schools* (Boston: Lockwood, Brooks, 1876), p. 193.

25. Packard, *Teacher Taught*, p. 87; Lloyd, *Teacher's Manual*, p. 82.

26. Both the social construction and the experience of adolescence are sensitively explicated in Joseph Kett, *Rites of Passage: Adolescence in America, 1790 to the Present* (New York: Basic Books, 1977). Karen Halttunen discusses contemporary fears of the city in her insightful *Confidence Men and Painted Women: A Study of Middle-Class Culture in America, 1830–1870* (New Haven: Yale University Press, 1982). Barbara Welter and Carroll Smith-Rosenberg have pointed out, however, the extent to which historical and contemporary discussions of adolescence have been based on male experience. See Welter, "Coming of Age in America: The American Girl in the Nineteenth Century," in *Dimity Convictions: The American Woman in the Nineteenth Century* (Athens: Ohio University Press, 1976), pp. 3–20; and Smith-Rosenberg, "Puberty to Menopause: The Cycle of Femininity in Nineteenth-Century America," *Feminist Studies* (Winter 1973), pp. 58–72. Gerald Strauss's revealing analysis of Lutheran schooling during the sixteenth century offers a much-needed corrective to the notion that adolescence was a nineteenth-century discovery: *Luther's House of Learning: Indoctrination of the Young in the German Reformation* (Baltimore: Johns Hopkins University Press, 1978), pp. 55–56.

27. Address of Divie Bethune, in Philadelphia Sunday and Adult School Union, *Fifth Annual Report* (Philadelphia, 1822), pp. 81 and 83; James Milnor, *Address Delivered before the Superintendents, Teachers and Pupils of the Sunday Schools attached to St. George's Church, Sunday, November 9, 1817* (New York: Published at the Request of the New-York Sunday-School Union Society, 1817), p. 5; *Religious Intelligencer* 3 (Dec. 5, 1818), p. 431; *Sabbath School Herald* 1 (May 1829), pp. 76–77; Lloyd, *Teacher's Manual*, p. 82.

28. D. P. Kidder, ed., *The Sunday-School Teachers' Guide* (New York: Lane and Tippett for the Sunday-School Union of the Methodist Episcopal Church, 1846), pp. 252–53. See also Anne M. Boylan, "The Role of Conversion in Nineteenth-Century Sunday Schools," *American Studies* 20 (1979), pp. 35–48.

29. "Western [New York] Sunday School Union," *Religious Intelligencer* 13 (Nov. 15, 1828), p. 390; Packard, *Teacher Taught*, p. 88; O. P. Eaches, "The Perilous Period," *Sunday School Times* 12 (Jan. 8, 1870), p. 27.

30. Lydia Bacon to Elizabeth C., Feb. 15, 1821, in *Biography of Mrs. Lydia B. Bacon* (Boston: Massachusetts Sabbath School Society, 1856), pp. 115–16.

31. Barck, *Letters from John Pintard*, June 2, 1830, vol. 3, p. 151; [Abby Farwell

Ferry], *Reminiscences of John V. Farwell* (Chicago: Ralph Fletcher Seymour, 1928), vol. 1, p. 123; letter of Charles C. Curtis in *Semi-Centennial of the Sunday School of the First Presbyterian Church of Utica*, pp. 46–47.

32. Isaac Ferris, *Semi-Centennial Memorial Discourse of the New-York Sunday School Union, 25 February 1866* (New York: n.p., 1866), pp. 54–55. For examples of "auxiliary" teachers, see Philadelphia, Fifth Baptist Church Sunday School Teachers' Association, Minutes, 1855–1882, Dec. 2, 1867, American Baptist Historical Society, Rochester, N.Y.; and Philadelphia, North Tenth Street Presbyterian Church Sunday School Teachers' Association, Minutes, 1870–1880, April 15, 1870, PHS.

33. "New-York Sunday-School Union Society," *Religious Intelligencer* 5 (Dec. 2, 1820), p. 444; *Semi-Centennial of the Sunday School of the First Presbyterian Church of Utica*, pp. 39–40; J. E. Blake, comp., "History of the South Baptist Sabbath School, Boston," 1871 (MS at Andover Newton Theological Seminary Library), unpaginated; Brooks, *Diary of Michael Floy, Jr.*, Apr. 2, 1834, p. 74; "Sunday-School Prospects," *Sunday-School Journal* 21 (Mar. 6, 1850), p. 37; "Immaturity," *The Baptist Teacher* 8 (Apr. 1, 1877), p. 49.

34. Clifton Hartwell Brewer, *Later Episcopal Sunday Schools* (New York: Morehouse-Gorham, 1939), p. 55.

35. *Sunday-School Facts*, pp. 10–11; New-York Sunday School Union, *Fifteenth Annual Report* (New York, 1831), appendix; *Thirty-First Annual Report* (New York, 1847), appendix; New York, Seventh Presbyterian Church Sunday School Teachers' Association, Minutes, Nov. 27, 1839; May 26, 1843; and May 27, 1853, PHS; Philadelphia, First Presbyterian Church [Kensington] Sabbath School Association, Minutes, 1817–1840, 1817 and July 1826, PHS; "Norwich, Ct., Sabbath-School Union, Sixth Annual Report," *American Sunday-School Magazine* 7 (1830), p. 304. The Indiana survey is mentioned in David I. Macleod, *Building Character in the American Boy: The YMCA, the Boy Scouts and Their Forerunners* (Madison: University of Wisconsin Press, 1984), p. 44. The American Sunday School Union counted 20,910 male and 22,454 female teachers in its *Eighth Annual Report* (Philadelphia, 1832), p. 51. Although men still outnumbered women as common-school teachers in the early nineteenth century, by the end of the century most teachers were female. See David B. Tyack, *The One Best System: A History of American Urban Education* (Cambridge: Harvard University Press, 1975), pp. 59–65.

36. Barbara Welter, "The Feminization of American Religion, 1800–1860," in *Clio's Consciousness Raised: New Perspectives on the History of Women*, ed. Mary Hartman and Lois W. Banner (New York: Harper and Row, 1974), p. 138; Catharine Beecher, *Evils Suffered by American Women and Children* (New York: Harper and Bros., 1846), p. 10; General Protestant Episcopal Sunday School Union, *Fifth Annual Report* (New York, 1831), p. 63. See also Ruth C. Linton, "To the Promotion and Improvement of Youth: The Brandywine Manufacturers' Sunday School, 1816–1840" (Master's thesis, University of Delaware, 1981), pp. 66–80. Many historians have discussed changes in women's relationship to the evangelical sects in the nineteenth century; see esp. Ann Douglas, *The Feminization of American Culture* (New York: Alfred A. Knopf, 1977), pp. 17–139; Nancy Cott, *The Bonds of Womanhood: "Woman's Sphere" in New England, 1785–1835* (New Haven: Yale University Press, 1977), pp. 126–59; Kathryn Kish Sklar, *Catharine Beecher: A Study in American Domesticity*

(New Haven: Yale University Press, 1973), pp. 84–93 and 174–77; Mary P. Ryan, *Cradle of the Middle Class: The Family in Oneida County, New York, 1790–1865* (New York: Cambridge University Press, 1981); and Blauvelt, "Society, Religion, and Revivalism," pp. 180, 212–28.

37. New York, Seventh Presbyterian Church Sunday School Teachers' Association, Minutes, May 27, 1853, PHS; Boston Society for the Religious and Moral Instruction of the Poor, *Eleventh Annual Report* (Boston, 1827), p. 20; Brooks, *Diary of Michael Floy, Jr.*, July 6, 1836, p. 244. See also Providence Association of Sabbath School Teachers, Records, July 17 and August 21, 1837, RIHS, for a detailed discussion of how to recruit male teachers and students.

38. *Biography of Mrs. Lydia B. Bacon*, pp. 88–89; Brooks, *Diary of Michael Floy, Jr.*, Mar. 29, 1834, p. 74 (quotation); May 14–18, 1834, pp. 84–85 (description of his visits to the dying student and the child's death). For another example of a male teacher's emotions, see Andrew Lester Diary, vol. 2, Apr. 2, 1843, New-York Historical Society.

39. McKendrean Female Sabbath School Society Minutes, Nov. 3, 1831; Nov. 1, 1828; Oct. 4, 1836; Oct. 16, 1837; and Oct. 1, 1838, LLMM.

40. Macleod, *Building Character*, pp. 42–44; Packard, *Teacher Taught*, p. 162; report of Christ Church Sunday School, Middletown, Conn., in General Protestant Episcopal Sunday School Union, *Fifth Annual Report* (New York, 1831), p. 41.

41. Female Union Society for the Promotion of Sabbath Schools, *Second Annual Report* (New York, 1818), pp. 30–44; S. M. to Joanna Bethune, Mar. 22, 1818, ibid., p. 44; Female Union Society for the Promotion of Sabbath Schools, *Fourth Annual Report* (New York, 1820), p. 28. For a list of books the society printed, see the *Second Annual Report* (New York, 1818), p. 19; on anniversaries, see "Second Anniversary of the Female Union Society for the Promotion of Sabbath Schools," *Religious Intelligencer* 2 (May 2, 1818), p. 780; on annual budgets, see Female Union Society for the Promotion of Sabbath Schools, Minutes, 1825–1828, Dec. 18, 1827, Brooklyn Historical Society, Brooklyn, N.Y.; on 1821 statistics, see *Sunday School Facts*, p. 11.

42. Philadelphia Sunday and Adult School Union, *Third Annual Report* (Philadelphia, 1820), pp. 44–56; Philadelphia Sabbath School Association, *Annual Report* (Philadelphia, 1859), pp. 6–10. On separate "departments," see Female Union Society for the Promotion of Sabbath Schools, *Second Annual Report* (New York, 1818), p. 6. On officers of coeducational schools, see Philadelphia, North Tenth Street Presbyterian Church Sunday School Teachers' Association, Minutes, Apr. 15, 1870, PHS. For one exception, see Linton, "To the Promotion and Improvement of Youth," pp. 70–75. Opinions on whether schools should be segregated by sex varied. Frederick Packard (*Teacher Taught*, p. 93) argued against "promiscuous classification" of the sexes on the grounds that "unavoidable mischief attends it." James W. Alexander agreed (John Hall, ed., *Forty Years' Familiar Letters of James W. Alexander* [New York: Charles Scribner, 1860], vol. 1, p. 292). John Todd, however, in *The Sunday School Teacher*, pp. 254–58, argued that coeducational schools were preferable because "the sexes . . . modify and benefit each other, even from infancy" and because men were better qualified than women to make public addresses and lead public prayers.

43. McKendrean Female Sabbath School Society, Minutes, Aug. 4, 1821, LLMM; Asbury Sunday School Society, Minutes, June 29, 1829; Feb. 15, 1825 (quotation); and Oct. 1, 1835, LLMM; McKendrean Female Sabbath School Society, Minutes, Oct. 1843

(quotation); Asbury Sunday School Society, Minutes, Jan. 7, 1845, and Oct. 6, 1845 (on merger).

44. Copy of letter in Female Union Society for the Promotion of Sabbath Schools, Minutes, Feb. 19, 1826, Brooklyn Historical Society, Brooklyn, N.Y.; negotiating sessions reported in minutes of Mar. 8, April 3–4, and April 3[0], 1826; problems and dissolution of female union reported in minutes of July 11, 1827, and Feb. 13, 1828. On the reorganization of the New York Sunday School Union, see Board of Managers, Minutes, 1865–1875, Oct. 16, 1873, PHS.

45. McKendrean Female Sabbath School Society, Minutes, Oct. 16, 1837, LLMM; Louise T. Knauer, "Foot Soldiers in the Kingdom of God: Backgrounds and Motivations of Single Women Missionaries" (unpublished paper delivered at the Third Berkshire Conference on the History of Women, Bryn Mawr, Pa., June 9–11, 1976). The incoming correspondence in the Frederick A. Packard file, Gratz Collection, HSP, contains letters from some of the most prolific women writers for the American Sunday School Union, as does the Packard Correspondence in the American Sunday School Union Papers, PHS. See also Edwin W. Rice, *The Sunday-School Movement, 1780–1917, and the American Sunday-School Union, 1817–1917* (Philadelphia: American Sunday-School Union, 1917), pp. 209–10.

46. E. D. Jones, *The Benton Street Mission Sunday School* (St. Louis: n.p., 1868), pp. 20 and 23; Although advice writers frequently referred to teachers as substitute fathers, ministers, and pastors, I have found only one specific reference to teachers as substitute mothers: R. G. Pardee, *The Sabbath-School Index*, p. 11. On the general issue of women's separate institutions, see Estelle B. Freedman, "Separatism as Strategy: Female Institution Building and American Feminism, 1870–1930," *Feminist Studies* 5 (Fall 1979), pp. 512–29.

47. Blanche Glassman Hersh, *The Slavery of Sex: Feminist-Abolitionists in America* (Urbana: University of Illinois Press, 1978), pp. 136–38 (quotation, 137). See also Nancy A. Hewitt, *Women's Activism and Social Change: Rochester, New York, 1822–1872* (Ithaca, N.Y.: Cornell University Press, 1984), pp. 40–47; and Anne M. Boylan, "Women in Groups: An Analysis of Women's Benevolent Organizations in New York and Boston, 1797–1840," *Journal of American History* 71 (December 1984), pp. 497–523.

48. New York State Sunday School Teachers' Association, *Proceedings of the Eighth Convention* (Troy, 1863) and *Proceedings of the Twenty-Third Convention* (Albany, 1878), appendices; Kentucky State Sabbath School Association, *Proceedings of the Tenth Convention* (Lexington, 1875) and *Proceedings of the Thirteenth Convention* (Lexington, 1878), appendices; Illinois State Sunday School Convention, *Proceedings of the Ninth Annual Convention* (Decatur, 1867), pp. 117–36. For a fuller discussion of women's role in Sunday school work, see Anne M. Boylan, "Evangelical Womanhood in the Nineteenth Century: The Role of Women in Sunday Schools," *Feminist Studies* 4 (Oct. 1978), pp. 62–80.

49. Rev. James Pierce Root, "Woman's Work in the Sabbath School," *National Sunday School Teacher* 6 (Aug. 1871), pp. 281–84; J. W. Willmarth, "Women and Men in Sunday Schools," *Baptist Teacher* 5 (Oct. 1874), pp. 110–11; Jesse L. Hurlbut, *The Story of Chautauqua* (New York: G. P. Putnam's Sons, 1921), p. 77.

50. Ned Harland Dearborn, *The Oswego Movement in American Education* (New York: Teachers' College, Columbia University, 1925), pp. 34, 68–71, 94–100.

51. Miss Sara J. Timanus, "Pestalozzi in Sunday-School Work," *Sunday School Journal* 3 (Dec. 1871), pp. 266–67; idem, "Questioning," *National Sunday School Teacher* 6 (July 1871), pp. 245–49; idem, *The Infant School: Hints on Primary Religious Instruction* (Chicago: Adams, Blackmer, and Lyon, 1870); Herbert L. Westgate, "Official Report of the National Sunday School Teachers' Assembly," in Methodist Episcopal Sunday School Union and Tract Society, *1874 Yearbook* (New York, 1874), pp. 227–31; *National Sunday School Teacher* 9 (July 1874), p. 275, (report of her marriage). Matilda H. Kriege, "Kindergarten and Sunday School," *National Sunday School Teacher* 6 (Feb. 1871), pp. 41–43; "The Religious Training in Froebel's Kindergarten," ibid. (Sept. 1871), pp. 321–22; "Kindergarten and Sunday School," ibid. 7 (June 1872), pp. 208–10.

52. Boylan, "Evangelical Womanhood," pp. 75–76.

53. Jennie Fowler Willing, "Sunday-School Temperance Work," *National Sunday School Teacher* 4 (1869), pp. 293–94; "The Temperance Problem and who can Solve it," ibid. 12 (April 1877), pp. 142–44; Westgate, "Official Report," pp. 116–18; Helen E. Tyler, *Where Prayer and Purpose Meet: The WCTU Story, 1874–1949* (Evanston, Ill.: Signal Press, 1949), pp. 11–28; National Woman's Christian Temperance Union, *Minutes of the Second Convention* (Chicago, 1875), pp. 66–67; *Minutes of the Fourth Convention* (1877), pp. 202–03; *Minutes of the Fifth Convention* (1878), pp. 87–89; and *Minutes of the Sixth Convention* (1879), pp. 81–89. See also, Mary Earhart Dillon, "Frances Elizabeth Caroline Willard," *Notable American Women,* ed. Edward T. James, Janet Wilson James, and Paul Boyer (Cambridge: Harvard University Press, 1971), vol. 3, pp. 613–19; Theodore L. Agnew, "Jennie Fowler Willing," ibid., pp. 623–25; and Paul R. Messbarger, "Emily Clark Huntington Miller," ibid., vol. 2, pp. 541–42. (Miller was the sister-in-law of Lewis Miller, one of the founders of Chautauqua.)

54. Hurlbut, *Chautauqua,* pp. 77–79; Ruth Bordin, *Frances Willard: A Biography* (Chapel Hill: University of North Carolina Press, 1986), pp. 11 (quotation) and 86.

55. Cott, *Bonds of Womanhood,* pp. 126–59; Welter, "Feminization of American Religion," pp. 137–57; Douglas, *Feminization of American Culture,* pp. 17–69.

56. See also John G. Cawelti, *Apostles of the Self-Made Man* (Chicago: University of Chicago Press, 1966), chap. 2; and Lois W. Banner, "The Protestant Crusade: Religious Missions, Benevolence, and Reform in the United States, 1790–1840" (Ph.D. diss., Columbia University, 1970), chap. 7.

57. McKendrean Female Sabbath School Society, Minutes, Nov. 3, 1821, LLMM; New-York Sunday-School Union Society, *Hints on the Establishment and Regulation of Sunday Schools* (New York, 1817), p. 8. There is good evidence that teachers themselves saw their work primarily as emotional; see Andrew Lester Diary, vols. 2 and 3, 1843–1847, New-York Historical Society.

58. E. T. James, *The Sabbath School Teacher's Guide* (Philadelphia: Philadelphia Sunday and Adult School Union, 1818), p. 49; Todd, *Sabbath School Teacher,* pp. 105 and 113; Lloyd, *Teacher's Manual,* p. 65; Kidder, *Sunday-School Teacher's Guide,* p. 111–20; *Kindling; or A Way to Do it: By a Sabbath School Teacher* (New York: Published by the Author, 1856), pp. 21–31.

59. American Sunday School Union, *Directions for the Formation of Sunday Schools* (Philadelphia, 1829), p. 7; *Sabbath-School Treasury,* n. s., 5 (May 1841); Lloyd, *Teacher's Manual,* chap. 2; Erwin House, *The Sunday-School Hand-Book: A Companion for*

Pastors, Superintendents, Teachers, Senior Scholars, and Parents (Cincinnati: Hitchcock and Walden, 1868), pp. 19–22.

60. Hiram Peck Diary, December 31, 1830, New-York Historical Society; Sklar, *Catharine Beecher,* pp. 151–67; Carl Kaestle, *Pillars of the Republic: Common Schools and American Society, 1790–1860* (New York: Hill and Wang, 1983), p. 66.

61. Todd, *Sabbath School Teacher,* pp. 81–82 and chap. 3; "Marks of a Good Sabbath-School Teacher," *Sunday School Advocate* 1 (1841), p. 21; American Sunday School Union, *Directions for the Formation of Sunday Schools,* pp. 6–7; Daniel Wise, *Sunday-School Organization* (New York: Nelson and Phillips, 1857), pp. 23–29; Packard, *Teacher Taught,* pp. 84–86.

62. On converted as opposed to unconverted teachers, see Todd, *Sabbath School Teacher,* pp. 81–82; and Robert Baird, *Religion in America* (1844; New York: Harper and Row, 1970), p. 155.

63. J. H. Vincent, "The School System," *The Normal Class* 2 (Dec. 1876), p. 531.

64. Articles by William S. Palmer and Henry Clay Trumbull, *National Sunday School Teacher* 4 (Sept. 1869); S[ara] J. T[imanus], "Sunday-School Gleanings," ibid. 6 (July 1871), pp. 276–77.

65. Westgate, "Official Report," pp. 110–13 (address by Bishop Janes); pp. 250–52 (competitive examination).

66. Bishop Thomson address, Sunday School Union of the Methodist Episcopal Church, *Annual Report* (New York, 1869), p. 33; *The Normal Class* 1–2 (1875–76). A typical issue of the *Normal Class* (January 1876) contained a Scripture lesson, a guide for "older scholars" studying it, Hebrew readings from the Old Testament, and an article entitled "Greek in a Nutshell," as well as Sunday school news and correspondence. For other examples of attempts to promote normal classes, see E. D. Jones, "Normal Classes," Missouri Baptist Sunday School Convention, *Proceedings* (Glasgow, Mo.: n.p., 1872), pp. 26–27; and John Hall, et al., *Preparing to Teach: For Study by Sabbath-School Teachers and Training Classes* (Philadelphia: Presbyterian Board of Publication, 1875). Bullard's comment is from *Fifty Years with the Sabbath Schools,* p. 115. Bullard, who had been secretary of the Massachusetts Sabbath School Society for years, was critical of the trend toward making teacher qualifications "so high and imposing that many of our most devoted and successful superintendents and teachers have shrunk back abashed and discouraged at the solemn array of responsibilities and duties of this work. . . . None but theological professors could possibly attain to the standard presented" (p. 112).

67. R. G. Pardee, "The Best System of Teaching," *Sunday School Teacher* 3 (Dec. 1868), pp. 359–60.

68. One rare reference suggests paying those who conducted institutes and convention classes: "A Delicate Subject," *Sunday School Workman* 1 (Nov. 5, 1870), p. 356.

5. CONVERSION AND CHRISTIAN NURTURE

1. Philadelphia, First Presbyterian Church [Kensington] Sabbath School Association, Minutes, 1817–1840, Constitution, 1817, PHS; John Henry Hobart, *The Beneficial Effects of Sabbath Schools Considered* (New York: New York Protestant Episcopal Sunday School Union, 1818), p. 10; "Sabbath Schools at Whitehall, New York," *Religious Intelligencer* 4 (June 26, 1819), p. 63.

2. Rhode Island Sabbath School Association Records, 1825–1862, Apr. 5, 1826, RIHS.

3. McKendrean Female Sabbath School Society of Baltimore, Records, 1816–1843, 1816, LLMM; New-York Sunday-School Union Society, *Hints on the Establishment and Regulation of Sabbath Schools* (New York, 1817), pp. 1–10; Edwin W. Rice, *The Sunday-School Movement, 1780–1917, and the American Sunday-School Union, 1817–1917* (Philadelphia: American Sunday-School Union, 1917), p. 297; Frank Glenn Lankard, *A History of the American Sunday School Curriculum* (New York and Cincinnati: Abingdon Press, 1927), p. 134.

4. New-York Sunday-School Union Society, *Hints on the Establishment and Regulation of Sabbath Schools,* p. 13; Albert Mathews, "Early Sunday Schools in Boston," *Publications of the Colonial Society of Massachusetts* 21 (1919), pp. 268–70, 274; New-York Sunday-School Union Society, Methodist Branch Minutes, 1816–1818, Mar. 15, 1816, NYPL.

5. On infant schools, see Dean May and Maris A. Vinovskis, "A Ray of Millennial Light: Early Education and Social Reform in the Infant School Movement in Massachusetts, 1826–1840," in *Family and Kin in Urban Communities, 1700–1930,* ed. Tamara K. Hareven (New York: Franklin Watts, 1977), pp. 62–99. On the presence of very young children in common schools, see Carl Kaestle and Maris A. Vinovskis, "From Apron Strings to ABCs: Parents, Children and Schooling in Nineteenth-Century Massachusetts," in *Turning Points: Historical and Sociological Essays on the Family,* ed. John Demos and Sarane Spence Boocock (Chicago: University of Chicago Press, 1978), pp. 39–80; and Joseph F. Kett, "Curing the Disease of Precocity," ibid., pp. 183–211. For statements encouraging formation of infant classes, see American Sunday School Union, *Nineteenth Annual Report* (Philadelphia, 1843), pp. 14–16; and Methodist Episcopal Sunday School Union, Board of Managers, Minutes, 1827–1833, Dec. 7, 1829, and Jan. 12, 1830, NYPL. For examples of infant classes, see Providence Association of Sabbath School Teachers, Records, 1827–1854, May 19, 1834, RIHS (5 of 11 schools in the association had infant classes); New York, Seventh Presbyterian Church Sunday School Teachers' Association, Minutes, 1830–1869, Nov. 25, 1835, PHS; *Semi-Centennial of the Sunday School of the First Presbyterian Church of Utica* (Utica: The Church, 1866), p. 42 (infant class started in 1839); Lynn, Massachusetts, First Methodist Episcopal Church Sunday school, Minute-book, 1839–1877, Sept. 1839 (infant class with 41 students), Apr. 18, 1852 (infant department with 43 students), Boston University School of Theology Library; Boston, Bromfield Street Methodist Episcopal Sunday school, Records, 1867–1872, Jan. 2, 1867 (infant department with 45 pupils under age 5), Boston University School of Theology Library.

6. *Sunday School Repository* 2 (Dec. 1818), pp. 161–63; Divie Bethune speech, in Philadelphia Sunday and Adult School Union, *Fifth Annual Report* (Philadelphia, 1822), p. 81; Gregory T. Bedell speech, ibid., p. 85.

7. *Semi-Centennial of the Sunday School of the First Presbyterian Church of Utica,* p. 114; McKendrean Female Sabbath School Society, Minutes, Nov. 3, 1821, LLMM; "The Example of Christ Recommended to Sunday School Teachers," *American Sunday-School Magazine* 1 (Oct. 1824), p. 104.

8. American Sunday School Union, *Third Annual Report* (Philadelphia, 1827), p. xxvii; *American Sunday-School Magazine* 2 (Mar. 1825), p. 68; Asa Bullard, *Fifty Years*

with the Sabbath Schools (Boston: Lockwood, Brooks, 1876), p. 52; *Union Questions* 5 (1835), pp. iii–iv. See also Lankard, *Sunday School Curriculum,* pp. 142–49, and George Herbert Betts, *The Curriculum of Religious Education* (New York and Cincinnati: Abingdon Press, 1924), pp. 98–106.

9. McKendrean Female Sabbath School Society Minutes, Nov. 3, 1827, and Nov. 1, 1828, LLMM; "A Conversation," *Sabbath-School Treasury* 4 (Sept. 1831), p. 18.

10. New York, Seventh Presbyterian Church Sunday School Teachers' Association, Minutes, Nov. 26, 1834, PHS; "Revival in a Sabbath School at Lewis, New York," *Religious Intelligencer* 4 (May 6, 1820), pp. 770–71; "Sabbath Schools," ibid. 10 (Jan. 21, 1826), p. 533; *American Sunday-School Magazine* 2 (July 1825), p. 216; "Early Religious Education of Children," *Religious Intelligencer* 13 (Sept. 13, 1828), 252–253.

11. Gerald Strauss, *Luther's House of Learning: Indoctrination of the Young in the German Reformation* (Baltimore: Johns Hopkins University Press, 1978), pp. 136–78.

12. *Union Questions* 2 (1829), p. 8; "Little Lessons for Little Folks," *Youth's Companion* 1 (May 11, 1833), p. 20.

13. *Account of the Death of Franklin Bryant Howard, A Scholar of Grace Church Sunday School, Boston* (Boston: n.p., 1840); *Youth's Companion* 1 (May 11, 1833), p. 22; "The Dead Scholar," ibid., p. 21.

14. Daniel T. Rodgers, *The Work Ethic in Industrial America, 1850–1920* (Chicago: University of Chicago Press, 1978), p. 128.

15. E. P. Thompson, *The Making of the English Working Class* (New York: Pantheon, 1964), p. 378; Arlie Hochschild, *The Managed Heart: The Commercialization of Emotion in Twentieth-Century America* (Berkeley: University of California Press, 1983).

16. For a statement on the ideal school curriculum, see Frederick A. Packard, *The Teacher Taught: An Humble Attempt to Make the Path of the Sunday-School Teacher Straight and Plain* (Philadelphia: American Sunday-School Union, 1861), pp. 92–100. On graded divisions in the schools, see Lynn, Massachusetts, First Methodist Episcopal Church Sunday school, Minute-book, July 2, 1865, and May 13, 1866; and Boston, Bromfield Street Methodist Episcopal Church Sunday school, Records, Jan. 2 and Dec. 29, 1867, Boston University School of Theology Library. On adult classes, see Rhode Island Baptist Sabbath School Convention, *Minutes of the Fourteenth Anniversary* (Providence: n. p., 1854), p. 10.

17. D. B. Nelson to Maurice A. Wurts, Oct. 25, 1867, American Sunday School Union Papers, PHS. See also William Stavely to Rev. S. A. Clark's Church, Oct. 4, 1857, ibid.

18. On summer retrenchment, see Philadelphia, Spruce Street Baptist Sunday School Society, Minutes, 1851–1860, June 17, 1858, American Baptist Historical Society, Rochester, N.Y. Figures on attendance at the Brandywine school are available at the Hagley Library, Wilmington, Del.

19. Sheldon Norton to F. W. Porter, Feb. 22, 1831 and Charles Grosvenor to F. W. Porter, Feb. 13, 1830, both quoted in Ralph R. Smith, Jr., " 'In Every Destitute Place': The Mission Program of the American Sunday School Union, 1817–1834" (Ph.D. diss., University of Southern California, 1973), p. 163.

20. On nineteenth-century child rearing advice, see Peter G. Slater, *Children in the New England Mind in Death and in Life* (Hamden, Conn.: Archon Books, 1977); Anne L. Kuhn, *The Mother's Role in Childhood Education: New England Concepts, 1830–*

1860 (New Haven: Yale University Press, 1947); Nancy F. Cott, "Notes Toward an Interpretation of Antebellum Childrearing," *Psychohistory Review* 7 (1977–78), pp. 4–20; and Bernard Wishy, *The Child and the Republic: The Dawn of American Child Nurture* (Philadelphia: University of Pennsylvania Press, 1968). Joseph F. Kett points out that nineteenth-century biographies devoted increasing amounts of space to the subjects' childhoods; see his *Rites of Passage: Adolescence in America, 1790 to the Present* (New York: Basic Books, 1977).

21. "The Power of Religion," *Sabbath-School Magazine* 1 (May 1, 1832), p. 67.

22. "Philadelphia Association of Male Sunday School Teachers," *American Sunday-School Magazine* 1 (Oct. 1824), p. 101; William A. Alcott, *The Young Mother: or, Management of Children in Regard to Health,* 2d ed. (Boston: Light and Stearns, 1836), p. 326.

23. Richard Albert Edward Brooks, ed., *The Diary of Michael Floy, Jr. Bowery Village, 1833–1837* (New Haven: Yale University Press, 1941), Sept. 6, 1835, p. 182; *Sunday-School Repository* 2 (June 1818), p. 76; "The Blessings of Early Piety," *Sunday-School Advocate and Journal of Christian Education* 2 (Mar. 14, 1832), p. 41; Providence Association of Sabbath School Teachers, Records, June 17, 1833; June 17, 1839; and May 17, 1847, RIHS. See also [John Hall], "The Duty of the Church in Relation to Sunday Schools," *Presbyterian Review* 4 (1832), pp. 377–80.

24. W. F. Lloyd, *The Teacher's Manual: or, Hints to a Teacher upon Being Appointed to the Charge of a Sunday School Class* (Philadelphia: American Sunday-School Union, 1825), pp. 47–48; Boston Society for the Moral and Religious Instruction of the Poor, *Third Annual Report* (Boston, 1819), p. 11. See also "Superior Importance of Moral and Religious Instruction," *Sunday-School Repository* 2 (Dec. 1818), p. 163; Packard, *Teacher Taught,* p. 37; John Todd, *The Sabbath School Teacher: Designed to Aid in Elevating and Perfecting the Sabbath School System* (Northampton, Mass.: n.p., 1837), pp. 25–26; Basil Manly, Jr., "A Sunday School in Every Baptist Church," *The Baptist Preacher,* n. s. (July 1852), p. 127; and Kuhn, *Mother's Role,* pp. 18–22.

25. "Sabbath Schools at Whitehall, New York," *Religious Intelligencer* 4 (June 26, 1819), p. 63; Massachusetts Sabbath School Union, *First Annual Report* (Boston, 1826), p. 6. Karen Halttunen has pointed out how prevalent the theme of "firm principles" was in antebellum advice literature; she has also noted the ubiquity of navigational metaphors. See *Confidence Men and Painted Women: A Study of Middle-class Culture in America, 1830–1870* (New Haven: Yale University Press, 1982), pp. 25–26.

26. Providence Association of Sabbath School Teachers, Records, Apr. 15, 1833, RIHS; John S. C. Abbott, *The Mother at Home: or Principles of Maternal Duty,* 2d ed. (Boston, 1833), p. 141.

27. Lydia Maria Child, quoted in Slater, *Children in the New England Mind,* p. 151; Kuhn, *Mother's Role,* pp. 90–101.

28. The Calvinist view of childhood is fully examined in Sandford Fleming, *Children and Puritanism: The Place of Children in the Life and Thought of the New England Churches, 1620–1847* (New Haven: Yale University Press, 1933), esp. pp. 54–76. William G. McLaughlin has written an incisive analysis of the child-rearing views of one strict Calvinist in the nineteenth century: "Evangelical Child Rearing in the Age of Jackson: Francis Wayland's Views on When and How to Subdue the Willfulness of Children," *Journal of Social History* 9 (1975), pp. 20–43. See also, Slater, *Children in the New England Mind,* pp. 128–52.

29. On Beecher, see Fleming, *Children and Puritanism*, p. 190, and Slater, *Children in the New England Mind*, pp. 81–84. On Taylor, see Slater, *Children in the New England Mind*, pp. 77–87; George Stewart, Jr., *A History of Religious Education in Connecticut to the Middle of the Nineteenth Century* (New Haven: Yale University Press, 1924), p. 321; Sidney Earl Mead, *Nathaniel William Taylor: A Connecticut Liberal* (1943; New York: Archon Books, 1967), pp. 171–99; and George M. Marsden, *The Evangelical Mind and the New School Presbyterian Experience: A Case Study of Thought and Theology in Nineteenth-Century America* (New Haven: Yale University Press, 1970), pp. 46–52.

30. Gardiner Spring, *A Dissertation on Native Depravity* (New York: Jonathan Leavitt, 1833), pp. 3, 8, 10, 17, 11–12, 36–37, 68–69, 88–92. See also McLaughlin "Evangelical Child Rearing," pp. 20–30; and Slater, *Children in the New England Mind*, p. 87.

31. Jehudi Ashmun, *Memoir of the Life and Character of the Rev. Samuel Bacon* (Washington, D.C.: n.p., 1822), pp. 113–14; "A Conversation," *Sabbath-School Treasury* 4 (Sept. 1831), pp. 17–18; McKendrean Female Sabbath School Society, Minutes, Oct. 1843, LLMM; Providence Association of Sabbath School Teachers, Records, Nov. 15, 1847, RIHS.

32. Daniel T. Rodgers, "Socializing Middle-Class Children: Institutions, Fables, and Work Values in Nineteenth-Century America," *Journal of Social History* 14 (Spring 1980), pp. 354–67; Donald M. Scott, *From Office to Profession: The New England Ministry, 1750–1850* (Philadelphia: University of Pennsylvania Press, 1978), chap. 4; Halttunen, *Confidence Men*, p. 26.

33. Horace Bushnell, *Views of Christian Nurture*, 2d ed. (Hartford, Conn.: Edwin Hunt, 1847); Rev. M. S. Hutton, "Importance of Early Conversion in Children," in American Sunday School Union, *Twenty-Seventh Annual Report* (Philadelphia, 1851), pp. 6–8.

34. Bushnell, *Views of Christian Nurture*, pp. 195 and 8.

35. Rev. Stephen Olin, quoted in Addie Grace Wardle, *History of the Sunday School Movement in the Methodist Episcopal Church* (New York and Cincinnati: Methodist Book Concern, 1918), pp. 114–15; Rev. Thomas Curtis quoted in Jessie Dell Crawford, "The Status of the Child in American Baptist Churches" (Ph.D. diss., Yale University, 1940), p. 317a; Rev. Thomas Robinson, "Religious Life in Childhood," *The Presbyterian at Work* 1 (Sept. 1873), p. 1; Henry Ward Beecher, "Child Christians," *Sunday School Times* 12 (Oct. 8, 1870), p. 644. See also B. K. Peirce address in *Our Sabbath Home: An Account of the Services Connected with the Dedication of the North Avenue Sabbath School Chapel, Cambridge, October 31, 1852 . . . with a History of the School* (Boston: n.p., 1853), pp. 33–45; and Thomas H. Skinner, *The Early Regeneration of Sabbath-School Children* (Philadelphia: Presbyterian Board of Publication, 1870), pp. 8–10.

36. Horace Bushnell, *"God's Thoughts Fit Bread for Children." A Sermon Preached Before the Connecticut Sunday-School Teachers' Convention, March 2, 1869* (Boston: Nichols and Noyes, 1869), pp. 24–25.

37. Rev. William Hague, "A Child's Religion, the True Religion for Men and Women," *National Sunday School Teacher* 5 (Jan. 1870), pp. 4–6.

38. Henry Ward Beecher quoted in *The Well-Spring* 14 (Oct. 30, 1857), p. 175; Bushnell, *Views of Christian Nurture*, pp. 291–99; "The Religion of Childhood," *Sunday-School Journal* 28 (Nov. 18, 1857), pp. 169–70.

39. Rev. A. J. Rowland, "Variety vs. Routine," *Sunday School Teacher* 2 (June 1867), p. 162; "Editor's Table," ibid. 3 (July 1868), p. 221; Frank P. Guernsey, "Children's Troubles," *National Sunday School Teacher* 4 (Jan. 1869), p. 14; R. G. Pardee, "Teachers, Study Your Scholars," *Sunday School Teacher* 2 (Sept. 1867), pp. 257–58; "Social Entertainments for Sunday-Schools," *Sunday-School World* 1 (Nov. 1861), p. 130.

40. Bushnell, *Views of Christian Nurture*, pp. 151–74. The Old School Presbyterian theologian Charles Hodge applauded Bushnell's ideas because they reinforced his own anti-revival sentiments and placed renewed emphasis, in Hodge's view, on the church tradition of the covenant. See Hodge, "Bushnell on Christian Nurture," in *The Princeton Theology, 1812–1921: Scripture, Science and Theological Method from Archibald Alexander to Benjamin Breckinridge Warfield*, ed. Mark A. Noll (Grand Rapids, Mich.: Baker Book House, 1983), pp. 176–84. On childhood, see Rodgers, "Socializing Middle-Class Children," pp. 354–67.

41. Robinson, "Religious Life in Childhood," p. 1; Rev. Thomas Murphy, "The One Thing Needed," *Presbyterian at Work* 1 (Jan. 1873), p. 1.

42. "A Dangerous Mistake," *The Baptist Teacher* 3 (Feb. 1, 1872), p. 13. See also D. T. Morrill, "Immediate Results Sought and Expected," Missouri Baptist Sunday School Convention, *Minutes* (Glasgow, Mo.: n.p., 1872), pp. 20–22; and "Wresting the Scriptures," *The Baptist Teacher* 5 (June 1874), p. 61.

43. Rice, *Sunday-School Movement*, pp. 101–20; Lankard, *Sunday School Curriculum*, pp. 179–80.

44. "Josiah's Early Piety" in: *Sunday School Magazine* 8 (Apr. 1878); *Sunday School Times* 20 (Mar. 23, 1878); *Sunday School Journal* 10 (Apr. 1878); *Baptist Teacher* 8 (Apr. 1878); *National Question Book, I, For Older Scholars* (Boston: Congregational Publishing Society, 1877), pp. 54–57; *Westminster Question Book* (Philadelphia: Presbyterian Board of Publication, 1877), pp. 48–51.

45. Rev. J. M. Gregory, "The Seven Laws of Teaching," *National Sunday School Teacher* 9 (May 1874), pp. 171–72; Joseph Alden, "Truth: How Acquired," ibid. 7 (Apr. 1872), pp. 130–33; Rev. C. H. Fowler, "Mental Philosophy," *Sunday School Journal* 7 (Jan. 1875); Sara J. Timanus, *The Infant Class: Hints on Primary Religious Instruction* (Chicago: Adams, Blackmer, and Lyon, 1870), pp. 28–54; Ned Harland Dearborn, *The Oswego Movement in American Education* (New York: Teachers' College, Columbia University, 1925), pp. 42–44.

46. Bushnell, *Views of Christian Nurture*, pp. 195 and 8. Edmund Morgan discusses the concept of Puritan "tribalism" in *Visible Saints: The History of a Puritan Idea* (New York: New York University Press, 1963), pp. 137–38. See also Lewis Schenck, the *Presbyterian Doctrine of Children in the Covenant* (New Haven: Yale University Press, 1940), pp. 2–11; Fleming, *Children and Puritanism*, pp. 27–35; Crawford, "Status of the Child," pp. 69–78; and Skinner, *Early Regeneration*, p. 11.

47. "Jesus as a Worker," *Sunday School Times* 12 (Feb. 19, 1871), p. 117; "Editor's Table," *Sunday School Teacher* 3 (Nov. 1868), pp. 349–50. The quotation is from "The Study of Child-Nature," *National Sunday School Teacher* 8 (July 1873), p. 246.

48. "Real Conversation," *Youth's Penny Gazette* 3 (Dec. 3, 1845), pp. 98–99; George L. Prentiss, *Life and Letters of Elizabeth Prentiss* (New York: Anson D. F. Randolph, 1882), pp. 12–13; "Uncle John's Letter-Box," *The Standard* 16 (1869) and 21 (Feb. 12, 1874).

49. New York, Seventh Presbyterian Church Sunday School Teachers' Association, Minutes, Nov. 23, 1836 (account of the death of a nine-year-old), PHS; Philadelphia, Northern Liberties Central Presbyterian Church Sunday School Association, Minutes, 1837–1850, 1862–1867, July 5, 1842, PHS; Brooks, *Diary of Michael Floy, Jr.*, May 14–19, 1834, pp. 84–85.

50. "The Converted Child," *Presbyterian Sunday School Visitor* 1 (June 15, 1851), p. 46; Miss H. C. Knight, "George and His Bible," *The Well-Spring* 1 (January 12, 1844), p. 5.

51. American Sunday School Union, *Twenty-First Annual Report* (Philadelphia, 1845), p. 30; Brooks, *Diary of Michael Floy, Jr.*, Jan. 26, 1854, p. 54; McKendrean Female Sabbath School Society, Minutes, Nov. 5, 1825, LLMM; New York, Seventh Presbyterian Church Sunday School Teachers' Association, Minutes, May 23, 1838, PHS. See also, "Evidences of Early Piety," *The Well-Spring* 1 (Jan. 12, 1844), p. 5.

52. *Semi-Centennial of the Sunday School of the First Presbyterian Church of Utica*, pp. 65–67; Ruth C. Linton, "The Brandywine Manufacturers' Sunday School: An Adventure in Education in the Early Nineteenth Century," *Delaware History* 20 (1983), pp. 179–80.

53. Caroline Cowles Richards, *Village Life in America, 1852–1872* (New York: Henry Holt, 1912), Mar. 20, 1853, p. 30; Nov. 23, 1853, pp. 36–37; Nov. 1853, p. 37; Feb.–Mar. 1854, p. 40; [?], 1854, p. 41. A writer for the *Baptist Almanac* in 1864 echoed Anna's view: "My early impression from Sunday-school books was that religion was very unhealthy. It seemed a terrible distemper that killed every boy or girl that touched it." Quoted in Crawford, "Status of the Child," p. 525.

54. Edwin O. Gale, *Reminiscences of Early Chicago and Vicinity* (Chicago: Fleming H. Revell, 1902), pp. 369–70. Temperance leader Mary A. Livermore recalled her childhood religion in similarly anguished terms, but attributed her religious fears to her father's instruction, not to her Sunday school experiences: *The Story of My Life* (Hartford, Conn.: A. D. Worthington, 1898), pp. 52–64.

55. Brooks, *Diary of Michael Floy, Jr.*, Sept. 9, 1835, pp. 182–83.

56. J. W. Vail to John W. Dulles, Mar. 6, 1856; William Bulkley to Maurice A. Wurts, Nov. 1, 1870 (both in American Sunday School Union Papers), PHS. See also "Our Question Drawer," *Sunday School Teacher* 1 (Feb. 1866), p. 59.

57. New York, Willett Street Methodist Episcopal Church Sunday School Society, Minutes, 1857–1872, Sept. 10, 1866, NYPL; New York, Bank Street [Methodist Episcopal] Mission Sunday school, Minutes, 1865–1868, July 10, 1865, NYPL; E. D. Jones, *The Benton Street Mission Sunday School* (St. Louis: n.p., 1868), p. 53.

58. See, for example, New-York Sunday-School Union Society, *Fourth Annual Report* (New York, 1820), pp. 3–4 (on anniversary gatherings); William H. Seward, "Sunday-School Celebration," in *The Works of William H. Seward*, ed. G. E. Baker (Boston, 1884), vol. 3, pp. 208–10 (Fourth of July celebrations); Jones, *Benton Street Mission*, pp. 53 (picnic), 34–35 (Christmas and anniversary celebrations); Charlestown, Mass., Union Methodist Episcopal Sunday school, Records, 1847–1871, Boston University School of Theology Library, Dec. 2, 1868 (handbill and program for "a grand exhibition"); New York, Willett Street Methodist Episcopal Church Sunday school, Minutes, Oct. 4, 1868, NYPL (a missionary from India "displayed pictures of heathen gods and some of the ornaments worn by the women"); Shepherd Knapp, *A History of the Brick Presbyterian Church in the City of New York* (New York: Trustees of the

Church, 1909), pp. 219–20, 229–30 (Fourth of July, anniversary, and magic lantern show).

59. Brooks, *Diary of Michael Floy, Jr.*, Mar. 23, 1834, pp. 71–72, and Jan. 26, 1834, p. 54; New York, Seventh Presbyterian Church Sunday School Teachers' Association, Minutes, May 23, 1868, PHS; New York, Willett Street Methodist Episcopal Church Sunday school, Minutes, Dec. 25, 1864, NYPL.

60. *Semi-Centennial of the Sunday School of the First Presbyterian Church of Utica*, p. 174; *Semi-Centennial of the Congregational Sabbath School of Wethersfield, Connecticut* (Hartford: n.p., 1867), p. 24. On Sunday schools in southern cities, see John Wells Kuykendall, *Southern Enterprize: The Work of National Evangelical Societies in the Antebellum South* (Westport, Conn.: Greenwood Press, 1982), chap. 2; and Rice, *Sunday-School Movement*, p. 65. On Tyng's activities, see Henry Anstice, *History of St. George's Church in the City of New York, 1752–1811–1911* (New York: Harper and Bros., 1911), pp. 199–205; and Stephen H. Tyng, *Forty Years Experience in the Sunday Schools* (New York: Sheldon, 1866), pp. 10–14.

61. Anstice, *St. George's Church*, pp. 87–89; Lynn E. May, Jr., *The First Baptist Church of Nashville, Tennessee, 1820–1970* (Nashville: The Church, 1970), p. 55.

62. For examples of schools under church authority, see General Protestant Episcopal Sunday School Union, *Fifth Annual Report* (New York, 1831), pp. 6–10. On Brick Church, see Knapp, *Brick Presbyterian Church*, pp. 222–26. On the Seventh Presbyterian Church, see New York, Seventh Presbyterian Church Sunday School Teachers' Association, Minutes, Nov. 24, 1843, PHS. See also Clifton Hartwell Brewer, *A History of Religious Education in the Episcopal Church to 1835* (New Haven: Yale University Press, 1924), pp. 210–15.

63. *Sunday School Times* 12 (June 4, 1870), p. 360; Philadelphia, Fifth Baptist Church Sabbath School Teachers' Association, Minutes, 1855–1882: Apr. 21 and Dec. 15, 1856; and Spruce Street Baptist Sabbath School Society, Minutes, 1851–1860: Apr. 25, 1852, both at American Baptist Historical Society, Rochester, N.Y.

64. Robert W. Lynn and Elliott Wright, *The Big Little School: Sunday Child of American Protestantism* (New York: Harper and Row, 1971); General Protestant Episcopal Sunday School Union, *Fourth Annual Report* (New York, 1830), pp. 20–21; Providence Association of Sabbath School Teachers, Records, July 26, June 21, and Aug. 16, 1847, RIHS.

65. Rice, *Sunday-School Movement*, pp. 128–29; "Parental Instruction," *Sunday-School Journal and Advocate of Christian Education* 2 (Mar. 14, 1832), p. 42; A. Jones, Jr., *The Training of Children, and the Influence of Properly Conducted Sabbath Schools* (Nashville, Tenn.: Southern Baptist Sabbath-School Union, 1859), p. 18. On changes in the ministry, see Scott, *From Office to Profession*, chap. 4; on family life, see Mary P. Ryan, *Cradle of the Middle Class: The Family in Oneida County, New York, 1790–1865* (New York: Cambridge University Press, 1981).

66. Crawford, "Status of the Child," pp. 380–400; Joseph H. McCullagh, *"The Sunday School Man of the South." A Sketch of the Life and Labors of the Rev. John McCullagh* (Philadelphia: American Sunday-School Union, 1889), pp. 99–109; Robert Frederick West, *Alexander Campbell and Natural Religion* (New Haven: Yale University Press, 1948), pp. 12–16; Bertram Wyatt-Brown, "The Antimission Movement in the Jacksonian South and West: A Study of Regional Folk Culture," *Journal of Southern History* 36 (Nov. 1970), pp. 501–29.

67. Wardle, *Sunday School Movement in the Methodist Episcopal Church,* pp. 54–55, 87–90; Fleming, *Children and Puritanism,* pp. 27–35, 51–56; Schenck, *Children in the Covenant* pp. 2–11; Crawford, "Status of the Child," pp. 69–78, 204–26; Stewart, *Religious Education in Connecticut,* pp. 263–93; Methodist Episcopal Church, South, *General Conference Journal* (Nashville, Tenn., 1854 and 1858); Clifton Hartwell Brewer, *Early Episcopal Sunday Schools (1814–1865)* (Milwaukee: Morehouse-Gorham, 1939).

68. "Editorial Miscellany," *National Sunday School Teacher* 9 (July 1874), p. 269; John McClintock, "The Sunday School in its Relation to the Church," *Methodist Quarterly Review* 29 (Oct. 1857), p. 529; Newark, N.J., High Street Presbyterian Church Sabbath school, Records, 1841–1887, 1858, PHS.

CONCLUSION

1. Thomas W. Laqueur, *Religion and Respectability: Sunday Schools and Working-Class Culture, 1780–1850* (New Haven: Yale University Press, 1976), pp. 1–13, 21–25, 63–65, 193–201.

2. Ibid., pp. 63 (quotation), 87–89.

3. Ibid., pp. 42–60.

4. Ibid., pp. 95–112 (quotations, 96 and 101).

5. Ibid., pp. 169–72.

6. Ibid., pp. 75–81, 83–86 (quotation, 80).

7. Ibid., pp. 36–40.

8. Laqueur, *Religion and Respectability,* pp. 155–58, 241–45.

9. See Gerald E. Knoff, *The World Sunday School Movement: The Story of a Broadening Mission* (New York: Seabury Press, 1979).

BIBLIOGRAPHICAL NOTE

I will not attempt here to list all the sources used in writing this book; they are fully covered in the footnotes. Rather, I will offer some general comments on the major types of sources used, giving examples of each.

The most important manuscript materials for this study were the voluminous papers of the American Sunday School Union and the records kept by Sunday school organizations and by individual schools. The American Sunday School Union Papers, deposited at the Presbyterian Historical Society in Philadelphia (and now available on microfilm) include the records of the Philadelphia Sunday and Adult School Union, numerous minute-books of the managers and their committees, and the union's complete incoming correspondence since 1817. There is also some outgoing correspondence, especially for the years after 1860, and the period 1817–1824. The collection is a veritable treasure trove for historians; moreover, it is well organized for scholars' use. The Presbyterian Historical Society also has very valuable minute-books of other Sunday school organizations, including the First Day Society (1790–1940), the Male Adult Association of Philadelphia and the Auxiliary Evangelical Society (1815–1822), the Philadelphia City Sunday School Union (1826–1829 and 1840–1852), the Philadelphia Association of Male Sunday School Teachers (1824–1831), the Missionary Committee of the Philadelphia Sabbath School Association, and the New York Sunday School Union (1865–1875).

Records of Sunday school organizations and individual schools are scattered and vary widely in content and usefulness. Some school records simply list the number of students and teachers present every Sunday or the order of events at teachers' meetings, while others provide intimate views of a school's operation. Often such records are kept by individual congregations, but many are collected at archives and available for historians' use. The New York Public Library's Division of Archives and Manuscripts possesses a fine collection of Methodist Sunday school records from nineteenth-century New York City, as well as minute-books of both the Methodist Branch of the New-York Sunday-School Union Society (1816–1818) and the Methodist Episcopal Sunday School Union Board of Managers (1827–1833). The Presbyterian Historical Society has an unparalleled group of Sunday school records, covering Presbyterian schools across the nation, though it is especially strong on the Northeast. Both the American Baptist Historical Society at Colgate-Rochester Divinity School in Rochester, New York, and the Andover-Newton Theological Seminary in Newton, Massachusetts have a small number of Baptist school records, and the New England Methodist Historical Society at the Boston University School of Theology Library possesses a small collection of Methodist records from schools in Boston and Lynn. The minutes of the Massachusetts Sabbath School Society (1841–1882) are at the Congregational Library in Boston. The Rhode Island Historical Society in Providence has two very useful sets of minute-books: the records of the Rhode Island Sunday School Union (1825–1862) and the records of the Providence Association of Sabbath School Teachers (1827–1854). And the Brooklyn Historical Society has a slim volume, "Minutes of the New York Female Union Society for the Promotion of Sabbath Schools," 1825–1828, that offered many insights into the demise of this early women's organization. Finally, at the Lovely Lane Methodist Museum in Baltimore I used two very rich sets of minutes: those of the McKendrean Female Sabbath School Society (1816–1845) and of the Asbury Sunday School Society (1817–1877).

Printed church and Sunday school histories were also an important source for this study. Like manuscript records, these vary widely in approach and utility, but the best of them are extremely valuable. Shepherd Knapp's *History of the Brick Presbyterian Church in the City of New York* (New York, 1909), Nathan E. Wood's *History of the First Baptist Church of Boston (1665–1889)* (Philadelphia, 1889), and Henry Anstice's *History of St. George's Church in the City of New York, 1752–1811–1911* (New York, 1911) are models of their type, offering a wealth of detail on the history of each church, its Sunday school, and its members. *Semi-Centennial of the Sunday School of the First Presbyterian Church of Utica* (Utica, N.Y., 1866) is an excellent school history, containing pupil and teacher reminiscences as well as details of the school's past. The school with perhaps the best-preserved history is the Brandywine Manufacturers' Sunday School, which is part of the Hagley Museum outside Wilmington, Delaware. Not only are the school's records available for research, but historians and Hagley Museum volunteers have diligently documented the school's history and researched the backgrounds of its students. Of particular importance to understanding this school is Ruth Linton's master's thesis "To the Promotion and Improvement of Youth: The Brandywine Manufacturers' Sunday School, 1816–1840" (University of Delaware, 1981) and her article "The Brandywine Manufacturers' Sunday School: An Adventure in Education in the Early Nineteenth Century," in *Delaware History* 20 (1983), pp. 168–84. Full of interesting details on the lives of Sunday scholars is the unpublished research report edited by Sarah H. Heald, "Report on the Biographical Research for the Brandywine Manufacturers' Sunday School." It is available at the Hagley Museum.

Annual reports of various national, state, and city Sunday school societies proved very useful as sources of promotional rhetoric, missionary information, and statistics, as were the published reports of national and state Sunday school conventions. Among the most useful of such published reports were those of the American Sunday School Union and its predecessor, the Philadelphia Sunday and

Adult School Union (1817–1880); the Methodist Episcopal Sunday School Union (1847–1880); the New-York Sunday-School Union Society (1817–1847); the New York Female Union Society for the Promotion of Sabbath Schools (1817–1825); the Massachusetts Sabbath School Union and the Massachusetts Sabbath School Society (1826–1868); the national Sunday school conventions held in 1859, 1869, 1872, 1875, 1878, and especially 1905; the Illinois State Sunday School Convention (1866–1880); and the New York State Sunday School Teachers' Association Convention (1862–1879).

Periodicals for teachers and pupils provided insights into popular attitudes and teaching advice. Their titles notwithstanding, two antebellum publications of the American Sunday School Union, the *American Sunday-School Magazine* (1824–1832) and the *Sunday-School Journal and Advocate of Christian Education* (1830–1858), were general interest religious periodicals that were read by people other than Sunday school workers. Later, the union published the *Sunday-School Times* (1859–1860) and *Sunday-School World,* beginning in 1861. After being sold by the union, the *Sunday School Times* became an independent weekly; as such it was a useful guide to trends in Sunday school circles, particularly among Congregationalists and Presbyterians. The postwar era saw a proliferation of teachers' magazines, each denomination starting its own periodical. The most popular postwar journal was the *National Sunday School Teacher,* which, although nondenominational in theory, reflected the strong influence of Methodist writers and editors.

Sunday school magazines published for children in the antebellum era were not very age specific, but most seem to have been designed for youngsters from ten years of age to young adulthood. The American Sunday School Union, for example, published the *Youth's Friend* (1823–1842) and then the *Youth's Penny Gazette* (1842–1858), both of which defined "youth" broadly. The *Young Reaper* was a Baptist publication for children and youth; the *Well-Spring* was a Congregationalist periodical; the *Sunday School Advocate* was put out by the Methodist Episcopal Sunday School Union; and the *Sunday School Visitor* was issued by Southern Methodists beginning in 1851. After the Civil War, the volume and variety of such periodicals increased, and new publications, such as *Kind Words* (Southern Baptist) and the *Sunbeam* (Presbyterian) were directed at younger children.

Teaching guides and advice-books for teachers were legion in the nineteenth century. Among the most representative were the following: C. R. Blackall, *Our Sunday-School Work* (Philadelphia, n.d.); W. F. Crafts, *The Ideal Sunday School* (Boston, 1876); W. F. Lloyd, *The Teacher's Manual* (Philadelphia, 1825); New-York Sunday-School Union Society, *Hints on the Establishment and Regulation of Sunday Schools* (New York, 1817); Frederick A. Packard, *The Teacher Taught* (Philadelphia, 1839); John Todd, *The Sabbath School Teacher* (Northampton, Mass., 1837); and H. Clay Trumbull, *Teaching and Teachers* (Philadelphia, 1884).

In chapters 3, 4 and 5, I drew on some very useful diaries, autobiographies, and reminiscences of Sunday school pupils, teachers, and supporters. *The Diary of Michael Floy, Jr., Bowery Village, 1833–1837,* edited by Richard Albert Edward Brooks (New Haven, 1941), not only provided delightful reading but also offered detailed comments from Floy on his weekly classes. The manuscript diaries of

Hiram Peck (1830–1847) and Andrew Lester (1836–1888) at the New-York Historical Society also gave interesting insights into the lives and ideals of a teacher and a superintendent. Caroline Cowles Richards's *Village Life in America, 1852–1872* (New York, 1912) was rich with detail from the standpoint of a pupil who became a teacher. Miron Winslow's *Memoir of Mrs. Harriet L. Winslow* (New York, 1840) contained many excerpts from a teacher's diary and letters, as did Bradford K. Peirce's *One Talent Improved: or, The Life and Labors of Miss Susan B. Bowler, Successful Sunday School Teacher* (New York, 1845). Lewis Ashhurst's Journal, 4 vols., 1834–1874 (Richard Ashhurst Papers, Historical Society of Pennsylvania) was very important for understanding the mind-set of American Sunday School Union workers, as was *Forty Years' Familiar Letters of James W. Alexander, D.D.*, edited by John Hall (New York, 1860). "The Autobiography of Bishop Vincent," in *Northwestern Christian Advocate* 58 (April 6–November 2, 1910) revealed a good deal about John H. Vincent's background and motivations.

A variety of published and unpublished secondary works shaped my thinking and provided important background information for this study. Among studies of American Sunday schools, the standard work has long been Edwin W. Rice's *Sunday-School Movement, 1780–1917, and the American Sunday-School Union, 1817–1917* (Philadelphia, 1917). It is very accurate and informative, particularly in discussing the American Sunday School Union, of which Rice was a long-time official. Marianna C. Brown's *Sunday School Movements in America* (New York, 1901) should be read in conjunction with Rice, however, to correct its lack of coverage of denominational unions. *The Encyclopedia of Sunday Schools and Religious Education*, edited by John T. McFarland, Benjamin S. Winchester, R. Douglas Fraser, and J. Williams Butcher (3 vols., New York, 1915) is a useful reference guide, particularly for biographical information on nineteenth-century religious educators. The best recent study of American Sunday schools is *The Big Little School: Sunday Child of American Protestantism* by Robert W. Lynn and Elliott Wright (New York, 1971), which, although designed for a general audience, is based on thorough historical research. Ralph R. Smith's Ph.D. dissertation, " 'In Every Destitute Place': The Mission Program of the American Sunday School Union, 1817–1834" (University of Southern California, 1973) is very good on the union's early years. John Wells Kuykendall's *Southern Enterprize: The Work of National Evangelical Societies in the Antebellum South* (Westport, Conn., 1982) is a well-done scholarly study of the American Sunday School Union and other national benevolent societies.

E. Morris Fergusson's *Historic Chapters in Christian Education in America* (New York, 1935) is an interpretive history of considerable merit, particularly in its treatment of the Sunday school conventions. For the history of curricular changes and the uniform lesson plan, Frank Glenn Lankard's *History of the American Sunday School Curriculum* (New York, 1927) is a good starting point. The best studies of denominational religious education are Addie Grace Wardle's *History of the Sunday School Movement in the Methodist Episcopal Church* (New York, 1918), Jessie Dell Crawford's "Status of the Child in American Baptist Churches" (Ph.D. dissertation, Yale University, 1940), and Clifton Hartwell Brewer's three books on Episcopal history: *A History of Religious Education in the Episcopal Church to 1835*

(New Haven, 1924); *Early Episcopal Sunday Schools (1814–1865)* (Milwaukee, 1933); and *Later Episcopal Sunday Schools* (New York, 1939). A very good state study is *A History of Religious Education in Connecticut to the Middle of the Nineteenth Century* by George Stewart, Jr. (New Haven, 1924). Thomas Laqueur's fine study of the English Sunday school, *Religion and Respectability: Sunday Schools and Working Class Culture, 1780–1850* (New Haven, 1976) provides essential background for understanding the American version.

Many more general secondary works on American religion, education, and society helped me clarify my ideas or understand particular developments. Robert T. Handy's *Christian America: Protestant Hopes and Historical Realities* (New York, 1971) is an excellent, brief introduction to historical issues in American religion. Three insightful works on nineteenth-century religion, revivalism, and benevolence are Carroll Smith Rosenberg's *Religion and the Rise of the American City: The New York City Mission Movement, 1812–1870* (Ithaca, N.Y., 1971), Lois W. Banner's "Protestant Crusade: Religious Missions, Benevolence, and Reform in the United States, 1790–1840" (Ph.D. dissertation, Columbia University, 1970), and Martha Tomhave Blauvelt's "Society, Religion and Revivalism: The Second Great Awakening in New Jersey, 1780–1830" (Ph.D. dissertation, Princeton University, 1975). For guidance on educational issues, I relied on Stanley K. Schultz's *Culture Factory: Boston Public Schools, 1789–1860* (New York, 1973) and two books by Carl F. Kaestle: *Pillars of the Republic: Common Schools and American Society, 1780–1860* (New York, 1983) and *The Evolution of an Urban School System: New York City, 1750–1850* (Cambridge, Mass., 1973). Peter G. Slater's *Children in the New England Mind in Death and in Life* (Hamden, Conn., 1977) is indispensable for understanding early nineteenth-century ideas about childhood.

As for general American social history in the nineteenth century, the list of important works is lengthy indeed. Among those I found most helpful were: Paul Boyer's *Urban Masses and Moral Order in America, 1820–1920* (Cambridge, Mass., 1978), Anthony F. C. Wallace's *Rockdale: The Growth of an American Village in the Early Industrial Revolution* (New York, 1978), Bruce Laurie's *Working People of Philadelphia, 1800–1850* (Philadelphia, 1980), Daniel Walker Howe's *Political Culture of the American Whigs* (Chicago, 1979), Daniel T. Rodgers's *Work Ethic in Industrial America, 1850–1920* (Chicago, 1978), Donald M. Scott's *From Office to Profession: The New England Ministry, 1750–1850* (Philadelphia, 1978), Joan Jacobs Brumberg's *Mission for Life: The Story of the Family of Adoniram Judson* (New York, 1980), Bertram Wyatt-Brown's *Lewis Tappan and the Evangelical War against Slavery* (Cleveland, 1969), Joseph Kett's *Rites of Passage: Adolescence in America, 1790 to the Present* (New York, 1977), Mary P. Ryan's *Cradle of the Middle Class: The Family in Oneida County, New York, 1790–1865* (New York, 1981), Nancy F. Cott's *Bonds of Womanhood: "Woman's Sphere" in New England, 1785–1835* (New Haven, 1977), and Kathryn Kish Sklar's *Catharine Beecher: A Study in American Domesticity* (New Haven, 1973).

INDEX